An Unholy A.

Thomas and Henry

By

Mike Inkster

Acknowledgements

Paula Lane, my long suffering partner, who now probably knows far more about Thomas of Canterbury than she ever wanted to. Thanks to her also for making the Family Tree of Henry II and drawing the plan of Canterbury Cathedral as it was in 1170 at the time of 'murder'.

Nick, 'Brindle' Brown, who read the drafts and made erudite comment and suggestions where he thought they were relevant.

Douglas Howe for his expertise and help in the design of the cover.

Steve Wilks for reading and commenting on some early drafts.

To all the writers, past and present, of the life and times of both Thomas of Canterbury and King Henry, the second of that name, to whom I looked for information to help me write my story. Any mistakes in chronology and the facts you might find are mine. This was written as a novel and not a history book so I have not attached a bibliography.

For my dad Ike who was one of life's great storytellers

Contents

Family tree of Henry II

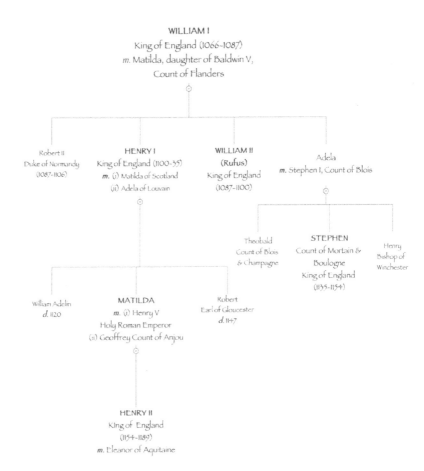

WILLIAM I
King of England (1066-1087)
m. Matilda, daughter of Baldwin V,
Count of Flanders

Robert II
Duke of Normandy
(1087-1106)

HENRY I
King of England (1100-35)
m. (i) Matilda of Scotland
(ii) Adela of Louvain

WILLIAM II
(Rufus)
King of England
(1087-1100)

Adela
m. Stephen I, Count of Blois

Theobald
Count of Blois
& Champagne

STEPHEN
Count of Mortain &
Boulogne
King of England
(1135-1154)

Henry
Bishop of
Winchester

William Adelin
d. 1120

MATILDA
m. (i) Henry V
Holy Roman Emperor
(ii) Geoffrey Count of Anjou

Robert
Earl of Gloucester
d. 1147

HENRY II
King of England
(1154-1189)
m. Eleanor of Aquitaine

Part One

Chapter 1

Mont-St-Sulpice

"Come on, if we leave now, we've got time for a coffee at the terminal before we get the train" David shouted up the stairs to his wife.

"Keep your hair on," she shouted back, "I'm just coming and anyway," she added, "we've got loads of time."

David Hartigan was comfortably ensconced as a professor of Archaeology at the University of Kent and his wife, Estelle, a systems analyst on the same campus, were confirmed Francophiles. Over the last seven years they had spent as much of their leisure time as they could arrange exploring the French countryside.

Retirement day had come and today they were leaving Canterbury to start a new chapter in their lives. Their searching for a new home had found them just what they were looking for in the hamlet of Mont-St-Sulpice in the Yonne region of north central France. Their house in Canterbury was to be let out to bolster their income whilst in France and also to act as a bolthole should the French adventure not work out as they hoped. Leaving the historical spires of their hometown Cathedral silhouetted by the sunset behind them, they joined the rush-hour trail to Folkestone and the Channel Tunnel rail terminal.

"You got the tickets, passports, wallet, 'phone," he asked as they got into the car. He did it every time. It was part of his 'leaving home' routine. "I've checked all the doors and windows."

"Yes and I've got the laptop and the charger and the international plug and all the other stuff we take every time we do this," she said.

"Right then, off we jolly well go and round the corner with a ho, ho, ho." Where he'd got that from she never did find out. No doubt something he'd picked up from his equally odd father.

They drove out of Canterbury on the A2, turned off at Barham and headed for Folkestone. The Elham Valley was beautiful and David sometimes wondered what the attraction of France was over the beautiful countryside they were already surrounded by. "It's the space," he'd concluded. France was five times less densely populated than England, especially in the rural areas. "Fewer people to get annoyed with and more room to breathe."

As well as a new home in a tranquil and picturesque environment in which they could enjoy their retirement, David had wanted somewhere with what he described as "a bit of history attached to it." He had the notion if they had somewhere like that, he could continue, quite literally, to dig around in the past whilst still being at home. "It would be nice to have my cake and eat it," was how he explained it to anyone who asked, "a bit of a busman's retirement."

They'd been through the tunnel enough times not to be excited by it. In fact, as the train whisked them under the Channel at 100 miles an hour, they sat in the cocoon of their car and had the picnic Estelle had prepared before they left.

For almost two years, they'd looked for the perfect place. Then, they found what they'd been searching for. When they'd driven into the small village of Mont-St-Sulpice they had immediately liked the environment. It had the feeling of the rural France that they'd been looking for.

"The house I'm taking you to look at is about a mile outside the village," the agent had told them as they drank their coffees in the small café in the village square whilst they took in the pleasant, relaxed atmosphere of their surroundings. "It's a bit run-down but definitely habitable. I think it's well worth you having a look at it. It won't need loads of renovations and I think it might just be what you're looking for. Just to add interest for David, the locals tell me that the place has history. Been in the village for hundreds of years in one form or another."

They'd bumped down an un-metalled track through a small stand of trees and there it was.

An old farmhouse faced them. It showed signs of its age which was hardly surprising as it had been there since the fifteenth century. Over the years, bits had been added to it and a collection of old farm buildings stood around an open courtyard in the middle of which was a well with a rickety, gabled roof.

Estelle gasped. "Oh David, it's just beautiful." Six weeks later, it was theirs.

David was intrigued by the name; "'Ferme du Prieuré', 'Priory Farm'. D'you know where the name comes from?" he'd asked the agent.

"The local legend is that there was apparently an old priory on the land but if it's true then it was a very long time ago. There's been a farm here since at least 15 something. That's all I know. I'm sure if you asked around there will be all sorts of tales to tell."

Estell had seen David's eyes light up. Nothing he would like better that being able to dig around in his own back garden looking for ancient ruins.

It had taken over a year to get their new home in France ready to live in permanently for when they decided the time was right. In the meanwhile the plan was to use it at every available opportunity for long weekends and holidays. The more they thought about it, the more they wondered why they continued to work in the jobs they were in just waiting for retirement to come around.

They were having dinner one evening when David said, "I've been thinking about it. Officially I've got two more years to go but I've accumulated as much pension as I'm going to get so why not go now? You're in pretty much the same position. Let's just bite the bullet, sell up here and move to France now."

"I'd like that," she said in reply, "but even with our decent pensions I'd feel safer if we had a second income if we needed it and whatever you say, you're not going to be happy sitting on your bum looking out of the window all day and come to think of it, nor will I."

"I've thought about that. We'll let this house to give us extra security 'til we're confidant we're going to survive. But, how about this for a plan? We've got spare rooms in the main house and we could create more in the outbuildings. Before you tell me you don't want to run a hotel, that's not what I was going to suggest. My plan would be for me to run residential archaeology courses whilst you could run residential IT courses. We could get someone from the village to do the housekeeping and the cooking so we'd be seen as providing some employment in the area. What do you think?" Estelle's answer had been in the affirmative.

The Hartigans had been running their courses for 2 years and by 2019 their season was fully booked.

David had used all his professional expertise and skills to research the area in general and stories of a priory on their land in particular. He discovered fairly quickly that there had indeed been a religious institute on the site and was, most probably, a small Cistercian brotherhood. From then on, the focus of David's courses had centred on discovering more about the Priory, where exactly it had stood, who had lived there and what the everyday life of the people who had lived there had been like.

David had always thought it possible, in fact, likely, that there would have been burials somewhere in close proximity to the farm. Sure enough, in late spring of 2019 a shout went up.

"David," one of his novice digger's shouted, "come and look at this." The obvious excitement in the digger's voice had David hurrying over. The outline of what looked like it might be a coffin, or at least, fragments of it, were just visible.

David could hardly contain his excitement at the find. All the other members of the course were gathering round to see what the excitement might be all about. David took over in the trench and sure enough, as he carefully scraped at the soil, what would prove to be an almost complete skeleton began to appear.

From that point on, each stage of the process was being meticulously recorded with drawings, measurements and video filming of everything as it happened. No detail was to be lost. David contacted his old colleagues in Canterbury and also the Society of Antiquaries of France based in the Louvre in Paris for more technical help in identifying and dating the new find.

Over the following days, teams of archaeologists had arrived from Canterbury and Paris and what would transpire to be the complete skeleton of a man were reverentially recovered from the ground. Samples were taken and sent to Paris for dating.

As if the discovery of an almost complete skeleton wasn't exciting enough, between its feet was a lead box.

"D'you think it's treasure?" one of the younger students had asked.

"Any find is 'treasure'," he was chided.

"But it must be something really special to be buried in a sealed-up metal box don't you think," he protested.

"Well, we'll have to wait and see," David told his eager young pupil. "We'll get it recovered and sent to the lab with the other samples for dating and see what they make of it all.

They didn't have to wait long for the dating results to come back. David gathered everyone at the dig site together and made the announcement. "Very exciting news. The body has been dated to around 1180 to 1195. That means that our man would appear to have been here for almost a thousand years. They've done some tests on the box we found with him and that's from the same period. Putting it in perspective, he was buried at about the time Richard the Lionheart would have been going on Crusade and Philip II was king of France. I think we should give ourselves a round of applause."

It was some weeks later that David was updated on the box his team had found in the grave. The team at the Louvre had opened it in sterile conditions and found it to contain sheets of manuscript written in what appeared to be archaic Latin. Two specialists from Canterbury would join the team at the Louvre and make a start on finding out what secrets the writing might hold.

Part Two

Chapter 2

The Chronology and Making of an Unholy Alliance

The year is 1178. In a priory in Cambridge, the Prior asked one of the novices to go and find Brother Edward and bring him to him. "You will most likely find him either in the scriptorium with his fingers covered in ink or in the library poring over a book."

The novice hurried off to carry out his task. He found Brother Edward as the Prior had suspected he would, in the library. "Brother Edward, I wish you good day," he started but got only a gruff response from the older monk.

"Can you not see that I am busy boy?"

"I am sorry to intrude Brother but Prior Luc wishes to speak with you and has sent me to find you. I had no wish to interrupt your reading," explained the young messenger.

"Prior Luc wishes to see me does he? Then best I close my book and attend to his command." With which, Brother Edward closed his book, placed it back in its place on one of the library shelves and shuffled off to see his superior with the novice trailing behind.

"Ah Brother Edward thank you for coming to see me. Please, be seated," the Prior said, when the old monk entered. "I have a task I would like you to undertake on behalf of the Priory for which there is no-one better suited. Let me explain what I would like you to do."

Brother Edward leaned forward to hear the Prior more clearly, his hearing not being as acute as it had been in his younger days. Added to which, his eyes were rheumy from the long hours he spent writing by candlelight in the scriptorium.

"I wondered", Prior Luc enquired, "have you ever seen the King?"

"No, never," Brother Edward answered.

Prior Luc said, "I have seen him only twice. I knew at once he was a man I would not forget. He seemed to me handsome, his complexion freckled and his grey eyes set off by his close-cropped tawny hair."

"Why do you ask", Brother Edward wanted to know.

"As you are no doubt aware, Brother, books written in our own scriptorium could be a useful source of income for our Priory. It occurs to me that in you, we have a valuable resource which we should make use of. I would like you to write of times in the not-too-distant past so that we might learn from your experience and knowledge. I am of a mind to believe that a society that does not know its history is like a tree without roots; easily blown over by any passing wind.

"Since the tragic events in Canterbury, of which you were an eyewitness and indeed, have the scars to prove it, added to the subsequent canonisation of our beloved Thomas, it seems to me that you would be the ideal person to write of what happened."

The old monk smiled at him. "You give me more credit than I am due. True I have lived a long life but whether my knowledge and experiences will be of use to you or anyone else is doubtful. Are you sure you want me to write my account of that dreadful day in the Cathedral?"

"Absolutely," Prior Luc replied. "Who better?"

Brother Edward sat quietly for what seemed an age before replying. "It would not make much of a book," he said eventually, "there would not be enough to fill a chapter, never mind a book and anyway, the King still lives and might not take kindly to my telling of an event he would perhaps far rather was forgotten."

"But" responded the Prior, "your story is but the end of a much bigger story that needs to be written. You spend most of your days in the library soaking up knowledge that puts everything into some kind of perspective. Why not put all that knowledge on parchment for future generations so that they may know the story in its entirety long after we who have lived through those times are gone? A work like that could only reflect well on the standing of our Priory. What do you think? Will you do it?"

Again, Brother Edward said nothing for a while. Then he spoke. "If you are truly interested then I will be happy to write the story," Brother Edward replied.

"Then so be it," the Prior said, "begin your task without delay."

As the old monk took his leave and shuffled off into the cloister, his useless arm hanging limp at his side, he gave the Prior some requests to enable him to carry out his task. "I will need a good quantity of writing materials, peace and quiet to work and someone to bring me food and drink whilst I work should I need it. There is much to write if the whole story is to be told and hopefully the good Lord will allow me to live long enough to finish the volume." Brother Edward was smiling to himself as he went and the sun came out to warm his walk to the scriptorium which, despite him being a man of God, he took as an omen of good fortune for his project.

The agreement having been made, the Prior gave orders that Brother Edward be given all he needed and the old monk set to work.

The scriptorium was a room to one side of the priory library and there, on a dull morning with the rain pouring down, Brother Edward sat at his writing desk to begin his book.

For several hours he sat, not writing but thinking to himself. "I know how the story ends but where should it start if it is to make any sense? To understand how it came about that I lost the use of my arm, it must, like all good stories, start at the beginning. My book will culminate with one of the most dramatic moments in our history, not only for the horrific nature of the event itself, but because it shows what happens when the interests of Church and State collide at the highest level. Furthermore, any ignorance of recent history and politics amongst our people and especially the young, is also something that I must endeavour to remedy. It really will not do for the young minds of the future to be ill-informed as to their past. My fear however is that to talk of such things, which concern a king who still lives, could be counted as sedition. Although I will seek to tell a true account of events, I have no desire to end my days in a dungeon for writing things that may offend the King's majesty."

Chapter 3

Brother Edward's Tale

The Paths to Power

Brother Edward sharpened his quills, filled his inkwell, ruled his parchment, made himself comfortable on his bench and began his tome thus:

In the year of our Lord 1100, England was to have a new King. As so often in history it is the ability to strike when an opportunity presents itself that leads to victory and as the youngest son of King William, the first of that name, Prince Henry was no different, which was why, against all the odds, he was about to come to the throne.

It was a warm, sunny day in August 1100 and a group of aristocratic huntsmen had cornered a stag in a clearing in the New Forest. The hounds were baying and the horses stamped the ground. The stag was terrified.

An arrow was loosed but instead of hitting the stag, it buried itself deep in the chest of one of the riders. A great gout of blood sprang from the man's mouth and he toppled from his horse. When he hit the ground, the arrow was driven right through his body so that its gore covered tip and shaft exited through his back. He was probably dead before he hit the ground.

This was no ordinary huntsman. This was William Rufus, King of England and also a son of King William, the first of that name. There was, as can be imagined, stunned shock amongst those in the hunting party.

One of the nobles rode forward and looked at the body on the ground where the blood was beginning to soak into the grass around it. He looked down at the body appalled. He dismounted and went to his knees looking for any signs of life. Perhaps a bubble of breath from the lips, a rise and fall from the arrow-pierced chest. Nothing.

"He's dead. There's nothing to be done here," the noble said and with that and in order to avoid any suspicion of foul play that might attach to them, he and his high-born companions galloped off. They left the King's body where it lay until some of the servants of the royal household threw a cloth over it and loaded it on to a cart belonging to a local charcoal burner named Purkis. The cart had been meant for the stag. Not a very dignified end for a King.

The man who had looked at the body and made the decision to ride off was the dead King's younger brother, Henry. Although there was nothing to be achieved by his staying in the forest other than out of respect for his brother, he knew full well that a great opportunity had just presented itself.

"We need to ride to Winchester with all haste," he ordered his entourage. Henry was wasting no time in getting from the forest to Winchester where, as soon as he arrived, he seized control of both the castle and the royal treasury. Once he had done that, he proclaimed himself King before his other brother, Robert Curthose, could do the same. Fortunately for Henry, Robert, at the time, was still on his way home from his triumphs in the Holy Land where his forces had played a leading part in the capture of Jerusalem.

"Hmm," Brother Edward mused as he wrote, "I do not suppose that Henry's rapid retreat from the site of his brother's demise has done anything to assuage the contention that it was perhaps not so much an accident as an assassination." Putting this treasonous thought to one side he continued:

It is this Henry, now the first king of that name in England, who will be our leading character in this first part of the story. He was born in England just two years after his father had beaten the Anglo-Saxon Harold Godwinson at Senlac Ridge in 1066. As soon as the battle was won, the father, William, snatched the English throne to become King William, the first of that name. Some still thought of him as William the Bastard being, as he was, the illegitimate son of Robert I, Duke of Normandy, by his mistress Herleva. Few, if any, would dare to call him 'Bastard' to his face.

It could be said with reasonable certainty that William was the progenitor of the whole sorry mess that was to follow his death and then last for at least the next 50 years. Put simply, all that was to follow resulted as a consequence of the way William, the first of that name, had divided up the territories he ruled between his three sons following his death.

That young Henry was born into a troubled and a dysfunctional family there can be no doubt. His older brothers, Robert, known as Curthose and William, the one known as Rufus, fought constantly with their father while he was alive and latterly with Henry who was much younger than them. Despite their lifelong animosity, to look at physically, Henry resembled his older brothers being as he was, short, stocky and barrel-chested.

In his will, their father William, had followed the Norman system of inheritance and had left his eldest son, Robert, the Duchy of Normandy and the middle son, William, he of the red hair, the throne of England. A fourth son, Richard had already died in a hunting accident so had not figured in the sharing out of William's lands and possessions.

"And what did the Bastard leave me?" Henry would rave for years afterwards. "The ability to read and write and a meagre pay-off of money but no land and no power, unlike my brothers who were given both."

But he showed them soon enough who was the better of the three brothers. He might not have had the power and the money to begin with but he had the brains and the ambition to better the other two. Henry was also due lands owned by his mother, Matilda, in Buckinghamshire and Gloucestershire but as soon as brother William was on the English throne, he made sure that his little brother never got his hands on them. That just served to added fuel to the fire in Henry's belly.

The three brothers spent years fighting and squabbling with each other. Robert disagreed fundamentally with William over their father's inheritance. He felt he should have and been given both the Duchy of Normandy and the throne of England. Following their father's death, William had been too quick for Robert and following the aforesaid ability to strike when an opportunity presents itself had scuttled off to England and had himself crowned King before Robert could stop him. They argued and fought for years amongst themselves, made and broke alliances with each other and against each other and each would besmirch the other whenever an opportunity presented itself.

Henry would tell anyone who would listen, "I had no choice but to stay in Normandy with big brother Robert because had I not, he would probably have confiscated what little money the 'Bastard' had deigned to leave me. Because I did that, brother William took the opportunity presented by my absence and sequestered my new estates in England. That is the kind of nice close family we were.

"I was taught to read and write, including in Latin, as I am sure my parents thought they might foist me off on the church as it was obviously not intended that I would be given any temporal power. Mind you, I did get some military training from a man called Robert Achard, and my father knighted me in 1086 shortly before he died. Luckily therefore, I was not a complete novice when it came to the business of war."

Time went by with no decrease in animosity between the siblings but then two things happened that changed both the future of Henry and of England.

Firstly, after mortgaging himself to the eyeballs to fund it, his eldest brother Robert went off to the Holy Land on Crusade thereby absenting himself from the centre of family activity. A significant error. Secondly, in 1100, King William of England, the second of that name, as I have already related, was shot by an arrow through the chest whilst out hunting.

Now, as we know and fate would have it, his younger brother Henry just happened to be in the same hunting party. Was that just fate or was it by design? Was it a hunting accident or a convenient murder? No-one will ever know. A mis-aimed arrow that changes the course of history? What is a matter of record, is that Henry, sticking to family tradition, struck when the opportunity presented itself and wasted no time in hastening to Winchester where he secured the royal treasury and then equally speedily got himself to London where he had himself crowned King. All while his dead brother's throne was still warm. Henry was sticking to the family creed of, "The quickest way to have power is to take it."

21

Of course, when Robert got back from crusading in 1101, he was much chagrined to find that his youngest brother had out manoeuvred him and had grabbed the throne of England which he had always thought should have been by right, his.

"That scheming, duplicitous little turd has pushed his luck too far this time," he thought to both himself and out loud to anyone who would listen. "I will soon show him who is in charge" and with that, he launched an invasion of England to teach Henry the error of his ways. Robert's efforts at getting himself installed as the King of England failed miserably and he ended up making a humiliating, negotiated settlement with his younger brother and instead of dislodging him from the throne, was forced to confirm him as the King.

Even then that was not to be the end of it. The rancour between them ran deep and any peace was predictably short-lived. Robert, who was now back in his Duchy of Normandy, decided once again to stir up trouble for his younger brother. To foil him, Henry invaded Normandy in 1105 where he defeated his brother Robert once and for all at the **Battle of Tinchebrai in** September of the year 1106.

"I'm not giving him any more chances to contest my rights to both the Kingdom of England and the Duchy of Normandy," Henry told his confidants. "I shall put him somewhere where his trouble making days will be at an end." Henry was as good as his word and after Tinchebrai he kept his brother Robert imprisoned for the rest of his life, which lasted for another 26 long, lonely, miserable years."

The light in the scriptorium had faded and the candle had nearly burned down. Brother Edward had been writing for hours. His back ached as did his eyes and his stomach rumbled. "Enough for today," he thought to himself, although he had actually said the words out loud. "Time for supper and then bed. Early prayers and then another chapter tomorrow." The candle died.

Chapter 4

King Henry Marries off his Daughter

Brother Edward settled himself on his bench. He had brought a fleece with him to make a cushion between his sparse buttocks and the hard wood of the seat. "If I am to be here," he thought, "there is no requirement that I need be any more uncomfortable than is necessary."

He began again:

The story now moves on to the year 1105 and although he could not know it at the time, King Henry was being drawn into what we know as the Lay Investiture Controversy. If any young fellows do not have knowledge of what that was then I will enlighten them as to its meaning as it plays a crucial part in what was to come. This 'controversy' would store up trouble not just for Henry himself but for future English monarchs and particularly, almost 50 years later, his grandson who is our present King Henry, the second of that name. At the time, this problem was the most important conflict to arise between secular and religious powers both here in England and across the Channel in Europe. Put simply, the question was one of who would control the appointment of bishops? The King or the Pope? Did bishops owe their loyalty firstly to their king or was it the other way around? Did the Pope in Rome take precedence and our King only come second? That was the nub of the falling-out for that is what it soon became.

Now at the time, one of Henry's closest confidants and advisors was Robert of Meulan who although by now, an old man, was much trusted by his King. Henry was seldom at rest but on this rare occasion when the King was sitting in a chair rather than on horseback, he was glad of the opportunity to speak with the old and trusted counsellor.

"You served both my father and brother well," Henry told Robert as they sat together in the king's private chambers at his palace at Westminster. Candlelight flickered in the room. "I believe you to be one of the wisest men of our age. You are eloquent and learned and three kings in this land have valued your counsel."

"My Lord King, your words do me much honour and are appreciated," Robert gave a small bow in the direction of Henry.

Henry had created Robert the Earl of Leicester. Whether this was purely as a reward for his valued wisdom and loyalty or because Robert was one of the few men who were with Henry in the woods on the fatal day that William Rufus had been killed by that 'stray' arrow, the truth of which, only Henry would ever know. What could be said with certainty was that Earl Robert was one of the last men alive to have fought at the battle on Senlac Ridge against Harold and his Anglo-Saxons in 1066. He was a living link to William the Conqueror.

"A man can't serve two masters," Henry was saying, "I rule in my lands and I will decide who will be bishops and who will not. They must owe loyalty and obedience to me for their secular powers and may defer to the Pope for matters spiritual but they will, first and foremost, obey me. This cannot be otherwise. Whilst I accept and support the theory that 'religion is what keeps the poor from murdering the rich', I want to control what goes on with the religion in my own country."

Robert was nodding his agreement but his advice to the king would lead him into deep, dark waters. As soon as the Pope, Paschall II, heard that Robert was advising Henry to continue selecting his bishops in opposition to the canons of the church he excommunicated him. While he was at it, Paschall threatened Henry with the same treatment if he continued to disobey him by investing and appointing bishops without his papal approval.

Henry was furious but needed to ere on the side of caution. "They have me in a cleft stick," he thought to himself. "My ability to govern all that I have is intimately bound up with the church and the Pope knows that only too well. He knows that the key to having the ability to be in many places at once, which my realm requires of me, is to have an administration system that can function in my stead when I'm not able to be there in person.

That needs people who can read and write and that means clerics and clerics need bishops. What I don't need, is the bishops being controlled and chosen by the pope in Rome and not by me in England and Normandy."

Henry remembered when Archbishop Anselm had returned from exile after hearing that William Rufus, who had exiled him, was dead and that Henry had taken the crown in his place.

"And do you know what the man did as soon as he was back," Henry asked himself rhetorically, "he told me he would be adhering to the Pope's ruling that the clergy should not give homage to their local temporal rulers but only to their spiritual leaders. Well I showed him."

When the argument could not be reasonably resolved between the two men, Anselm went into exile once more to avoid possible retribution from an enraged new King. Henry confiscated the revenues of all his estates.

"If he thinks absconding to France or wherever he has fled to, gets him off the hook then he has made a big mistake." Henry was getting a reputation for harshness. He had, without doubt inherited some of his father's less likeable traits but no-one respects a king they were not afraid of.

Anselm fought back. He did, after all, have the support of the Pope in Rome, a not inconsiderable ally in time of trouble. From exile, Anselm once again threatened Henry with excommunication and in July 1105 the two men finally agreed to a compromise and negotiated a solution. A distinction was to be drawn between the secular and ecclesiastical powers of the prelates. Under the agreement Henry gave up his right to invest his clergy but, he retained the custom of requiring them to come and do homage to him for their lands. With this arrangement in place Henry continued to play a major role in the selection of new bishops and Archbishops both English and Norman. Thus, he somehow managed to avoid the ever-present threat of excommunication. Of course, he carried on appointing many of his secular officials and friends to bishoprics despite the agreement with Anselm. In fact, Henry's chancellors and those of both his queens, became bishops of Durham, Hereford, London, Lincoln, Winchester and Salisbury.

The result was what Henry wanted, which was a cohesive body of administrators through which he could exercise careful influence, mainly through people he had chosen personally, over his domains.

"Robert," Henry addressed the older man. "I would value your advice on something that has been exercising my mind for some time now."

"I am flattered my Lord that you think so highly of my thoughts. Please enlighten me as to your thinking."

"Well," Henry replied, "what if we could kill two birds with one stone? It occurs to me that Henry of Germany has also been having similar problems over this question of the investiture of bishops and is currently involved in much acrimony with the Pope. How would it be if we were able to make some alliance with him for the future so that the Pope would be contending with two adversaries rather than one? At the same time, the Germans are no lovers of the French and it would be useful for us to have an ally pushing at Louis' other border. I hear that German Henry has been looking around for a bride and it further occurs to me that we might have just the person. My daughter is still but a child but a true king can be neither husband nor father; he must consider his throne and nothing else."

"You are as always my Lord King as astute a politician as you are a fearsome warrior." Robert had not survived as long as he had around Norman kings without knowing how to flatter them.

Shortly afterwards, negotiations were opened and Henry of England agreed to pay Henry of Germany the extraordinarily high sum of 1500 pounds of silver as dowry for his daughter Matilda. In return, the marriage would enormously increase his prestige and give England the continental alliance he was seeking as well as a confederate against the Pope.

It would seem that unlike his fellow monks in the priory Brother Edward's day was less dictated by the needs of the spiritual than of the temporal. He attended services as he was required to do for he could not do otherwise but spent most of his time in the chapel thinking about what he was to write next rather than his prayers. The needs of his stomach were what really dictated the rhythms of his day. He would write until his stomach told him it was time to eat rather than listen to the priory bells.

"I know not where he puts it," one of his fellow Brothers commented. "he eats like a man starved but stays as thin as an under-fed herring."

Chapter 5

Matilda is betrothed

"Now," Brother Edward thought, "where did I leave off yesterday? Ah yes, with Henry's plan to marry his daughter Matilda to the German King. I must," he reminded himself, "make sure that somewhere further on to make it clear which Matilda is which in order to avoid confusion. I already have three making an entry to the plot and there is another to come later. William, the Bastard of Normandy and then King of England was married to a Matilda who was Henry's mother, Henry as we will see married a Matilda of Scotland who is the mother of the young Matilda who will be a major, on-going character in the coming story." Having cleared his mind of that small problem and making sure his quill was properly sharpened he started:

We are now in the year 1110. She was a child, only eight years old but on a cold, windy day in February in the year 1110 she stood looking out across the grey, wild sea of the English Channel. Crossing the English Channel at any time of the year was always a risk. During the winter the risk was greater than ever.

This child was Matilda, the same Matilda that Henry and Robert of Meulan had been discussing. She was young and afraid but had no choice in the matter. Like all daughters of kings, she was merely a pawn in the power games that their fathers played. She was going across the waves to a land she knew nothing about with a language she could not speak and to a man she had never met and who was fifteen years older than her. Putting it bluntly, she was a broodmare whose only valued function in life was as a bargaining chip in the business of politics. Her sole purpose was to provide her future husband, King Henry V of Germany with heirs and her father with a strong alliance on the continent to aid in his struggles against both the Pope and the French. This king of the Germans was soon to become an Emperor but that is part of another story.

This marriage was to be Matilda's destiny; to become an Empress, hopefully with a bright, exciting future in front of her. As she stood on that cold day watching the sea roiling and crashing, being an Empress was probably the furthest thing from her mind. She just hoped she could contain her tears and would not be too sick.

Before she left, her mother, whom as we have already discovered, was, confusingly, also a Matilda, had spoken to her daughter about her destiny. The mother, Matilda of Scotland was the daughter of Malcolm II of Scotland and his Anglo-Saxon queen Margaret. Her marriage to Henry, the first of that name, of England in 1100 thus brought to Henry, the descendant of the conquering Normans a direct and politically desirable link to his wife's Anglo-Saxon ancestor Alfred the Great.

"You must always remember who you are," the mother told her young daughter as they stood waiting for the ship. "You are the daughter of a king as am I: you are the granddaughter of two kings and are the descendant of Ango-Saxons kings. You are a royal princess of the highest pedigree and you should never forget it. Let no-one treat you otherwise. Always do your duty with dignity and honour and never forget God." Her mother was a devout woman who had instilled the love of and duty to God in her daughter. "He will protect and guide you in all things." These words lodged in the young Matilda's spirit for the rest of her life. As she kissed her young daughter's cheek and bade her farewell at the Channel's shore, she could not know that she would not see her again.

Likewise, although she could not know it at the time, the young Matilda would inherit the outstanding talents of a mother who had been educated at the exclusive convents of Romsey and Wilton. In the matter of ruling, Matilda's mother was an important and active part in the administration of her husband Henry's realm when she served as a member of his Royal Court and on occasion, acted with what amounted to vice-regal authority in England while Henry was in Normandy.

These were all familial traits, both male and female that come into would come to play an important part in the coming life of this small child.

Chapter 6

Thomas Enters the Story

"Now," Brother Edward said to himself, "time for a new and important character to enter the story." He took up his jug and had a healthy drink of his small beer and a piece of bread and cheese to go with it. It was, after all, at least another hour before the mid-day meal would be ready. No need to starve to death. A man needs to keep up his strength.

In 1118 on 21 December a child was born, in London, in a house on the north side of Cheapside between Ironmonger Lane and Old Jewry which was within earshot of the busiest street market in the city. Against all the odds and through a remarkable chain of events this middle-class Londoner's child will rise to a position where he will become the equal of barons and knights, converse with kings and popes, and one day come to defy a king.

The house, like those around it, was built of wood and limestone with narrow, unglazed windows which would let in the sounds and smells of the city. The main living area was an open hall warmed by a central, stone hearth, with a private chamber to the side where the family lived, slept and entertained their closest friends and relatives. The house was approached via a gatehouse and was provided with an outdoor lavatory flowing into a cesspit.

The servants, who waited on the family and prepared their meals, slept in the hall. Beneath the house was an undercroft serving as a warehouse to store goods. The kitchen was outside in an annex to minimize the risk of fire. Water for cooking and washing was drawn from their private well. Soap, if it was ever used, was made from ashes and the occupants cleaned their teeth using green hazel shoots before polishing them with woollen cloths.

It was beginning to get dark, on that late winter's day afternoon when the child's first cry was heard. The father,

Gilbert called for wax candles to be lit and for the fire to be stoked up against the cold.

"Today is the feast day of St Thomas the Apostle" Gilbert announced to the household, "so we shall call my new son Thomas."

Gilbert Beckette, the new born's father had come to London from France some years before to carry on his trade as a cloth merchant. The Beckette family had originally come from the area around Rouen. Gilbert's wife, Matilda, the new born's mother was also of Norman ancestry, coming as she did from Caen. So it was that Thomas was brought up in a household that spoke mostly French rather than English although as he grew older Thomas would speak English more and more.

When he was a very young boy, Thomas had asked his father where his name of Beckette came from. "Was it because you lived near a town called Bec," he asked? His father had told him, "no, it was because one of our ancestors supposedly had a very small nose and was given the name 'Small Beak' as a joke and the name had stuck ever since but was now Beckette." Even at a young age, Thomas wasn't sure he should believe the story but he liked the tale non-the-less and would repeat it in years to come to amuse guests in his company. Thomas was showing early signs of the ready wit that would be a recognisable trait throughout his life. For what was to come, he would need a sense of humour.

"As men of the cloth," Brother Edward thought, "we should not believe in auguries and dreams as did the pagans of old but before he was born, some say Thomas' mother dreamed the river Thames was flowing through her body. Obviously, a strange, misguided woman, she dreamed that her baby was already out of her womb and as he lay on a purple blanket, looking up at the roof, the blanket unfolded by itself, overspilled the bed, then overspilled the room. She then found herself walking backwards, holding the hem of the blanket until she was walking to the rim of the universe among the moon and stars. Some say this was a dream foretelling that the greatness of her child would spread across the whole world.

"I think perhaps she had too much cheese before bedtime," the scribe mused.

Brother Edward interrupted this strange train of thoughts, thinking to himself, "I must put Thomas to one side for a time and come to an event that would have far reaching consequences for his future and that of all the others in the coming saga. This happened in the year 1120 when Thomas was only two years old, far too young to realise how what was about to happen would alter both the course of his future life and eventual death."

Chapter 7

The White Ship

"Picture the scene," he wrote. "On the bitterly cold but dry afternoon of 25th November 1120 Henry, the first king of England to bear that name, was in Barfleur along with his entourage waiting to take ship to England. The ground was still covered by a hard frost.

This was the main port in Normandy from which the crossing to England was and still is routinely made. It was reputed to be the port where the first Vikings to invade that part of the Channel coast had landed. They settled and gave the area its name, 'Norseman's Land'. It was the port from which Henry's father, the then Duke of Normandy, had launched his invasion of England 54 years before and it was a rock in the seas just outside Barfleur harbour that would change the course of both English history and that of Thomas of London along with it.

With the arrival of the royal caravan, it was a scene of bustling activity both on the quayside and on the water. The town's taverns and hostelries were doing good business. Stall holders and hawkers cried their wares to the throng of incomers in the hope of making as much from them as they could. Urchins and beggars pleaded for largesse from the richly robed nobles and their attendants and were mostly met with a boot for their troubles. The air was redolent with smells of the sea, people, horses, fish and cooking food.

"I wonder," thought Brother Edward, "if while he was standing on the dock at Barfleur, Henry reflected on how far he had come in the last few years? One brother hastily buried 'neath the soil in Winchester, another locked away safely in Devizes Castle, the lands of England and Normandy divided between those two brothers when his father had died now, united under his single rule. He must have felt pleased with himself." He went back to his writing:

Some would say it was a little late in the season to be crossing the Channel but the crossing had been made so many times that it had been deemed to be safe. Anyway, a crossing was what Henry wanted and he always got what he wanted. He was the King and not a man to be disagreed with if you valued your eyesight or testicles, as blinding and castration were two of his favourite forms of punishment for those who were rash enough to disobey his orders. Although he'd been given the soubriquet of the 'Lion of Justice' he routinely and frequently blinded or executed rebels and castrated thieves. He had even encouraged the governor of a castle to slit the noses and put out the eyes of two of his own granddaughters who had disobeyed him. Henry was not a man whose desires and orders were to be taken lightly. Like his father, Henry had a cruel streak but as we will see, a King who is to be successful needs that characteristic.

Henry's son and only legitimate heir, William Adelin, sometimes called 'the Atheling', the current Duke of Normandy, an ebullient, spoilt, fun-loving teenager, just seventeen and recently married, accompanied his father. They were in exuberant mood after a hard, but successful few months, quelling a rebellion caused by quarrelsome Norman nobles whilst at the same time, battling the land hungry King of France, Louis VI. The military campaign had resulted in an advantageous peace with King Louis and Henry was well pleased with the way things had gone. William, at just 17, had proved himself on the battlefield. His youthful, good looks and fine physique had made him the hero of the time. Someone to be seen in the company of. William was indulged by his father which only made the young man more precocious and self-confident than ever.

In a moment of unsolicited praise, his father had told him, "you have done well William, you will make me a worthy heir." William pretended nonchalance but was inwardly elated with such an accolade from his father.

"Thank you, father. I will do all I can not to let you down or fall short of the expectations you have for me." William knew that the future of the Norman line rested on his shoulders. Fortunately, they were broad and well-muscled.

Inwardly, William wanted his father on board a ship and gone. After the previous months of fighting, this was the time for

35

a celebratory party and as soon as his father was out of the way, he would make sure that the party began.

"We shall go on ahead in the Mora," Henry told his son as they stood on the quayside. "You and your friends can follow in the White Ship." He pointed to the sleek ship in the harbour. "I have spoken with her captain, Thomas FitzStephen, who tells me that he's the son of Stephen FitzAirard who piloted the Mora when it carried my father William to England and victory on Senlac Hill in 1066. He has offered his services and his new ship to me but I will sail in the Mora as did my father but I have granted him permission to take you and your friends across the channel for its maiden voyage. He assures me that she is the latest thing in sea-going transport, fitted with all the devices known to the shipbuilders of today. He boasts that she is the fastest ship on the seas so even if you leave after us, you will likely arrive before us. Whatever the case, we will see you in England."

The King and his party boarded the Mora and set out for the English coast. It would be the last time Henry spoke to his son.

As had been his plan all along, William chose not to leave immediately. "We'll have a drink and some merriment before we leave," he told his coterie of young, aristocratic friends. "We've got plenty of time to catch up with the royal party once we get to sea." When Prince William had arrived at the dock and being the celebrity he was, he was greeted with raucous cheering. The sailors had asked for drinks with which to toast him and William, being mightily flattered, obliged. He ordered three barrels of wine brought aboard to be shared between the crew. The casks of wine were soon opened and began to flow freely among not only the crew but also the party of armed soldiers who were to travel on the ship. As the party atmosphere began to take over, most of the passengers joined in the fun.

Young men, being young men, especially when showing off to the young ladies in the gathering, were soon indulging themselves to the full and set about the drinking with full gusto. Sailors, being sailors and being given access to as much free alcohol as they wanted, followed suit. Toast followed counter-toast as acts of bravado in battle, real or imagined, were recalled and it was late evening by the time William and his entourage were ready to give up the delights of Barfleur and set out across the Channel for home.

"All aboard," William was shouting, "onward to England." Some of the more sober, slightly older members of the party decided that the ship was too over-crowded with riotous and headstrong youths for their liking or indeed, their safety and decided to take different ships. Even then, in addition to the full complement of sailors and oarsmen, some 160 knights, nobles, ladies and all their servants were crowded onto the White Ship. All in all, by the time all the passengers were on board it was late in the evening and the White Ship was carrying almost 300 people when she left the harbour.

At the last moment, just before the ship sailed, William's cousin, Stephen of Blois, said he was suffering from diarrhoea and left for the shore with two of his men at arms. "Tell my cousin that I'm feeling too unwell to face the Channel and that I will follow later when I feel better," was the message he left as he descended the gangplank. The message never did get passed on and amidst the crush William certainly had not noticed Stephen leaving.

Stephen's bout of diarrhoea was to change the course of English history.

As was the custom, some priests had arrived and wished to bless both the assembly and the ship before she sailed but they had been mocked and insulted by the drunken passengers. They gave up trying and disgusted by the behaviour of the Prince's friends, took their leave. Thus, an unblessed White Ship sailed away from Barfleur harbour.

In their drunken state, the passengers were by now exhorting the oarsmen to overtake the Mora. "Come on you sailors, let us see what the ship can do or is all the talk of being the fastest ship afloat just a lot of hot air. Surely you can overtake an old scow like the Mora." The Captain, Thomas FitzStephen, his normal good senses and skills drowned in too much free wine ordered his crew to take up the challenge. His was the newest, fastest, sleekest ship afloat and he was going to prove it.

The oarsmen needed little encouragement and the White Ship sped across the water.

The night skies were clear and moonlit but it had become bitterly cold. The stars were clear and bright and Captain Fitz

Stephen could easily have set an accurate course using the Pole Star. Had fitzStephen not been as drunk as the rest of the crew, the White Ship would have, as usual, safely navigated the infamous waters around Barfleur harbour with its strong currents, submerged rocks and fast tidal stream. With a drunk captain and crew and the ship going at full speed they had managed less than a mile through these obstacles before disaster struck.

The safe passage out of Barfleur harbour is directly to the north-east, which should have been straightforward had the helmsman steered correctly. But urged on by both his captain and the passengers and in his haste to cut the corner, he steered too far north. The ship was caught on the notorious Quillebeuf Rock. With a terrible sound of splintering and smashing of timbers, the port side of the ship impaled itself on the submerged rock which ripped a huge hole in her side below the water line. Sailors tried to free the vessel with their boathooks, but the prow was stuck fast. Sea water poured in and within minutes, the ship was capsizing. Bodies were flung into the water. People had started to scream in terror. Few could swim. Panic ran through the stricken ship. Some in the water attempted to swim against the strong underwater current which swirled around the capsized ship and the submerged rocks. Most thrashed about helplessly in the maelstrom.

The water was freezing cold and weighed down with their clothes, most on board stood little chance of survival once they were in the waves. The night air was full of screams and cries for help but these were soon silenced as the sea claimed those to whom the voices belonged. Tales of mermaids and wild men of the sea or spirits lurking in the bodies of already drowned men filled the minds of the hopeless souls struggling to survive. The crabs and denizens of the deep would feast well for weeks to come.

Among all the panic, some sailors had managed to launch a single, small skiff. Somehow in the churning maelstrom it stayed afloat and miraculously its crew had managed to find Prince William clinging to a piece of broken decking. They hauled him aboard and started to row away. They were easily in reach of the shore if they pulled together and the heir to the throne would be saved but through the cries of the drowning souls, William thought he heard his half-sister's voice crying out for help.

"Turn back," he ordered the oarsmen, "we have to save my sister if we can." Turning back was the last thing the sailors wanted to do but if a royal prince commands you to do something, you do it. They did as they had been ordered and turned the small skiff about but as they once again came close to the capsized ship, survivors in the water and those clinging desperately to wreckage tried to climb into the small boat. It too capsized and was swept under the waves with all those in it.

At daybreak the next day, fishermen found only one survivor from the 300 people thought to have been on board clinging to a broken mast spar. He was a butcher called Berold who was owed money by one of the nobles on board and had gone on the ship to try and get his money back. He was just alive. He had survived the cold and the long dark night because he alone was clad in sheepskin and not the finery of others onboard. Once carried to safety and warmed before a roaring fire he was revived with soup and wine. He told his story of rescue to a large crowd and afterwards lived in good health for another twenty years.

Norman villagers scoured the beaches around Barfleur until they located the wreck. Using ropes, they managed to drag what remained of the White Ship ashore. Somehow, of all things, all the royal treasure the ship had carried was salvaged. No bodies. The search for survivors lasted over a week and in spite of generous rewards offered to experienced divers by the victims' relatives, few bodies were recovered for burial. But not that of prince William Adelin, Duke of Normandy. He was never seen again. Even then, after the creatures had feasted on them, most bodies could only be identified by their clothing.

On the south coast of England King Henry had landed around midday. It was getting dark and he was asking for news of the arrival of his children. "Where is prince William and his new wife," he wanted to know? "They should be here by now". He had no idea that disaster had struck his family.

Some of those who had friends and relatives on the White Ship had already heard the tragic news of the ship's sinking but were too afraid to give the news to the King so they kept their silence and the awful truth. Whilst they mourned and wept, they did so in seclusion and silence for fear that Henry would ask what ailed them. By the following day, the court knew that they could not keep the secret much longer as Henry was becoming more and more agitated, demanding news of his childrens' whereabouts.

Henry's nephew, Count Theobald IV of Blois-Champagne, using his initiative, arranged for a young boy to throw himself sobbing inconsolably at the king's feet. Henry, of course asked, "what ails you young man to sob so violently?" Then the truth was revealed. "I weep for your children Lord King. They are all drowned."

Henry was so traumatised and shocked by the boy's revelation that he fainted. He was carried by his attendants to his bedchamber, where he remained in seclusion for several days, grieving for his lost children, especially his only son and heir.

Once recovered from the initial trauma of his grievous loss, Henry knew he would now need to concentrate on a potentially catastrophic problem: after all his plans, all his work, there was now no obvious heir to the throne of England."

Brother Edward had written enough for the day and stopped at this point in his story. His eyes were drooping and his scrawny, bony backside, despite his fleece cushion felt like all the blood had been squeezed from it.

"At the end of his triumph, so recently enjoyed had come heartbreak at the hands of a jagged rock and youthful foolhardiness. His only legitimate son and heir swept to the cold depths of a grey sea to be eaten by the fish; a crown never to sit on his head. Even some of his unlawful children gone to the deep with their royal sibling. No-one left but a daughter to inherit that which he had so hard won.

"Tomorrow is another day and I will come to that part of the story when the lives of those living in England were turned upside down. A time when, as Thomas had been growing up happily in Cheapside in his loving mother's care, a crisis of national importance was brewing in Royal circles. The consequences for the country and everyone living in it were to be catastrophic."

Chapter 8

Who is to succeed Henry

After prayers and a decent breakfast Brother Edward was back at his bench. Prior Luc called in to see him.

"How goes it Brother?"

"Slow but sure," was the reply, "you can see from the sheets I have already written that progress is being made," Brother Edward pointed to the pile of manuscripts on the bench, "but I am only at the beginning. I am afraid it will be a long and sometimes tedious task so do not expect a finished book for some time yet."

"It will take as long as it takes," responded the Prior Luc as he left Brother Edward to his work.

"Now then, where was I? Ah yes, the White Ship."

After his only legitimate son William the Atheling drowned in the White Ship, Henry knew immediately that his royal succession would be in jeopardy. Who would succeed him as King of England and Duke of Normandy? What was Henry to do? Simple, within a year of the White Ship tragedy he had married Adeliza of Louvain who was young, attractive and hopefully, fertile. Although Henry was by now in his mid-fifties, he still thought himself more than capable of producing more children.

"God's teeth, I've fathered more children than I can count. Some say my bastards are as common as ticks on sheep, though not in my hearing, so fathering a few more, this time legitimate, will not be a problem. I suppose I should have produced more with my first wife instead of spreading my favours amongst all those others. Oh well, what is done is done. Let us get to it with a will. It is not, after all, an onerous task especially with such a young and willing bride." Henry was upbeat about his fecundity and was confident that he and Adeliza could soon solve the problem of the missing male heir.

This was not to be the case even although Adeliza accompanied Henry on all his journey around his domains in an effort to increase the opportunities for and chances of her getting pregnant. However hard they were trying the much-needed heir was not to appear. The situation was becoming desperate for Henry, forcing him to consider other options. Might there be a possible heir among his nephews? Whatever his thinking may have been, fate gave him a solution.

His only remaining, legitimate child was Matilda who for the last15 years had been with her husband in Germany and was now an Empress in her own right. As well as the genetics inherited from her astute and able parents, she had also learned the art of politics and of war at the side of and in the service of her husband, a skilled operator in the dark arts of political manouvering on all levels. She had served him in every way a faithful and loyal wife could; except in the most important. She had not provided him with the all-important son and heir.

Suddenly, Matilda's situation worsened in the worst possible way. In 1125, her husband, the Emperor, was wounded during a siege and died from his wounds. Now, overnight, with no children and thus no claims on the German throne, she became a spare part. There was nothing left for her in Germany and by the time she returned to England she had forgotten most of her native Anglo-Norman language and the customs of her land of birth were by now, all alien to her. For the second time in her life, she was a stranger to both the country and society fortune was forcing her to live in. To make matters worse, she and her father had not been on the best of terms but on her return to England there were efforts to make things better between them. They did not have much choice.

Within a year of Matilda's return, Henry had made a decision. Should he die without a male heir, then she, Matilda, was to be his rightful successor. Putting forward a woman as a potential heir was, to say the least, unusual and there was a good deal of opposition to the declaration. The conditioning and status of any woman was decided the moment a baby was pronounced as female! The situation was no different for Henry and Matilda no matter their royal blood.

Nobles, Barons and Bishops wondered if the king had lost his mind. "A woman in charge? Not while I breath," was the sentiment expressed by many. Henry was adamant and would brook no opposition to his wishes. To reinforce his will, he gathered all the Anglo-Norman barons together in Westminster during the Christmas of 1126 and made them swear individually, in public, that they would uphold Matilda as his legitimate heir. Equally importantly, they also swore at the same time, that they would recognise that any future legitimate children Matilda might have would be the next in line of succession after her.

The first to swear this oath of fealty to the king's wishes and to Matilda's right of accession was her cousin, Stephen of Blois.

This longer-term question of succession bothered Henry. He was now well aware of the problems caused by there being no obvious male heir. "You need a new husband, daughter," he told Matilda, "you can't remain single and childless. You must produce heirs to the throne. Therefore, I have decided that you will marry Fulk of Anjou's younger son, Geoffrey. I have every faith that he will provide you with the children you need."

Matilda was aghast. "You expect me to marry a mere boy of fourteen and only a Count to boot? I am 23 and an Empress do you really expect me to be bedded by a pimply youth. Apart from which, he will, as my husband, expect to become King of England when the time comes for me to ascend the throne as your appointed heir. Marrying this youth is beneath my Imperial dignity."

Henry had no inclination to hear any arguments. "You madam, Empress or not, will do as I, your King and father, command you. As for the possibility of the 'pimply youth' sitting on my throne I shall make it very clear that it will not happen. It will be your children who will be the heirs to my throne and not this Count of Anjou. Your husband he might well be but my heir, never."

The couple, despite Matilda's entreaties to her father, were married in 1128. The marriage, as Matilda had predicted, was not a happy one. The couple did not particularly like each other and within less than a year Matilda had left Geoffrey in Anjou and returned to Normandy. Fortunately for Matilda, her father Henry blamed the separation on her husband but by 1131 the couple were reconciled and as his reign was drawing towards its close, Henry himself was increasingly placing all his hopes on the birth of grandchildren.

Much to the pleasure and relief of Henry, Matilda then gave birth to two sons. Henry, named after his grandfather, in 1133 who was quickly followed by Geoffrey, named after his father, in 1134. King Henry was besotted by his new grandsons. He could see the security of his lineage made flesh and blood. The omens, however, were bad and during his final months, which he spent mainly hunting in Normandy, the chroniclers would record an eclipse of the sun, an earthquake and violent winds, all occurring within a few weeks leading up to the King's death, which they interpreted as a stark warning of evil times to come. How right they would prove to be.

The burning question of who was to succeed King Henry came to a head when he died on 1 December 1135. He had been on campaign throughout the autumn, strengthening the southern frontiers of his domains across the Channel against incursions by Louis of France and had then travelled to Lyons-la-Forêt in November to enjoy some hunting, still seemingly in good health. Once there, he fell ill apparently from eating too many Lampreys, a kind of fresh-water fish and was dead within the week."

"This seems like a good place to stop for the day," Brother Edward said, "I will leave it for another day to continue the saga. The next chapter in the story will be one of bloodshed and misery for the kingdom and its people."

Chapter 9

Stephen Grabs the Throne

It was some days later that Brother Edward was able to continue with his written history. He imagined an audience gathered in the cloister to hear the next part of his narrative. He spent so much time alone in the scriptorium that brethren passing by would often hear him mumbling to himself. In his head he addressed his imaginary audience. On his manuscript he wrote:

King Henry had declared his only legitimate daughter Matilda to be his heir. Despite his barons having sworn oaths to respect this, the succession was hotly disputed especially when Hugh Bigod, the Earl of Norfolk testified that Henry, on his deathbed, had released the barons from their oath to Matilda.

In contempt of their oaths to and the wishes of the now dead king many who had sworn the oath to uphold Matilda's rights to the throne now reneged on their promises. "A woman ruler?" they said, "ridiculous, it is only storing up trouble for the future. If you chose a Queen for England then you are also choosing a King for England. As a wife she must obey her husband: a woman must obey her husband, even if she be a queen. If we accept Matilda then we risk Geoffrey of Anjou sitting on the throne as our overlord. Never!" Opposition to Matilda taking the throne was growing.

Across the Channel in Normandy, Stephen of Blois, Henry's nephew and Matilda's cousin, hearing of both the King's death and the assertion that on his deathbed he had released those who had taken the oath to support Matilda, followed what now seemed an established family tradition. He wasted no time in sailing from Boulogne accompanied by his military household and with the help of his brother, Henry of Blois, who was the Bishop of Winchester, seized power in England. Crowds in London believing that he would grant the city new rights and privileges, proclaimed Stephen the new monarch and he had

45

himself crowned King on 22 December. His brother, the Bishop, completed the coup and delivered the all-important support of the Church.

"Although I have read in a chronicle," added Brother Edward, "that much was made of supposed bad omens when on the day Stephen disembarked in England there was 'a terrible peal of thunder, with most dreadful lightning, so that the world seemed angry at his arrival'.

"There is no getting away from the fact," Brother Edward continued, "that the simple reason for Stephen's success was that, since the death of Edward the Confessor seventy years before his arrival, the crown of England had been there for the taking each time the incumbent died. Anyone with a reasonable blood claim and the resources to back it up could make a legitimate attempt. As I have already said, being in the right place at the right time had worked before and it worked now. Stephen had all the advantages that came with being a legitimate adult male; and a legitimate adult male, moreover, who could talk smoothly, who could win people over with his genial and open-hearted nature, and who had influential supporters in the church. Still, the speed of his actions meant that there was a wealth of contemporary confusion about how events had transpired, and exactly what Stephen's justification had been. Perhaps the most obvious reason why Stephen was preferred by many of the bishops, earls and barons, who had originally sworn fealty to the king's daughter and her heirs, was simply that they could not bear the thought of submitting to the rule of a woman, whatever her lineage.

Matilda was not going to give up so easily. "My father gave his throne to me whatever that liar Bigod might say. I will not give up my birth right to England and Normandy which is rightfully mine to claim. I will not be cowed by deceitful, oath-breaking men. If they want my throne, they will have to fight me for it. I may be a woman but I am also an Empress who has been on campaign. I am no stranger to the battlefield. The usurper Stephen will pay for this treason with his head."

It would also have been in the back of Matilda's mind that Stephen had five legitimate children of his own, three sons and two daughters, so both England and Normandy would slip away from her father's line permanently if she did not take action.

Matilda appealed at first to the Pope against the decision that allowed the coronation of Stephen which she said had been illegal and then took more positive action by invading England from her base in Normandy to start what would become a prolonged civil war.

"But" Brother Edward asked himself, "what of our man Thomas whilst all this had been going on? I shall enlighten my readers so that they may know and understand that the path to sainthood is not always a smooth or easy one."

Chapter 10

Thomas, his early days

Taking up a clean sheet of parchment he continued with his writing:

The year would be about 1128 or so when our Thomas reached the age of ten and his father decided that it was time for the boy to leave the influence of his mother's apron strings. She was a devout and pious woman and Thomas doted on her but Gilbert, his father, knew that it took more than a religious, caring mother to prepare a boy for what he might face in the world outside the confines of the family.

"'Ere long Thomas you must make your own way in the world," his father told him. "I have been fortunate in business and have thus been able to accumulate some wealth and position."

They sat side by side in the house in Cheapside. Gilbert by this time, as well as his dealings as a cloth merchant, owned several properties in the city and the family were comfortably off thanks to the income those properties generated. In addition, he was a Sheriff of the City of London, a position which gave him much prestige.

They were speaking in Norman French, not only because his father and mother were both from Normandy but because French was the language of the better off classes. English was a tongue spoken by the Anglo-Saxon riffraff on the streets. "A good education will be your passport to success, so now that you have reached your tenth birthday your mother and I have decided that you will go to the school at Merton Priory in order that, that objective might be achieved."

"Thank you, father. I shall be a good and diligent pupil and endeavour not to disappoint you both." was young Thomas's reply. Inwardly the thought of leaving the comfort of his much beloved mother's side filled him with anguish. She spoilt and molly-coddled the boy and the thought of leaving that warm embrace was not one he enjoyed.

A few days after their talk and Thomas's feelings, not withstanding, Gilbert loaded his son's belongings onto the cart that was to take him off to his new life as a pupil at Merton Priory.

Until this point, Thomas's mother had been the driving force in his education and had, most likely, taught him to read before he left for Merton. He would not learn to write until he reached the Priory.

"God go with you my precious boy," his mother had cried, "be as one with the Lord and do not stray from the path of righteousness. Pray every day as will I." His father just waved and Thomas hid his tears and waved until his parents were lost to sight. He had never been away from home before and even more worrying, never away from his mother's care.

The Priory was an Augustinian establishment and had been founded by Gilbert, the Sheriff of Surrey, the year before Thomas's birth in 1117. It was only a journey of six or seven miles south-westwards from Cheapside. It rained all the way and young Thomas arrived soaked and miserable.

Thomas soon learned that the key to the Augustinian ethos was the pursuit of truth through learning. He studied the Trivium, which formed the syllabus of all formal learning, as it does now, consisting of Grammar, that being the art of inventing symbols and combining them to express thought. What we simply call writing. Logic, the art of thinking and Rhetoric, the art of communicating thought from one mind to another. Along with their theological studies these are the subjects that our young priory novices must learn to this day.

Thomas's masters were monks and as Thomas found to his cost, they most definitely believed that 'sparing the rod, spoilt the child'. Lessons were routinely and literally beaten into the pupils in their care. I think that the novices of our priory are lucky in that we are not quite so free with the stick as they are in some places but that does not mean that they will be spared a thrashing if they merit it."

Soon, Thomas had lost count of the times a monk would berate him with, "you, master Beckette, are a lazy boy who too often, neglects his lessons." The price to pay would follow swiftly and there is little doubt that Thomas was no stranger to corporal punishment during his stay at Merton Priory.

He told a friend one day, "I think I'm developing a leather arse." His comment was overheard by a passing monk who was quite happy to test Thomas's theory by beating him yet again.

Lessons were, of course, mainly in French but Latin was also in frequent use although Thomas was never particularly proficient at speaking it. Being a priory run by monks, church services were frequent throughout each day and were all in Latin as they are here so that although his conversational grip of the ancient Roman language was not good, his grasp of its meaning was sufficient to see him through.

Had he been at the school some five years earlier he would have had the pleasure of meeting Nicholas Breakespeare who was obviously a higher academic achiever than Thomas as he went on to be, thus far, our only ever English Pope when he took the Papal title of Adrian IV. He seemingly must have done better with his Latin and lessons at Merton than had Thomas.

Thomas did however meet one person at Merton who would be a thorn in his side for the remainder of his life and that person was Roger of Pont L'Évêque.

But now when he was a little older, perhaps 13 or 14 in the year about 1132, there was a downturn in the business affairs of Thomas's father's which forced him to remove his son from Merton Priory and move him closer to home. The school where he was now sent was in the precincts of St Paul's Cathedral where he was, once again, fed on an academic diet much the same as that which had recently been beaten into him at Merton. Whether his 'leather backside' situation improved or not we shall never know but he seems to have been happier being closer to home. More importantly, he was now able to see his mother on a daily basis so from that point of view, his day-to-day life improved dramatically.

After his return to Cheapside our knowledge of what happened to the now adolescent Thomas becomes a little more vague. Much of what I have related in my story has, up until now, been well documented by other writers of Thomas's life, most of whom it has to be said, have been clerks like our brothers here and which our novices are learning to become. Writing is a skill that will serve them well into the future and that is borne out by how Thomas progresses in his life in the near future.

There came a point in Thomas' life when he was about 16 or17, when he was sent to Paris for a short while to continue with his studies and in all likelihood it was not until he reached there that he learned to write skillfully. Where the money came from to fund this next part of his education is unclear and why he would go to Paris to continue his education in particular is also something of a mystery given how close he was to his mother. In this closeness to his mother and the concern she had for his moral well-being may lie the answer.

Rumours have abounded about this part in the young man's life and continue to this day. Although they are, to my mind at least," wrote Brother Edward, "all fabrication and an effort to besmirch the reputation of a saint who cannot now defend himself. But, as an historian, it falls to me to tell the story so that you as the reader can decide the veracity for yourselves.

It was at this time that Richer de l'Aigle, a Norman in his mid-to late thirties, came to stay in London to take care of some of his business affairs and while there, lodged with the Beckette's, having known Thomas' father when both had been in Normandy years before. Richer was of the aristocracy and it was his younger brother Geoffrey de l'Aigle, who had clung for his life to a spar when the White Ship capsized before succumbing to hypothermia and drowning. It was during the summer of what must have been about 1134 or 5 that he invited young Thomas to visit him at his country estate of Pevensey Castle in Sussex.

During diner one evening as the family sat around the table Gilbert made a point of introducing Richer to young Thomas.

"Well," Gilbert asked, "is he not a fine young man, well-educated and perhaps deserving of more than I, a merchant, can offer him in the future?" Was this Gilbert hinting at some possible preferment for his son?

Richer, with a glint in his eye that was not missed by Matilda, said he did indeed find Thomas to be a fine-looking boy who might enjoy spending some time at his castle learning some of the pleasures of the chase.

51

Thereafter, a friendship was struck up between the older man and the pubescent Thomas. Thomas it seems was dazzled by Richer, whose father had been a prominent courtier. Throughout one whole summer the two went out hawking and hunting together at Richer's castle at Pevensey, where they rode daily to the chase with hounds and hawks. It was without doubt here that Thomas got his first taste of the better things in life and pursuits that normally would be reserved for those of a higher status than a boy from Cheapside. Although his father was a Sherriff of the City of London and a successful businessman, he was not an aristocrat.

It would not be long before Matilda Beckette voiced her worries to her husband. "How can know for sure what the true nature of Richer's affections for our impressionable son is? What happens to our Thomas when he is at Pevensey under the influence of Richer? An older man, wise in the ways of the world and an adolescent boy. I am his mother and worry for my son's soul and do not want him corrupted and worry that the friendship may have become too intimate and their friendship become too intense."

"I think you worry needlessly my dear," Gilbert told his anxious wife, "but given the dramatic events that are taking place in not only in London but throughout England and that are rapidly reducing the country to chaos and added to the concerns you have for his welfare let us 'kill two birds with one stone' and remove the boy from both dangers. We can a afford it, so I suggest we send him to Paris to continue his education there."

Whatever his parent's reasons may have been for sending him to Paris, it was not that he should enjoy himself in the ways that he reportedly did. Despite his mother being a devout and pious woman and despite the fact that Paris boasted an idyllic setting on the banks of the Seine, it also had a much less wholesome side. It may be that his mother was removing her son from one set of temptations and introducing him to another."

"But" Brother Edward pondered, "how was Thomas able to live in Paris while he studied, surely the cost was more than a young man of his status could afford? Was Richer still involved somehow at a distance? But 'no' is the likely answer to that. The archives say his father paid for it all by way of giving his son an allowance whilst he studied abroad and would that not be a fine thing? To have a father able to afford that," Brother Edward said to himself and went back to his writing:

All good things must come to an end and in Thomas's case that happened when his father was forced to economise, perhaps even stop his son's allowance altogether. It would not have been cheap to keep his son in Paris. Thomas was supposedly in France to study but we know from John of Salisbury's writings and remember, he was there at the same time as Thomas, that like most young men he liked the good things of life and was determined to enjoy himself. Maybe during the time he had spent with Richer de l'Aigle he had acquired tastes that his father could no longer afford, especially hunting and falconry.

Although John of Salisbury, who became Thomas's lifelong friend, tells us that as a younger man his friend's character had been far from blameless. He had, John says, indulged in the rakish pursuits of youth, was proud and vain and unduly eager to be noticed. In the evenings students would meet to drink in the taverns which the locals called the 'devil's monasteries', where wine was served by the pot. Like most young men, and here, Brother Edward crossed himself at the thought of what he was about to write, sex was often on their minds and might readily be found in the taverns. "I do not like to believe that young Thomas would have allowed himself to be so corrupted by carnal desires even when he was younger. These would not be the traits I would want to associate with a man destined for sainthood. I do not like to think of him indulging in that depraved behaviour."

Although Thomas had potential, his quick brain and keen eye could not compensate for his laziness. For all his assets, whilst in Paris he appears to have been no more than a dilettante. Good-looking, smooth and ingratiating, he could be headstrong and a show-off. A Londoner born and bred, who considered the freedoms that he associated with civic life as a means of getting him from where he was to where he wanted to be, most likely after encountering Richer de l'Aigle, he had ambitions to put himself among the ruling classes. In his twenties and early thirties, he would still, in reality, be little more than a charmer: verging on the gauche, lacking ideals, mingling with the great and the good, imagining himself to be a young aristocrat whereas in reality, he was a newcomer and an outsider aspiring to be an insider.

Two years after Thomas had arrived in Paris, and when he was about twenty-one, a messenger came with the distressing news that his mother had died. These sad tidings brought Thomas back to London to be with the family.

Did he return to Paris you ask? The short answer to that question is no, at least not for a long time and when eventually he did, it would be amidst great pomp and ceremony.

By now his time in Paris and his sojourns with the wealthy Richer de l'Aigle had developed in him appetites for better things. In many ways it seems he had become somewhat foolish and vain and was intent on having fashionable clothes and manners that would mark him out from those around him. He adopted an air of refinement above his station in the society in which he was now living.

"You cannot go on like this Thomas," Gilbert admonished him whilst they sat in the garden at Cheapside. "You've been back from Paris for almost a year now so loafing about at home any longer than you already have done is not an option. Even if you wished to continue your studies and return to Paris it would be impossible for me to support you as I did before. The simple fact is that I am now retired and living only on the income from my rental properties, which after all these disastrous fires we have had in the city recently, leaves money short indeed. Thomas, you must grow up and take responsibility for yourself and get a job."

As it had been up until this point in his life, family came to the rescue once again. A relative, albeit a distant one, heard that Thomas needed employment and as it happened, he needed an employee who could both read and write. His name was Osbert Huitdeniers.

"Well Thomas, what do you think?" Osbert asked him, "your father tells me you would make me a capable secretary and clerk, of which I have need. My business is in finance, something it would do a young man no harm in learning. I may not be the most popular man in London at this time as it is known that I support the cause of the Empress Matilda over that of Stephen which is contrary to the position held by most Londoners. Be that as it may, it is a fair position which I offer you and you will learn much of value should you accept."

Thomas was in no position to turn down either the offer or the opportunity and accepted the offer without demur.

"This," Brother Edward reminded himself, "is another lesson in life which I would do well to remember. It is often, not how much you know as who you know, that will gain you advantage and position. In the case of Thomas, it was a family connection that supplied him with this first position. Without the shadow of a doubt, a degree of nepotism was likely to have been in action. Life has ever been thus."

"By now a young man, a contemporary account which I have read," Brother Edward continued, "describes Thomas as being tall and thin, with dark hair and a pale face that flushed red when he became excited. It is said that he had a memory which was both tenacious and prodigious, and that he excelled in both argument and repartee. He is also reported as having had a slight stammer which, when I met him much later in his life, I did not notice. Perhaps he had cured himself of it by then."

As I have already said, anyone who would have known Thomas at this time in his life would have thought him an extremely poor prospect for sainthood at any time in the future. Yes, he was bright and likeable, witty and charming with a taste, some thought, for things above his current station in society. Was he 'saintly' though? That is the question. At this time in his life the answer would have been, definitely not.

By now, the day was drawing on and the priory bell was sounding to bring the brothers and the novices to evensong. "I must stop for another day but whilst life was moving on for Thomas, ground-shaking events were taking place in the country and that is where my story will go on the morrow." Brother Edward dusted his manuscript and shuffled off to his devotions and his supper.

Chapter 11

Matilda Stakes her Claim

Brother Edward took up his story once again:

In the year 1135, the peace of Henry's reign that had been enjoyed by the people of England and Normandy for 35 years was dead and gone and it would be in very short supply for the next fifteen years as the English crown lost control of its territories. To add insult to injury, the Scots and Welsh used the opportunity to raid deep into England and capture or regain territories they had long coveted.

The ordinary man and woman in the land didn't really much care who was king, or for that matter, queen. The biggest problem with any civil war is that the protagonists on both sides devastate the lands and lives of the very people over whom they seek to rule. Most of the people in England and Normandy at the time and as they do now, live at a very basic level. In most cases, just surviving. Any damage done to lands and crops by marauding war bands has a significant, detrimental effect on their everyday lives. Added to which, there is no doubt, that what little money they might have was subject to regular extortion and theft. Any lack of stable government was just a signal for opportunistic and general lawlessness to abound. Which is exactly what happened.

"We peasants just get on with life as best we can which is never an easy task at the best of times but it gets a lot more difficult if we're forever being pillaged and burnt out by greedy, land-grabbing lords intent on self-aggrandisement," might have been a common thought at the time if peasants were allowed to have any thoughts of their own. Which they were not. Again, then as now, most were happy if they were left alone to deal with life the best they could.

When Henry had died, supposedly from eating too many lampreys, those fish which he had been told were not good for him, his legitimate daughter, Matilda, should have succeeded him. Despite the fact that the barons and bishops had all sworn an oath to uphold Henry's wishes that Matilda would have the throne on his death, many now reneged on their promise. Especially as Hugh Bigod, whose older brother William had perished on the White Ship, maintained that Henry had absolved the barons from their oath to Matilda on his deathbed. where Hugh said he had been present.

"Bloody Bigod," Matilda exploded when she'd heard that piece of news, "I'm told he wasn't even there but I suppose all the men will chose to believe that which most suits them most." Unsurprisingly, Empress Matilda was not to the liking of many of the powerful barons who preferred Stephen of Blois, now the wealthiest man in England, Henry's nephew, Matilda's cousin and hypocritically, the first to have sworn the Oath of Fealty to her in public.

Matilda knew full well that both in England and in western Europe, there were plenty of examples of women wielding power at high level but they had to approach matters differently from that of their male counterparts. The fly in this particular ointment was that while women could exercise authority, they had to do it on behalf of and with the permission of male relatives. This is what Matilda had done on many occasions for her now deceased husband, the Holy Roman Emperor, Henry V. Matilda had spent her entire life in royal courts and was not stupid. In many ways, she was already much more experienced in the qualities required of a monarch than Stephen.

Importantly, this was not what Matilda was attempting to do. She was, in effect, intending to be not a 'Queen' but a female King, something that had never happened in England before.

She wanted to succeed to the throne in her own right, to claim and exercise sovereignty on her own behalf as she maintained was what her father had wanted her to do. This disconcerted many of her male contemporaries mightily. Even a queen, it seemed, was incapable in their minds of being more than a political bargaining chip between kingdoms and a brood mare to bear the heirs of Kings or in Matilda's case Emperors which she had failed to do.

The one way in which Matilda could be sure of her position as queen, or indeed as a female king, was to have a crown set upon her anointed head in England, just as she had in Mainz back in 1110 and in Rome in 1117 when she had become both a queen and an empress.

She certainly made efforts to suppress her identity as the wife of a mere Count. She made her position clear and unambiguous to anyone who would listen.

She told her half-brother, Robert of Gloucester, who was to be her greatest supporter, "first and foremost, I am an Empress and will be recognised as such, even though to some this might hinder my cause and leave me, as a woman, standing alone and not one in the shadow of a husband or any other man. I will not refer to myself in any official document as the Countess of Anjou. I know this is a completely alien concept to the majority of magnates and churchmen around me and a difficult, if not impossible one for many of them to understand. The positive side is that it might help to alleviate the potential threat and any fears they may harbour of Geoffrey of Anjou ever ruling over England. While we talk of it, let no-one be under the false illusion that I am claiming the throne in the name of my son Henry of Anjou as a future heir. I will have the crown in my own right. The crown is mine by the will of my father the old King, whatever that worm Hugh Bigod might have others believe. I am sure in my own mind of what it is I need to achieve. Women have to learn to harness their power. It may not be easy in this man's world but it is just learning not to take 'no' for an answer. If I cannot go straight ahead to achieve my goals then I must find another route. Any uncertainty will erode my strength and resolve the way waves gouge at the rocks of a cliff and cause it to fall." Matilda was certainly a woman who knew what she wanted, what she was entitled to and would accept nothing else.

As the on-off civil war continued over the next decade and a half, the unscrupulous barons took advantage of the chaos to seize new lands, build castles and even went as far as to mint their own coinage, a sure sign of the King's loss of control. Something like that would never have happened in Henry's time. When he had found that some mint owners were both 'clipping' the coinage and adulterating the silver content he called them altogether from throughout his realm. He then cut off their right hands just in case any were tempted to continue their fraudulent practices."

"Just think about it," Brother Edward considered, "a woman, perceived as weak in body and weak in will. Would she be able to rule the fractious, turbulent lands that England and Normandy had become? With all the perceived frailty of her sex, could she possibly rule?"

He added, "the answer to that question was that ultimately, she would fail in her first objective but would succeed in the second. There is much of the story to come but for now, as usual, my hunger and age get the better of me and I must leave more of the story for another day."

Chapter 12

Stephen Grabs the Throne

Brother Edward was warming to his task and knew that a good story is held together by one question: what happens next? He was now reaching a part in his story which he knew should keep future readers captivated. Battles, bloodshed and daring escapes!

He started. "I have reached the instalment where the two main protagonists are facing each other across the Channel so what was to come next? The answer is that two cousins, Empress Matilda on one side and Stephen of Blois on the other, would be waging war for the futures of England and Normandy and only one of them could win. We need to remember that as the story unfolds in England and Normandy, government ceased with the death of the King. The anointed King, Henry, the first of that name, is dead so with no King, there could be no King's peace to be kept. With the barons and magnates uncontrolled, anarchy will reign. From now on, bandits and ruffians would roam the land at will. Nowhere would be safe."

Now then, what do we know of Stephen of Blois? He had a very decent pedigree as grandson to King William, the first of that name and nephew to Henry. Of course, if William Adelin had not drowned in the seas around Barfleur and the White Ship had not sunk then Stephen would almost certainly never have been king.

Stephen was said to be good-looking, pious, chivalrous, and charming to everyone, even poor people. "If he wanted to rally sufficient support around him in the coming decades," Brother Edward surmised, "he would need all those qualities. As we already know and most importantly, he was able get to England and the vacant crown before any of the other possible candidates and that included Matilda who was still stuck on the southern borders of Normandy. Oddly enough, she was there because she had been helping her husband Geoffery fight against her father whose crown she was now laying claim to.

Stephen had set sail for England in an effort to strike while the proverbial iron was hot and seize power.

"It worked for Uncle Henry so there's no reason why it won't work for me," was his thinking. "The Magnates in both England and Normandy like me, I've got the money and most importantly, I'm not a woman."

Put simply, he was geographically closer than his main rival Matilda. The small matter of a very public religious oath having been given by him to support her were now seen as no obstacle. Stephen's younger brother Henry, who just happened to be the Bishop of Winchester, not surprisingly in order support his brother's claim, argued that King Henry had been wrong to have forced his court to take the oath and that brother Stephen was justified in ignoring it for the good of the realm.

"The fact that Bishop Henry would probably do very well out of his big brother being King no doubt swayed the argument somewhat." Brother Edward added.

"Stephen also managed to persuade the royal steward, who had been present at the old King's deathbed, to swear that King Henry had in fact changed his mind and made him, Stephen, his heir in place of Matilda.

When the steward's testimony was backed up by Bishop Hugh Bigod who said he had heard the King say the same thing, it was enough to persuade many of the English barons to join Stephen in reneging on their oaths and support him over Matilda. But Stephen's grab for the crown was not all going to be plain sailing.

Nonetheless, although Matilda and her husband Geoffrey could not immediately get to England they took the opportunity to march into southern Normandy and seize the key castles around Argentan that had formed Matilda's disputed dowry and while they were at it, they pillaged the surrounding countryside which, in turn, alienated much of the Norman nobility and pushed them into Stephen's camp. Matilda was by now also pregnant with her third son so this may well have been another reason for her staying in the south rather than hurrying to England.

61

If Stephen could spot an opportunity then so equally could King David of Scotland who just happened to be Matilda's uncle. Whilst Stephen was otherwise occupied in the South, King David invaded in the North hoping to add a swath of northern England to his Scottish realm. Stephen responded to the threat and marched with his army, meeting David in Durham. They, being practical men, decided that talking was preferable to fighting and came to an 'understanding'. David retreated north but kept Carlisle as a small bonus for his endeavours whilst Stephen returned south and immediately began securing his power base there.

At the same time and in a clever and astute political move, Stephen granted the church more powers and as a reward for this the Pope, Innocent II, confirmed him as King of England.

Chapter 13

Matilda Claims the Throne

By the time 1139 came along the road to war seemed unavoidable. Matilda was by now a mature, skillful and shrewd leader who had the staunch support of her half-brother, Robert Earl of Gloucester one of the richest men in England who as well as being a talented, if somewhat devious politician, was also a warrior and general of some repute.

Having already taken sizeable chunks of Normandy, Matilda, at the head of an invading force and with Robert at her side, was ready to face Stephen in England. In the interim, she had even appealed to the Pope to reverse his decision of granting legitimacy to Stephen but the Pope refused. Even so, this would help create doubt around Stephen's rule.

Matilda was not going to take this situation lying down. She was furious and determined to launch this invasion into England to remove Stephen from the throne she thought rightly hers. "Had her father not told her he wanted her to be his heir?" Brother Edward asked himself

Whilst Matilda and her brother had been busy marshalling their forces in northern France in preparation to cross the channel, on the other side of the water, Stephen had also been keeping himself busy. To make sure he kept his supporters happy, he had been creating new Earldoms for loyal supporters and removing those who threatened or opposed his rule, all the while preparing his own forces for war.

Plans were ready and the stage was set.

When she left, her husband Geoffrey focused on conquering Normandy whilst Matilda crossed to England to take the kingdom and the crown by force from her cousin. She landed in England near Arundel where she lodged herself in the castle there with her stepmother Adeliza, declared herself the lawful Queen and so began the civil war.

Once recruited to the cause of his half-sister, Robert of Gloucester had set about talking round nobles and knights, persuading them with flattery and bribes to support Matilda.

The joint efforts of Matilda and her three principal lieutenants, Miles of Gloucester, Brian fitzCount and Robert Earl of Gloucester had initial success. By the time she had been in England a month she had established a secure base for her campaign, welcomed to her side a group of powerful men who would form the nucleus of her party and set the groundwork for a long-term campaign. But now found herself besieged in Arundel Castle by Stephen who had marched his forces to meet her.

Bottled up in Arundel Castle, Matilda was trapped and although not actually captured by Stephen, the would-be queen was, to all intents and purposes, his prisoner all the time she was besieged in the castle in West Sussex.

Fortunately for Matilda, King Stephen was altogether of a different character than was usual in his family antecedents. He was in many ways, the very opposite of both his uncle, Henry I and his grandfather William the Conqueror. Stephen had an attractive personality and was good natured and courteous but he had a fatal flaw. He was weak-willed and lacked resolution. He seemed incapable of enforcing strong law and order and thus, anarchy was to be the unavoidable result.

On the other hand, Matilda was shrewd and had spent her entire life in royal courts and was savvy to their ways and idiosyncrasies. In many ways, she was already much more experienced in the qualities required of a monarch than was Stephen. She knew full well that in both England and Europe, there were plenty of examples of women wielding power at a high level but was equally aware that being women, they had to approach matters differently from that of their male counterparts.

Matilda could only take as exemplars the rulers who fell within her own experience. Had not Bernard of Clairvaux advised Melisende, Queen of Jerusalem, to be more like a man in order to succeed?

"Consider this," Brother Edward advised his readers, "that Matilda's male relatives had proven themselves successful over and over again by not being gracious and forgiving of weakness in adversaries. On the contrary, they instilled fear in their enemies. Stern authority and ruthlessness had worked for both her father King Henry and both her husbands, the Emperor Henry and Geoffrey the Count of Anjou. When any of the latter had ever exhibited any mercy or generosity to adversaries, it was because they could afford to do so.

Matilda had seen for herself the way in which Emperor Henry had wooed the rich and powerful Italians by offering concessions during his stay there in the 1110s. Might this strategy work if she offered similar concessions to the Londoners whose choice of who they wanted as their monarch could decide the issue? But husband Henry had been a strong and established man as well as an emperor. Had he been an inexperienced boy, who would have been a reasonable comparison to Matilda being a ruling woman, his actions may have been interpreted as weakness and taken advantage of accordingly. Matilda's gender was always going to be against her. If she acted like a strong, ruthless man she would alienate people and be called arrogant, cold and heartless. If she acted as society expected a woman should, then she would always been seen as weak and not fit to rule.

In emulating the style of control she had seen in her father and first husband, Matilda forever suffered from gendered barbs saying that "she became elated to an intolerable degree of pride" and acted "with all the spitefulness of a woman".

If any of these comments about Matilda were to have been aimed at Henry I, or even at Stephen, they would have sounded ludicrous. Who would dare to criticise a king for arranging matters according to his own will, for walking confidently, or for speaking with a voice of authority? What was acceptable in a King was obviously not acceptable in Matilda, who in some eyes, was failing to exhibit "the modest gait and bearing proper to the gentle sex". The hypocrisy of these views is clear to see when at the same time, Queen Matilda, Stephen's wife, was being praised for being "a woman of a man's resolution." Added to which there was an additional complicating factor for Matilda: if she referred to herself as Regina Anglorum, 'Queen of the English', she would simply be duplicating the title of Matilda of Boulogne, Stephen's wife, who used the same title based on her marital, rather than personal, status."

"Having said all that," Brother Edward wondered, "can anyone ever conceive of the English people having a 'Queen' as Matilda envisioned herself being, at any time soon or if at all in the future?" His question being rhetorical required no answer. All this writing had given him a thirst so he took a drink of small beer from the jug at his side.

"Another problem," he continued after taking his quaff, "was the question of Matilda's position as a married woman and the very real fear in the minds of her detractors that her husband, Geoffrey of Anjou could end up as the King of England purely because he was her husband. To avoid any misconceptions, Matilda made her position clear and unambiguous right from the start and made strenuous efforts to suppress her identity as the wife of a Count and refused to sign anything other than as an Empress."

"Now," Brother Edward said, "in a stupid act of chivalry, generosity and reasonableness, a trait which I alluded to in the previous paragraphs, Stephen had released Matilda from her incarceration in Arundel Castle and by doing so would pay for the decision for years to come. He no doubt expected Matilda to be grateful for his beneficence but that was the mistake that truly plunged the country into an all-out Civil War from the point of her release. To make matter worse for Stephen, his barons quickly recognised these weaknesses in their King and rapidly set about exploiting them to their own advantage. Robber barons became a law unto themselves and built unlicensed castles from which they would terrorise the populace. All the time Matilda and Stephen were at each other's throats, the barons and magnates made free with the land and its people.

For her part, as soon as she was free, Matilda, rather than giving up and returning to her husband in Anjou, as Stephen had hoped she would, established a rival court in south-west England and carried on the fight against her cousin.

The war swirled on between them throughout the year of 1139 each of the protagonists making gains and then losses. Alliances with varying factions were made and broken but neither gained any real advantage over the other.

Stephen meanwhile managed to alienate the Church by refusing to accept their advice and appoint their chosen candidate as the new Archbishop of York, preferring to keep the position and monies accruing to the See for members of his family. He continued to make matters worse when he ordered the arrest of the Bishops of Lincoln, Ely and Salisbury for refusing to surrender their castles to him."

"We as men of the Church," Brother Edward opined to himself, "understand what an unwise course of action it is to make an enemy of God's servants."

Chapter 14

Lincoln

Brother Edward continued:

Those of you who have been paying attention to the story thus far will recall that in 1136, King Stephen had made a treaty with King David of Scotland after the latter had invaded the north of England. As part of that treaty Stephen had granted lands belonging to Ranulph of Chester to the Scots. As the reader can easily imagine, Ranulph was not happy with the arrangement and from then on, allied himself with the cause of Matilda.

By 1141 the situation in the country, as we have seen, had moved on and Ranulf determined to take Lincoln on behalf of Matilda thus taking his revenge on Stephen for the loss of his lands in the north. Ranulf was canny and selecting a time when he knew from his spies that the garrison in Lincoln was widely dispersed around the country, he sent his wife to the castle under the pretence of a friendly visit. Sometime later, Ranulf and three of his Knights arrived, ostensibly to escort his wife home. Once inside the castle they killed the unsuspecting guards and allowed their own men to enter and take the castle.

To the south, Stephen, alerted by townspeople of Lincoln loyal to him, sped north and quickly captured the town but not the castle where Ranulf remained. In an act of desperation and bravado Ranulf managed to escape and went to seek the support of Robert, Earl of Gloucester, Matilda's half-brother. Ranulf was determined not to be out done by Stephen once again. Having joined forces with Robert of Gloucester, who in addition to all his knights and men at arms, brought with him a force of Welsh archers and together they returned to retake the castle.

Basically, Stephen now had two choices. He could either stand and fight at Lincoln, or he could retreat north and leave the city to his enemies. Although there were some amongst his Council of War urging retreat, most of his advisors favoured fighting. The 'fighters' won the argument and Stephen mustered his men for a battle. To support him, the city sent its militia.

Whatever his personal failings as a King may have been, Stephen was a skilled soldier and capable general. His royal army drew itself up in a defensive position to the west of the city, outside its walls, despite knowing it had come equipped for a siege, not for open battle."

Brother Edward took pause. He was coming to an important part of his saga. Once again, he took a drink from his jug as if to fortify himself for what was to come.

"I have read the history books written by some who say they witnessed the battle," he continued, "and we are told that Ranulf and Gloucester debated how to go about attacking Stephen's defensive position and who it would be that would lead the attack. Ranulf wanted that honour saying, "Since it is through me that you face this battle it is fitting that I should bear the brunt of it and be foremost in the attack upon this faithless king."

Gloucester replied to this assertion with hard-headed realism. "It is fitting that you should have the honour of striking the first blow, both on account of your high rank and your exceeding valour."

"I think Gloucester was applying some flattery here to sooth what he would say next," Brother Edward wrote.

Gloucester continued to address Ranulf, "If it were a question of rank alone, no one has higher pretensions than me the son and nephew of mighty kings; and for valour there are many here would stand among the most renowned to whom no man living can be preferred. But I am actuated by considerations of a very different kind. This king has inhumanly usurped the crown and by the disorder he has spread has caused the slaughter of thousands and by the example he has set of an illegal seizure of lands has destroyed the rights of property. The first onset ought, therefore, to be made by those who have lost most and with whom the God of Justice will co-operate and make them the administers of just punishment."

"In other words," Brother Edward told his readers, "Robert wanted the first attack to be made by those who were angriest with the king and who could therefore be relied upon to fight the hardest."

"Unbeknown to Robert or Ranulf," Brother Edward then added, "just after dawn, Stephen had attended mass in the cathedral to celebrate the Feast of the Purification of the Virgin. As is the custom he, as the senior lay person present, was holding a ceremonial wax taper while Bishop Alexander began the service. As Stephen passed the taper to the bishop it snapped in half and went out. This caused Bishop Alexander to fumble the pyx containing the holy wafer, causing it to fall sideways on to the altar. Some say that these were signs sent direct from the saints or even from God of impending ill fortune. A rustle ran around the church as men and women glanced at each other. Notwithstanding these portents let us go back to the unfolding battle."

On the other side of the battlefield and having got his men into a good defensive position, Stephen's next task was to make sure that everyone understood what was required of them by giving a rousing speech. However, Stephen had a weak voice so he asked Baldwin fitz Gilbert to deliver the address instead. Baldwin exhorted the army by referring to the justice of their cause, the true claims of Stephen to the kingdom and the feckless faithlessness of Robert of Gloucester and Ranulf of Chester before winding up by flattering the great valour and skill of his men in battle. Even as the royal troops listened to the exhortations of Stephen's lieutenant the advancing enemy was heard approaching.

Seeing that Stephen was still deploying his troops Robert launched his attack with a cavalry charge aimed directly at the Royalist frontline. Immediately, William of Ypres, Stephen's mercenary General, launched a counterassault on Robert's Welsh archers with his heavy cavalry and had some initial success, driving the enthusiastic but poorly equipped archers back. Alas for William of Ypres and his charging knights coming down the hill there was something they had not seen. Earl Ranulf and his men had been closely watching the unfolding events. When the royal knights were too committed to the charge to pull out, Ranulf let out a cry and led his own knights forward. Ypres' knights were scattered after their wild attack on the archers, their horses were blown and they were distracted by their desire to slaughter the Welsh. They did not see Ranulf and his heavy horsemen coming until it was too late. Ranulf led his mounted knights in a compact body to strike hard into the exposed flank of the royal knights. William of Ypres and his cavalry were routed and he and what remained of his force fled the field.

"Imagine the battle," Brother Edward asked of his readers, "the horrors of war all around, sparks from the clash of helmets and swords; the fearful hissing of arrows and terrifying shouts and screams re-echoing from the hills and city walls. Many were killed, some fearfully wounded, and others carried off as captives. No mercy was shown them.

Amidst all this slaughter and bloodshed stood the King.

Stephen and his remaining men were soon surrounded as Robert's army surged around them. Cut off from the city and with no mounted knights in support, Stephen's fate was clearly sealed. His faithless Earls had left the field whereas Stephen showed great personal courage even although he must have known the game was up. Attacked on all sides, we are told that he continued to lay about him with his sword until it broke. Still he would not give in. Someone passed him a battle-axe; a fearsome weapon in skilled hands and King Stephen had been taught from an early age how to use it.

These great double-handed battle axes take enormous strength to swing and great skill to use properly. In the hands of a master it is a murderous killing weapon and Stephen was a master. The axe head has a wide blade on the end of a haft nearly six feet long. It is swung overhead, swishing around in a lethal figure of eight loop with the momentum of its heavy head keeping it constantly in motion. Men, even those in armour and their horses, could be sliced in two by a skillfully used axe without it seeming to lose any speed as its deadly arc continued its lethal course. Nobody could say that King Stephen was not brave.

His men fell around him but, in the end, Stephen was felled by a stone that hit him on the helmet, stunning him for long enough to allow Robert's men to take him captive. Until Stephen was finally taken some of his more loyal troops had continued to fight at his side. This may, of course, have been simply because they had no other option but to fight for their lives. They were surrounded and so completely hemmed in that retreat was

71

impossible. Most were slaughtered but a few lucky ones were allowed to surrender.

There is little doubt that Stephen was honest, brave and honourable but found it difficult to recognise duplicity or treachery until it was too late. He had trusted men he should not have done and mistakenly assumed that everyone would fight as well and as bravely as he himself had. To his credit, Stephen would never abandon a friend in trouble but this trait could also be his undoing. Unfortunately, he was never able to understand that men he thought his friends would abandon him or change sides as circumstances suited them.

The Battle of Lincoln may have been over, but not the violence. Earl Ranulf clearly held a grudge against the citizens of Lincoln and the city was to pay the price for having had the temerity to throw him out. He decided to treat the city as if it were a foreign town in enemy territory that he had captured rather than a town in England. He stormed into the city and let his soldiers loose to plunder the houses and the population as much as they liked. Robert made an effort to restrain Ranulf and his troops but to little effect.

Chapter 15

Matilda and the Londoners

Matilda now had her nemesis where she wanted him and this would be the lowest point of Stephen's reign and, at the time, looked very much like it might be the end of it.

Robert of Gloucester was somewhat more lenient when it came to his treatment of Stephen than his half-sister Matilda would have been. The king, for such he still was, was escorted into Lincoln Castle with great honour just as if he were a guest rather than a prisoner but a prisoner he most assuredly was. Matilda must have felt triumphant.

To begin with, Stephen was taken off to Bristol and a reasonably comfortable confinement at Robert's castle there. But Stephen's comfortable and honourable imprisonment by Robert was not destined to last long. He was escorted to meet Empress Matilda in the city of Gloucester where she gloated over her cousin, the prisoner.

"You have the gall to title yourself King. You are nothing more than an oath breaker," she told him. "I should have your head removed for your treachery but that would be too quick. Put him in the deepest dungeon they have in Bristol Castle along with the rest of the rats and vermin. While you are at it", she ordered the gaolers, "I want him weighed down with iron manacles and chains." Which is what happened.

Languishing in his chains in Bristol Castle, Stephen must surely have been haunted by thoughts of his uncle Henry's lifelong incarceration of Robert Curthose after defeating him all those years ago at Tinchebrai. He must have wondered if he too was going to die in this dungeon. Left to rot away in the chains that bound him.

As it was, King Stephen was to spend the next six months as a prisoner, locked up and in chains in Bristol Castle and in the short term it looked as though the Matilda had won.

Imagine the misery of King Stephen's situation. Iron shackles at his hands and feet, locked in a deep, cold cell with the water dripping down the walls and only the rats for company. It was still early in the year and the cold must have been unbearable.

Meanwhile, now that her rival was safely out of the way, Empress Matilda had herself elected Queen whilst she was at Winchester as was the custom at the time and a month later, she was on her way to London to prepare for her coronation. Matilda had sent orders ahead that she was to be crowned in Westminster Abbey at Easter 1141 but Archbishop Theobald of Canterbury was not certain this was a good idea so he summoned a council of bishops and barons to discuss the situation. The claims of Matilda to the crown were, he said with some courage, not certain. A brave or perhaps foolish man. Without Theobald to do the anointing there could be no coronation. Imagine Matilda's rage when she heard that the Archbishop had put an obstacle in her way. She was, after all, her father's daughter and had, it seems, inherited his temper.

Whether Archbishop Theobald of Canterbury was merely sitting astride the fence by being unwilling to declare Matilda queen immediately or whether he genuinely felt that Stephen was still the rightful King can never be known. If Stephen was still the King then he would need to be consulted before the Archbishop could commit himself to the coronation of Matilda. What Theobald did, was take a delegation of clergy and nobles, to Bristol to see Stephen in his dungeon. Again, Stephen's lack of ruthlessness showed itself. He agreed that, given the situation, he was prepared to release his subjects from their oath of fealty to him thereby clearing the way for the new coronation.

If Matilda thought that she was at last going to become the Queen, as she had always asserted was her right then she was sadly mistaken. Forces loyal to Stephen and his wife Matilda had remained close to London making the citizens there fearful about being caught in the middle of the two warring factions. Londoners believed that there existed an ancient custom that allowed only them to choose who should be sovereign and that now was the time to assert their right. They claimed, 'it was their right and peculiar privilege that if their king died from any cause a successor should immediately be appointed by their own choice'. Unfortunately, Matilda had done little to endear herself to the citizens. They said that they had found her to be too self-interested, vain and aloof and feared she would impose taxes on them to pay for her wars which was another strong reason for not backing her bid for the throne. The Londoners made their feelings clear by taking direct action and in a popular uprising drove Matilda and her supporters out of the city and locked the gates behind her.

Matilda and her followers made a chaotic retreat from the city leaving behind them the proposed coronation and any thoughts of an end to the war. As soon as they were gone, London opened its gates instead to forces loyal to Stephen."

Chapter 16

Matilda escapes from Oxford

Brother Edward began again the next day in the scriptorium which had dawned fair and warm after a satisfying breaking of his fast and a leisurely walk through the cloister garden. He began:

By now the civil war was at its height yet neither party was able to gain an advantage over the other. Both had suffered from the vagaries of fate in the previous few years which had alternately put them ahead of, and then behind their rival. Stephen had been captured by Matilda's army at Lincoln and still languished in his dungeon at Bristol Castle. Matilda on the other hand had been recognised as "Lady of the English", but not as Queen and had then been chased out of London by its belligerent citizens. Throughout the country there was no doubt a common thought amongst the barons and bishops that with the King in prison and unlikely to get out again they had a free hand to do whatever they liked. Which they did. They raided and pillaged, continued to build illegal castles and some even minted their own coins. The country was in a complete sate of turmoil. It was said that "God and all His saints were asleep" during these grim years.

Matilda, after her escape from the London mobs had gone to Oxford and had chosen it as her new headquarters. It was a city well-defended with both rivers and walls protecting it and was also strategically important as it was at the crossroads of the country, east to west and north to south.

Now Brother Edward wrote: You will recall that William of Ypres had made a hasty withdrawal from the battlefield at Lincoln. He had, however, despite seemingly abandoning his leader to his fate, remained loyal to the cause of King Stephen. Having escaped Robert's clutches at Lincoln he used what remained of his mercenaries as the nucleus of a new army. What happens next is just an example of how confused and unreliable alliances and loyalties had become in this turbulent period.

After Lincoln fell to Robert and Matilda, Henry of Blois, the imprisoned king's brother and the Bishop of Winchester, had given his oath of fealty to Matilda. He did this in return for her assurance that she would give him control over the Church. Then, when Matilda was forced from London, Henry, the double-dealing bishop, once again changed sides and went back to his brother's cause. In retribution for this betrayal and duplicity, Robert and Matilda laid siege to Winchester where they in turn found themselves surrounded when William of Ypres and an army loyal to Stephen arrived.

Robert and his army made an attempt to escape the clutches of William's troops but as it sought to cross the River Test, Ypres attacked with skill and daring, destroyed most of the fleeing army and captured Robert himself. During the confused fighting Matilda somehow managed to make good her escape and made her way to Oxford

"As with the battle of Lincoln," Brother Edward wrote, "I have read eyewitness accounts of what has become known as the Rout of Winchester. This is the story they tell:"

There was chaos all around, shields and coats of mail and arms of every kind lying strewn on the ground; sometimes costly cloaks and vessels of precious metal, with other valuables, flung in heaps, offering rich pickings to those scavengers who appear on a battlefield as soon as the contest is over. The field was full of the dead and dying, too badly wounded to move, or just fainting from weariness and at their last gasp. These men lay at the mercy of the human vultures come to rob them and the crows and magpies come to eat them. Such a rout is terrible and wonderful at the same time.

Matilda must have returned to Oxford greatly shaken by the rout of Winchester and worn out almost to the point of utter collapse. Her fortieth birthday, which it was in that year, came and went in a much less positive manner than her thirty-ninth. She had lost her main source of support and military strength with the capture of her half-brother Robert so she took the risky but inevitable course of action by agreeing to the exchange of

Stephen for Robert. For the time being, the status quo was thus re-established.

Free once again and with Matilda thinking she was secure in Oxford, Stephen believed that all it would take to win the war decisively would be to capture Matilda herself. Having raised a large army in the north he moved south to put his plan into action.

Stephen's army approached Oxford in late September taking Matilda's small force by surprise. The approach to the city was blocked by rivers and waterways but not to be thwarted, Stephen swam his army across. Those defenders that were not killed or captured retreated into the castle where Matilda was now ensconced. Although Stephen now controlled the city, he knew he was unlikely to be able to take the castle by force and even with the latest in siege technology which he had brought with him, he knew it would be a long, hard wait before Matilda was starved out.

After nearly three months of siege, conditions for the garrison in the castle must have been dire, Matilda would have been cold, hungry and desperate. Most of Oxford had been reduced to a smouldering ruin, the bombardment from Stephen's siege engines was never ending, and the blockade was complete. Since the siege had started, no supplies had got through to the castle and food and fuel were running out. Matilda had been completely cut off from the outside world for months and had no idea whether help was on its way or not. Faced with these stark realities, it is not surprising that she should decide that there was nothing for it but to take matters into her own hands and escape if she could.

Brother Edward was coming to an exciting part of the story. Like most men, he enjoyed a good escape story of derring do and was eager to write as to whether Matilda was going to make it or not.

"He carried on writing:

It was early on a December evening that Matilda supposedly crept out of a postern gate in the castle wall and across the snow-covered fields and the frozen river. There is a story that says she escaped by shinning down a rope made of white sheets from Saint George's Tower.

Brother Edward thought to himself that this was overly romantic and most unlikely to be true.

However, it remains a fact of history that she did indeed escape. They say she was dressed all in white to camouflage herself in the deep snow that lay all around. Using stealth, she managed to pass through Stephen's lines undetected and made her way to Abingdon where she was safe. Oxford Castle surrendered to Stephen the following day. He was furious when he found his prey had escaped his trap.

With both antagonist free once again anarchy, turmoil and violence stalked the land. The civil war was far from over and would rage on for several more years yet.

"So much writing," Brother Edward said. As usual, he thought he was talking to himself but any passer-by would have heard him. "I am in need of a break from all this excitement, my backside is numb and my stomach is rumbling." Not much changed in his life.

As he cleared his desk he thought, "what of Thomas of London during these times of trouble? Where does he enter the story? Good and pertinent questions which I shall address on the morrow. I will begin to write on the progress and whereabouts of Thomas next time but now, as I said, my old bones need rest," and with that, he wandered off in search of first food and then sleep.

Chapter 17

The Anarchy Drags on

Last night when he had finished his day's work Brother Edward thought that it was now time to bring Thomas back into the story. On reflection, however, he realised that he must first tidy up the loose ends from where he had left the story the night before. Thomas of London would have to wait a little longer. Taking up his story of the war between Stephen and Matilda he wrote:

The war by now had degenerated into a stalemate with Matilda controlling much of the south-west of England, and Stephen the south-east and the Midlands. Both parties were rooted more or less in their original position, hardly different from the situation in 1139 when Matilda had first invaded: it was as if Lincoln, Winchester and Oxford had never happened. The town of Devizes was providing her with a centre of power and administration from where, acting as the rightful monarch, she granted charters and received vassals. She even continued to have coins minted that bore her image as Queen.

Large parts of the rest of the country were in the hands of local, independent barons acting as they wished and if she had not realised it before, she was certainly aware that after her narrow escape from Oxford it was highly unlikely that she was ever going to sit upon the throne herself.

"I suspect," surmised Brother Edward as he wrote, "that she might, by now, have admitted defeat, at least to herself in the battle over who would rightfully succeed her father Henry, bearing in mind that by this time, Stephen had occupied the throne for nearly a decade."

Now the question was not whether Matilda would ever be Queen but who would reign when Stephen died? In this cause, Matilda would fight to the end to make sure that it would be her son Henry FitzEmpress, soon to be Count of Anjou and Duke of

Normandy as and when his father Geoffrey died or chose to pass on the titles."

Whilst Matilda had been fighting for survival in England, Geoffrey had secured all of Normandy west and south of the Seine and by 1144, he had crossed the Seine and entered Rouen. It was here that he had assumed the title of Duke of Normandy. Matilda meanwhile had remained in Devizes but her half-brother Robert had gone to Normandy to fight alongside Geoffrey which is where he first met the young Henry.

"It is at this point in the story," Brother Edward announced to his readers, "that our present King, Henry, the second of that name, first visits these shores."

When in March 1133 Geoffrey and Matilda's first son was born at Le Mans, the capital of Maine, Henry's succession strategy seemed to have paid off. As we have seen, in honour of his grandfather, the baby boy was named Henry. The place of his birth was highly symbolic, given that the county of Maine lay at the heart of a long dispute between the ruling families of Anjou and Normandy. In this young boy lay the hope that enmity could be set aside, and peace be brought to the troubled region. Another male heir, Geoffrey, was born in June the following year and a third son, William, would appear after their grandfather's death in 1136. The oldest boy became known as Henry FitzEmpress and represented a more acceptable future option for the throne of England than his mother. Matilda though a formidable woman, was, still a woman. A powerful familial bastard in the shape of Henry's half-uncle Robert or the charming outsider, Stephen of Blois would always seem more acceptable options. Henry, the first of that name, was overjoyed at the birth of his grandson and spent some time at Rouen celebrating the birth where once more, he forced the barons to swear an oath recognising Matilda as his heir.

At this point, the chances of the infant Henry FitzEmpress fulfilling his grandfather's wish and succeeding to Normandy and England looked bleak, especially given that Stephen and his wife also had a son, Eustace, born in 1130. More pertinently, most of the cross-Channel barons clearly preferred being ruled by the House of Blois in preference to the House of Anjou and the pretender Geoffrey.

Now, compared to the 14-year-old 'pimply youth' that Matilda had married, Geoffrey had grown into a handsome, red-headed, jovial man and a great warrior. Here was someone who would give Stephen a stern challenge if he wanted to hold on to his territories in Normandy. All who met him agreed that he was charming and good company on the surface, but that his cheerful disposition was merely a mask that hid a cold and calculating character. He derived his nickname, 'Plantagenet', from a yellow sprig of Broom blossom that he wore in his hat. A plant known locally as the 'planta genet'.

From an early age, Henry FitzEmpress, as the boy was styled, was affected by his parents' struggles to win England and Normandy, as well as the fact that they spent little time together. Theirs was, after all, a marriage born out of diplomatic necessity that no one, including the couple themselves, were ever really comfortable with. For the first few years of his life, Henry was looked after in his mother's household, mainly in Anjou, although he would have been present during her attempts to win over the Norman barons. Once the succession crisis broke, it is probable that this young boy provided a more acceptable prospect as overlord to many of the Norman barons than did Matilda or Geoffrey.

When he was slightly older Henry undertook a formal education that included classical training, with knowledge of reading and writing in Latin and was based primarily in his father's court of Anjou. Then in 1142 or 1143, after the final conquest of Normandy had begun in earnest and Matilda had established a firm base in the south-west of England, Henry was invited to join his mother.

At about this time, Robert, the boy's half-uncle, had been sent on a mission to Normandy to try and persuade Geoffrey to supply Matilda with troops and arms with which he could return to England and once again, thus reinforced, take the fight to Stephen. In this, he failed but the one decision Geoffrey did make was to allow Robert to take the young Henry into his household and begin his training as a knight and future King. Although Henry was only nine years old when Robert returned to England, he took the boy with him to visit Matilda, where his arrival added a whole new dimension to the war for the crown.

This somewhat risky decision to take the boy to England was at the insistence of Geoffrey, although his mother Matilda would, in all likelihood, have been equally keen to have her son with her. Henry was a stark reminder to the barons of England that the old King, Henry, the first of that name, had a living, direct, legitimate, male descendant. Henry's stay in England was soon over and he returned to his father in Anjou. By the time he returned, his father had almost completed the conquest of Normandy.

It would have been during the period after Normandy had been captured that young Henry started to learn the art of government at first hand. Here he began to benefit from closer proximity to his father as he consolidated his hold on the Norman administration, watching and learning about the key figures at court in preparation for his own future career as its leader. Indeed, it is possible to detect some later character traits from influences in Henry's early upbringing in his father's court, such as a love of intellectual discourse, encouraged no doubt by his tutors, absorbing his military skills, flashing temperment and red hair from his father.

Brother Edward reflected on the difference between the nascent king's upbringing and his own. "Being the second son of a farming family, I was always destined to go into the Church. My oldest brother would get the land which only left the life of a clerk to me unless I wanted to become a squire to some local knight and work my way up from there. Never having been a lover of the martial arts, the peace and quiet of a clerics life had much more appeal. Now here I am having got my wish, sitting hunched over a parchment for hours on end, an aching nether region and failing eyes but still alive, clothed and reasonably well fed. On reflection, better than the other options, the life of a farmer being too arduous and that of a knight too dangerous. Anyway, enough about me. Back to the story."

Chapter 18

Henry and his Mother Disagree

Henry of Anjou now fourteen, which was the same age his father had been when he had married the widowed Empress Matilda. This fourteen-year-old had not only inherited his grandfather's name but also his stocky, thick-set build and fiery temper. From his father, as we have seen, he inherited red hair and an even quicker temper. Like both, he was strong-willed and full of boundless energy. He would rise before dawn to hawk, hunt and train at arms with his retinue of knights. His legs were already becoming bowed from long hours spent in the saddle. He was a young man in a hurry.

That day, when he came into his mother's presence, he'd been out riding and hawking since dawn and was dirty and smelly but that was not unusual. He was not a boy concerned with his looks or style of dress. Fashion meant nothing to him. Comfort and practicality are what were important. Noises of men-at-arms training in the courtyard came through the windows. The clash of steel-on-steel reminding them both that they lived in violent and troubled times.

By now, Matilda was world-weary! She'd endured almost 20 years of war and political mayhem and now she just wanted to live and die in peace. Stephen ruled and there was nothing she could do about it. It was now a waiting game.

Without preamble Henry told his mother, "I shall go to England and smash this usurper Stephen". She immediately disagreed.

"No, you won't" she said, "and I'll tell you why. You're fourteen and too young, you don't have an army and more importantly, you have no money so an invasion of England is a stupid, almost childish idea. I forbid it and that's final!"

Stung by the implied barb of 'childish', Henry snapped back at his mother, his face suddenly flushed and angry. "You will forbid me nothing!" She was aware of his volatile nature but the sudden outburst took her by surprise.

"Be calm Henry" she admonished, "you forget that I am both a Queen and an Empress and will speak as I choose, especially to an adolescent boy who is still but a prince. You would do well to remember that I have been fighting Stephen for years so I know what I'm talking about. In time you will be King but not yet. To attack Stephen now will only serve to antagonise him and may even prompt him to greater efforts to eradicate you as a future threat to his own son Eustace. I would live to see you become a king, not a corpse on a battlefield being picked at by the ravens. Stephen is a fearsome opponent with years of battle experience and has some of the greatest knights in all Europe to call upon to do his fighting for him. No Henry, you must curb your impetuosity and wait a while longer for your destiny to be fulfilled."

These were words that the young prince had no wish to hear. His mother may just as well have been talking to herself but she carried on anyway.

"Haste is the curse of youth and will only lead to misfortune. Be patient and think on your history. Learn lessons from that. Learn from your grandfather. He was known as 'Beauclerc' for good reason. He knew how to fight when he had to but more importantly, he knew how to use his brains to get him what he wanted. However, for all his brains, he wasn't perfect, if he had been, we wouldn't be in the mess we're in now, although the tragedy of his legitimate son William being drowned in the 'White Ship' when it sank in the English Channel can't be blamed on him. That can be blamed directly on stupid drunkenness and youthful folly, something I'm advising you to avoid.

"Had your grandfather not been so lax with disciplining his son and teaching him responsibilities instead of over-indulging him, I'd not be fighting to be Queen of England and you would be my undisputed heir but not to the throne of England. If fate had not played its hand and killed his only legitimate son, you would never be more than the Count of Anjou."

These were words Henry had no wish to hear. "If haste is for youth," Henry replied, "then waiting is for old men. I've heard all your stories of escaping from Oxford Castle in the dead of winter, of how you wore a white cloak to camouflage yourself in the snow as you crossed the frozen Thames, of all the battles you fought with the usurper Stephen and look where all that's got you. Cooped up in Anjou, just waiting for him to die. He's sitting on my throne which he's sat on for too long so whatever you might have to say about it, I'm not going to sit on my arse any longer doing nothing."

Matilda despaired of him. He had inherited both his grandfather's and his father's temperament, a toxic mixture and she realised that there was little she could do to control him. Her worst fears were shortly to be confirmed.

As she suspected, her words of wisdom had gone in one ear and out the other of Henry of Anjou. He had no intention of sitting still any longer and letting Stephen the Usurper, for that is how he thought of him, rule as King Stephen of England.

Chapter 19

Henry, the Count of Anjou Joins the Fray

There can be no denying that young Henry had a reckless side, something he had in all probability inherited from his grandfather which is why in 1147, still only fourteen-years-old, he defied his mother and decided to intervene in the war in England. He abandoned his studies, hired a band of mercenaries on the promise of future payment from campaign plunder and accompanied by his small household, sailed for England. Here he was, completely ignoring Matilda's wise advice and landing in England in command of a tiny army intent on removing the accursed Stephen from the throne. Apart from anything else, this was an adolescent youth, full of masculine rage taking on a mature, battle hardened warrior. It was only going to end one way. The meagre forces he had brought to accomplish his avowed task were wholly inadequate to challenge Stephen's established hold on the kingdom.

Within only a few weeks he found himself abandoned by his men mainly because he was unable to pay them but just as likely because the mercenaries he had hired now knew there was no chance of success, plunder or glory of any kind and the very real possibility of getting themselves slaughtered.

His first course of action was to appeal to his mother and then to his half-uncle Robert for the money he needed to get him out of the hole he had dug himself into. Both, unsurprisingly, refused him as neither were in favour of his hairbrained escapade in the first place and had told him so. He knew it would be waste of breath asking his father.

Then, in a touch of breath-taking cheek, Henry, instead of surrendering, showed some of the daring and determination that would later make him a great king. He simply sent a secret message to Stephen offering to withdraw to Normandy if the King would send him the money to allow him to do so. Even more surprisingly, Stephen, in yet another of the displays of the leniency and misjudgement that had allowed the Anarchy to take hold in the first place, took up the offer and paid for Henry's journey back from whence he had come.

Whether or not Henry was grateful for this show of magnanimity mattered not. He had got what he wanted and thus would live to fight another day.

"If Stephen was fool enough to let me off the hook then I'll make sure he lives to rue the day. Kings need to be ruthless and unmerciful otherwise they are taken advantage of, or worse still, taken for granted."

Henry would live to be both a ruthless and unmerciful King in the years to come and no-one ever took him for granted and got away with it.

Four months after Henry's return to Normandy, his half-uncle Robert, his mother's military commander and greatest supporter died. She decided that without his armed strength on which to rely there was nothing to gain by staying in England so in early 1148 she too left England and returned to Normandy.

Chapter 20

Henry Tries Again

From now on, if Henry wanted to claim what he believed was his rightful inheritance, the throne of England, he would have to fight for it himself which is why two years on he returned to England. The lessons of his first failed invasion had been learnt and this time he made Scotland his first point of landing where he made an alliance with his great uncle King David of Scotland.

Henry, as the potential heir to a kingdom needed, if possible, to be given the honour of being knighted by someone of royal rank. This, he rightly supposed, would mark his coming of age and once that objective had been achieved, he could no longer be treated as a boy. This then was the reason for going to Scotland where great-uncle, King David, duly obliged his young kinsman and knighted him. This formally brought him into the ranks of military commanders, and whilst he was at it, he made an alliance with Stephen's old enemy and adversary, Ranulf of Chester, he of the Battle of Lincoln where the Stephen had been captured. Henry was actively laying the ground for his undisputed accession to the English throne.

His goal of knighthood having been achieved over Whitsun at Carlisle, which great-uncle David had gained as part of his treaty with Stephen some years before, Henry was rubbing Stephen's nose in his previous miscalculations. "That should get Stephen's hackles up," Henry thought to himself and sure enough, Stephen immediately riposted by having his own son and heir, Eustace, knighted.

The chess game continued but early in 1150, Henry still lacked the necessary resources to strike a decisive blow against the King and found himself defeated once again by an army led by Stephen. Deciding that common sense dictated what should happen next, he beat a hasty retreat to Normandy where at the age of seventeen, he acquired his first territory.

Even if Henry's campaign had no discernible impact in England, his authority and leadership had impressed his parents. Geoffrey declared his son to be 'of age' and, with the support of Matilda, in whose name he had governed, he transferred the government of Normandy to Henry in a ceremony held at Rouen, and thereafter Henry adopted the traditional title of 'Duke of the Normans' as his great grandfather William, the first of that name, had done.

To say the least, King Louis VII of France was unimpressed by this handing over of power in Normandy. Instead of recognising Henry as Duke, Louis formally proposed that Stephen's son Eustace should be considered the lawful ruler of Normandy. Eustace did not then hesitate in joining forces with the king of France to wage war against Normandy and the Angevins. This long-drawn out war of succession had truly become a family affair.

On a hot summer's day in September 1151, Geoffrey travelled to his headquarters at Le Mans in the county of Maine where he stopped to bathe in the cool of a forest pond. Unfortunately, the welcoming coldness of the water led to a chill, and he died at the nearby Château-du-Loir. He was only 39 years old, a relatively young man. On his father's death, Henry inherited Normandy, Maine, Touraine, Brittany and Anjou and for the first time unified all these territories under one ruler and found himself head of the family.

"So," thought Brother Edward, "the family feud was now being continued by the younger generation." He dusted his manuscript, wiped his quill, blew out the candle and went, as usual, in search of food.

Chapter 21

An End to Anarchy

Duke Henry was in Normandy where he was making ever more threatening preparations to invade England but despite this, Stephen refused to give up on his plans to have his son Eustace confirmed as his successor to the English throne before Henry could act to foil him. To facilitate this, he summoned Archbishop Theobald and all the bishops in England to him in London in early 1152 and demanded that they crown his son in his place without delay.

Putting himself in severe danger of incurring the King's wrath, Theobald refused, politely, but firmly,.

Theobald was no doubt as acutely aware as was Stephen that Henry was imminently expected to arrive in England with his army. Theobald knew that if the church took sides now, it might not only prolong the coming conflict but more importantly, if it chose the wrong side, then it would be inviting the possibility of the victor's vengeance. It was also possible that the archbishop, being a man of wisdom, might have decided that it was time for the church to step back and keep out of the storm that looked likely to be coming. He could have been thinking that by not taking sides it might force Stephen and Henry to find some lasting resolution that would give them both what they wanted without any loss of face and thus bring an end to this hated pointless war.

King Stephen had the ability to make people like him but seemed incapable of making them obey him. This was not a trait for making him a strong, effective ruler. When it came to getting soldiers to fight for him it caused him severe problems. In the main, soldiers will fight out of fear, or rage, or greed for plunder but rarely because they find their leader a charming fellow. The result of this was that even though many owed Stephen their allegiance few were prepared to fight for him. If a King has no home-grown soldiers to fill his army then his only recourse is to hire expensive foreign mercenaries which is what Stephen did. Yet another course of action he would come to rue in the coming years.

To add to his woes, in May 1152, Stephen suffered a huge personal blow. His wife of twenty-seven years, Queen Matilda, died. She was only in her mid-forties and had been the King's greatest supporter throughout his reign. Her death was totally unexpected when she was taken by a sudden fever at Hedingham Castle in Essex. Stephen arranged for her to be buried at Faversham Abbey, which they had founded together some years earlier.

Brother Edward paused in his writing to reflect on what Stephen must have felt. "I grieve for the man," he thought, "I have never been married but to have someone so close to you taken without warning must have been hard for the man to bear. Imagine what a setback that must have been to a King struggling to keep a grip on his realm." Brother Edward, despite his brief empathy for Stephen, carried on with his task:

Stephen decided that he would pre-empt any invasion by Henry and take the fight to Henry's allies in England and the first target on his list was Wallingford, the castle to which Matilda had first fled when she escaped his clutches at Oxford. Since 1139 Stephen had already made two failed attempts to take the castle there and this would be his third attempt to reduce this stubborn outpost of Matilda and Henry's supporters.

The Castellan of Wallingford had been Matilda's staunch supporter Brian FitzCount. He had developed the fortifications at Wallingford making it one of the most powerful castles in England but Brian had recently died. His absence may have led Stephen to believe that the castle might now fall giving him a significant tactical victory before Henry could arrive to relieve the siege.

By now, Stephen knew the futility of attacking the fortress head-on having tried and failed twice before. Instead, he ordered the building of a counter castle across the river at Crowmarsh. Then blockaded the river Thames to prevent supplies from reaching Wallingford, and the siege was begun. Trapped inside the castle was Roger of Hereford, another of Matilda's allies, who tried to break through the blockade but without any success. Stephen settled down to starve the castle and its occupants into submission.

Eventually the castle garrison was unsurprisingly running very low on food and Earl Roger suddenly made Stephen an offer. He said he would transfer his allegiance to the king and fight tirelessly at his side if the king would help him recover his castle at Worcester from Waleran of Meulan. The prospect of gaining the allegiance of one of the principal supporters of Henry in England on the eve of the expected invasion was too much for Stephen to resist. Leaving some men to continue the siege of Wallingford, Stephen took the rest of his army to Worcester, where alongside Earl Roger, he laid siege to the castle

Once again, Stephen's own devotion to honour and chivalry had blinded him to the glaringly obvious. It was a trick. Roger, after leaving Wallingford with Stephen, immediately sent a message to Henry telling him that, "if he had any regard for his own supporters or cared at all to recover his kingdom, he should return to England with all speed". Stephen soon became aware of Roger's trickery, left the siege of Worcester and made a hasty return to Wallingford. Before he left he ordered some of his men to stay behind so that Roger could not claim he had been the first to break their pact. To add insult to injury, as soon as Stephen was gone, Roger negotiated with those inside Worcester and the castle surrendered to him.

In the second week of January 1153, Henry set sail from Barfleur for England intent this time on taking his kingdom. This would be different from his previous attempts. He was a man, no longer a boy. He was Duke of Normandy, Duke of Aquitaine, Count of Anjou and he was determined to be King of England before the year was out.

Brother Edward took a long drink of his small beer before continuing. All this writing was thirsty work. He continued to write of Henry's return:

On the feast of Epiphany a small squadron of ships appeared off the Dorset coast probably at Weymouth or perhaps Poole. Their exact point of landfall is not known. What is known for a certainty is that from this small fleet emerged young Henry and a fighting force of perhaps fifteen hundred men.

Rather than heading directly to relieve the besieged Wallingford Castle as had been expected, Henry instead went to Devizes and from there, struck at Stephen's important outpost at Malmesbury. As the townsmen flocked to defend the walls Henry's men began to undermine them whilst at the same time he sent others with ladders to scale them. His archers all the while firing volleys of arrows into the town to terrorise the citizens.

As Brother Edward wrote of what followed a chill ran down his spine at the thought of the carnage and sacrilege that was about to take place in a priory filled with monks much like himself. He calmed himself and wrote:

The walls were soon breached and Henry's troops rampaged into the town and began committing terrible atrocities. Many fled to a church which contained a priory of monks living according to monastic rule into which the attackers burst. Not only did they plunder everything they could lay their hands on, but they also murdered the monks and priests wherever they could find them. Not satisfied, they went on to pillage more churches, murdering anyone they could find in Malmesbury. Henry had just ordered the castle to be encircled and besieged when King Stephen arrived with his army in an effort to relieve the town and its castle.

By then, neither side it seemed wanted to carry on the fight and all that happened was a stalemate.

With the two opposing factions sitting looking at each other they somehow managed to open negotiations as to how they could resolve the stand-off. Finally and to everyone's relief, they arrived at the sensible conclusion that Malmesbury Castle was not worth spilling anymore blood over and should be demolished because they were no longer prepared to fight each other for it.

"The Lord does indeed work in mysterious ways," sighed Brother Edward as he wrote these lines. "Perhaps common sense does exist after all."

After Malmesbury, sometime towards the end of July or the beginning of August, Henry decided to move his focus to Wallingford to relieve the ongoing siege there as it had been almost six months since he had been begged for urgent assistance by those trapped within its walls. When he finally arrived, the first thing he did was assault the counter castle Stephen had built at Crowmarsh to blockade the river Thames and although successful, the weariness with the fighting experienced at Malmesbury by both sides persisted.

Although Henry and Stephen had finally met head-on and now faced each other with their armies on either side of the Thames at Wallingford they showed every sign of being happy to dance around each other rather than engage in a battle. It has even been mooted that Stephen and Henry had a private meeting at a narrow section of the river, away from prying eyes.

"I wonder," thought Brother Edward, "if they had both come to the conclusion that no-one could be trusted other than themselves and that the only way out of the impasse they found themselves facing was to talk to each other man to man?"

Suddenly, whilst the two armies stood looking at each other, everything changed. Stephen's son Eustace died unexpectedly and his death immediately and radically altered the face of the conflict. With Eustace gone, no longer a possible heir to Stephen, there was a glimmer of hope by which a final and lasting peace might be brought to England. Stephen had, after all, been fighting for most of his adult life and if he fought on, what would it be for? A throne for a son who was now dead? In the aftermath of the King's tragedy, Archbishop Theobald, saw a new chance of peace. He had always been considered neutral, and now made a serious effort to bring the two warring sides together in the hope that they could come to mutually agreeable terms for a cessation of hostilities.

At last, in November 1153, Stephen and Henry were finally persuaded to meet each other at Winchester to try and find a lasting, amicable solution to a situation that had lasted for almost 18 long and bloody years.

The agreement they reached was a simple one. In an assembly of bishops, earls and other magnates it was agreed that Stephen would rule the country for the rest of his life, and when he died Henry would succeed him. It was even suggested that Stephen formally adopt Duke Henry as his son. The treaty was to be guaranteed by the Church, which undertook to punish any breach of it with excommunication and at Oxford in January the English barons duly did homage to Henry whilst at the same time, reserving their allegiance to Stephen during his lifetime.

It must have seemed to everyone who heard the news coming out of Winchester that it was too good to be true. Could the Anarchy truly be over? Stephen and Henry went so far as to spend Christmas together in London, and after Stephen led Henry through the streets, the Treaty of Westminster was promulgated, giving final form to the agreements reached in Winchester.

Now in his late fifties, Stephen was at last able to enjoy his position on the throne unchallenged and it was said that 'it was as if he began to reign for the first time'. There were apparently some of Stephen's long-term supporters who feared for their positions once Henry eventually ascended the throne but the principal magnates were only too relieved that matters had been settled and order was now in the land.

Stephen made a triumphant progress through the north of England, but the unhampered enjoyment of his rule was to be short lived. In October he fell ill at Dover with a bowel disorder but in the end, he had probably just had enough of life. He was by now an old man. When it became clear that he was dying his old friend Prior Ralph of Holy Trinity, Aldgate, was called to Dover to attend him at the last.

As well as Prior Ralph, Archbishop Theobald seems to have also been in Dover as Stephen lay dying and when he died, it was Theobald who sent word across the Channel to Henry. Stephen's body was taken to the Cluniac abbey he had founded at Faversham and was buried there in the choir alongside his wife and son. Theobald then immediately travelled to London where he took over the temporary administration of the country while he waited for the return of the new King.

Henry appeared not to have learned, or at least not taken heed of his family's history at times like this. He made no immediate effort to return to England when news arrived of Stephen's death. It was a risky decision. His mother's late arrival had cost her the throne, whereas the speed of action of both his grandfather and that of his recent enemy Stephen, had gained them both a throne. Henry must have felt supremely sure of the security of his inheritance. Of course, he might have simply been waiting to see whether anyone would dare to challenge him. Was he daring possible enemies to show themselves now, or forever remain silent under his coming rule. Henry did not sail from Barfleur, the place where it all started, until 7 December. He was duly crowned at Westminster Abbey on 19 December 1154.

Now the second of that name, Henry was King of England, Duke of Normandy, Duke of Aquitaine and Count of Anjou. He now ruled over an empire that stretched from the Pennines in the north of England to the Pyrenees in the south of France. He was 18 years old.

"Well," Brother Edward congratulated himself, "that is a fine end to this part of the story and I can now move on to the next which is telling of the amicable and then terrible association of two men. One of these men we now know had become our King and indeed, still is. The other a lowly clerk working for Archbishop Theobald whilst that man had been negotiating with King's. None other than our man Thomas of London."

He put down his quill and rubbed his bleary eyes. "that will have to wait for the morrow to be told. Now I must eat.

Chapter 22

Thomas Begins Work for Theobald

Prior Luc once again enquired of Brother Edward how his writing progressed. The older man was somewhat annoyed by the question which he took, rightly or wrongly, to imply a criticism of the speed at which he was working.

"Do you fail to understand that it is a laborious process," he retorted with an edge of anger in his voice? "I am working as fast as I am able. My environment is ill-lit and mostly uncomfortable. It is an arduous task that you have assigned to me. Perhaps if you were to undertake it yourself you might better realise how difficult is the work. My back aches interminably and my eyes grew weaker by the day. Sometimes it feels like torture on my old body."

The Prior was taken aback by the outburst, "Brother Edward I assure you I meant no criticism. I was merely enquiring as to how the work progressed. If my question implied dissatisfaction with your work it was not meant thus and I beg you to accept my apology for any hurt you perceived."

Brother Edward looked slightly abashed. "No," he said, "it is I who should apologise to you for my surly response to your simple question but there is no denying that I find the work physically wearying. On the other hand, I find it mentally stimulating and have no desire to stop the work if you are happy to allow me to continue."

"Then," Prior Luc replied, "continue you shall and with my blessing," and with that, left the old monk to bring his story up to date.

Brother Edward started his new day with a new chapter. "Now I must bring Thomas of London back into the story after having concentrated so long on all that had been going on between Matilda and Stephen." He reflected on the fact that he had himself lived through the Anarchy and everything that it had wrought upon the land and thinking to himself of how the ordinary people suffered during Stephen's 19- year rule. He felt himself fortunate to have been spared most of the misery by being, as he was, cloistered in the Priory.

"In the days of Stephen," he remembered, "it felt like there was nothing but strife, evil and robbery throughout the riven land. How quickly the great barons and land-holders realised how mild and good- humoured Stephen was as a king. How slow he was to punish the transgressions they committed and failed to inflict retribution; they happily committed all manner of horrible crimes. Castles were built without his authority and the unhappy people of the country were forced to labour on those castles. When the castles were built, their owners filled them with private armies and mercenaries to terrorise the population even more. I heard stories," Brother Edward recalled, "of how anyone believed to have had money were seized, whether they were men or women and then tortured to get their gold or silver. Some they say were hung up by the feet and burned and smoked over open fires. They strung them up by the thumbs, or by the head, and hung coats of mail on their feet to stretch them beyond endurance. They tied knotted cords round their heads and twisted them until they entered the brain. They put them in dungeons where there were adders and snakes and toads and so destroyed them. All these things I have heard and of course, many thousands starved to death."

Brother Edward felt a great sadness as he thought of that part of his life through which he had lived. "I know not how to tell of all the atrocities nor of all the cruelties which were wrought upon the unhappy people of our country. I do know that never should a country endure such great misery and never did the godless act more vilely than they did."

Putting these thoughts aside, he returned to writing of Thomas:

When last we encountered him, he was a young man living in London with his parents but pushed into employment as a clerk to a friend of his father's, Osbert Huitdeniers. He would now be about 23 years old and the year about 1143. At this time in his life, he titled himself plain Thomas of London, son of a city merchant. He must have been in London at the time when Matilda arrived for her coronation and would have witnessed first-hand the population rising against her when she was forced out of the city. Perhaps he was even in one of the mobs that pushed her out although as we've seen, his employer, Osbert, was one of the Queens few admirers in London at the time so perhaps Thomas stayed his hand and remained neutral.

It would seem that young Thomas, by the time he had been in the employ of Osbert for two or three years, had begun to find the work humdrum and unexciting and once again, nepotism and fate would take a hand in his life. He got his next chance mainly through influence rather than by his own merits.

Sometime in 1145 two brothers from Boulogne, Archdeacon Baldwin and Master Eustace, both lodged with the Beckettes when they visited London. As a further quirk of fate, both worked for Theobald, who just happened to be the Archbishop of Canterbury. Friends in high places indeed.

It was said that it was that whilst staying with Beckettes they heard Thomas bemoaning his dreary situation. "All I do all day is fill in dusty old ledgers. I need to do something that stretches my capabilities more. I'm just not being used to my full potential." Even at this stage in his life, Thomas obviously had a high regard of his own worth. Perhaps being a clever and astute young man with burgeoning ambition, Thomas took the opportunity offered by the two brothers' presence in the house to advertise himself as someone looking for advancement.

The brothers took the offered bait. "Why not seek the preferment of the Archbishop?" Baldwin suggested. "My brother Eustace and myself could put in a good word for you. The Archbishop is always in need of bright, literate young men to surround himself with."

Thomas did not need telling twice and with the recommendation of the two brothers from Boulogne in his pocket, wasted no time in visiting Theobald at his manor of Harrow, only a few miles north of London. Amazingly, after a brief conversation, Theobald was so impressed by the charm and intelligence of the young Thomas that on the spot, he offered him a post as one of his ten or so clerks. In spite of his own confidence

100

in his abilities Thomas must have been surprised at this sudden turn of events as it was well known that the Archbishop's staff included some of the ablest scholars in the country.

Thomas had just made one of the most critical choices of his entire life. He was now going to be moving in a much higher circles, both academically as well as socially, than he had been accustomed to up until now. Did this upward move worry him? Probably not although he was no longer in his old world of fellow-Londoners, citizens, merchants and their employees. Now he would be rubbing shoulders with bishops, clergy, church courts and their officials. Besides his fellow-clerks, his immediate circle included the archbishop's cross-bearer, a chancellor, two monk-chaplains, a butler, a dispenser, a chamberlain and a steward. They were upstairs and below stairs were a master cook, an usher, a porter, a marshal and numerous minor functionaries such as grooms, purveyors, janitors, bakers, carters, washerwomen and carriers. The Beckettes in Cheapside no doubt had servants but nothing on the scale he would now be experiencing.

The surroundings in which Thomas now found himself, that of Archbishop Theobald's court, could be likened to a combination of a university, monastery and lodging-house all rolled into one for ambitious, talented, young men. Theobald himself has never been regarded as much of a scholar in academic circles but he was most certainly a generous patron of learning and clever in his choice of acolytes, who were for the most part, unlike him, extremely clever. However, he had spared no expense in equipping his staff of bright young things with a library regarded as one of the finest in the whole of Christendom.

To begin with Thomas must have found it a struggle to keep up and he appears to have made little or no attempt to hide the fact that, in comparison to those around him, he was not so well learned. "In fact," Brother Edward remembered, "I read somewhere that when he began his apprenticeship with the Archbishop he was 'raw and modest'. He certainly had a lot to learn, since while at Paris he had studied the liberal arts, he had not studied Roman or Canon law, the subjects he would need now if he were to advance. To rectify this, Theobald assigned him a tutor, most likely the same master he had employed to teach his nephews. Quite a privilege and accolade for one so recently employed.

But, Theobald, expected his clerks to work as a team, suppressing individual ambitions for the greater good of the whole. They were meant to be collegial and mutually supportive, whereas Thomas was naturally competitive, flamboyant and hungry to succeed. A difficult circle to square.

Even with this show of preferential treatment, Thomas began his new career at the bottom, assisting his fellow-clerks with the legal and administrative work in which they all shared. A novice in legal affairs, Thomas was most likely assigned tasks in the clerks' office that included filing documents and taking witness statements. "He must have sometimes thought that he might well have been back as a clerk to Osbert," thought Brother Edward as he stopped to replenish his inkhorn. Once that was done, he took up his quill and continued to write:

In spite of Thomas' fears, his new master clearly recognised that the 'new man' had more to offer, which was, after all, why he had offered him a position in the first place. He had obviously seen something in Thomas that greatly impressed him and had the young clerk marked out for greater things. For certain, Master Beckette had to acquire the basic skills Theobald thought he needed for his future. Therefore he wasted no time and sent him off to learn from the masters of the law schools at Bologna and Auxerre which is where he was to spend the next year.

Whilst he in Bologna it was rumoured that he had acquired a reputation as having a taste for ladies and a bit of a scoundrel although he was also considered a somewhat solitary man which is perhaps why it is difficult to get at the truth of what really went on while he was there. What we do know about him for sure is that later in life, it was common knowledge that he drank cider rarely and wine in moderation although he did develop a liking for fine wine when he did drink it. More usually, it would seem, he drank small beer or wine diluted by water. If he were under pressure, even these could upset his stomach which is maybe the reason he did not indulge in the copious quantities of alcohol that many of those around him did.

"This report of him being a womaniser seems strange," Brother Edward speculated, "as I have read in many accounts of him being described as chaste by which I take to mean he was free from all taint of lewdness or salaciousness. Primarily chaste implies that he refrained from acts or even thoughts or desires that were not virginal or sanctioned by marriage vows. Methinks that this adjective was being accredited to him after his sojourn in Bologna and not before." Whatever the veracity of his research into whether Thomas was or was not purer than driven snow Brother Edward continued with his narrative:

When he left Bologna Thomas travelled to Auxerre, near Sens in northern Burgundy where he continued his study of law and it was there, possibly for the first time in his life, he took his studies seriously. Throughout his life his severest and most unrelenting critic, of whom he went in fear, was himself.

"I suppose," Brother Edward surmised, "that fear of a return to Theobalds household and staff not having learned anything and with a reputation as a philanderer would have had a devastating effect on his career. In reality, it probably would have ended it and Thomas was sagacious enough not to let that happen so he threw his energies into the task of going back knowing a lot more than when he left."

Thomas was clever enough to know that the knowledge he would need to enable him to keep up with his contemporaries could not be assimilated in only twelve months so he probably took short cuts to getting what he needed.

Brother Edward thought he knew the answer as to what Thomas would have done. "We in the Priory use Summae or 'cribs' of classic textbooks such as Justinian's Institutes rather than reading the complete original which takes much longer. This is enough to give us the fundamental principles we are trying to learn and sometimes, by stripping out the refinements from the originals, makes it much quicker and easier to grasp." He felt sure that this is what Thomas would have done.

However accurate Brother Edward's thoughts may have been, Thomas returned to England a new man and over the next nine or so years, would come to witness and in part help to shape, a fundamental change in the relationship of King and Archbishop that was to influence him for the rest of his life.

As well as an increase in status and knowledge, as Theobald's clerk, Thomas had also gained admission to the higher social circles that had appealed to him since he had spent his school holidays in the company of Richer de L'Aigle at Pevensey.

"Since bishops and archdeacons often enjoyed hunting and hawking, and still do," Brother Edward thought somewhat primly, "it is a fair assumption that he began keeping his own falcons while living in the Archbishop's palaces and was beginning to get a reputation as someone with a liking for fine clothes and the grander things in life. None of which would have endeared him to his peers or many of those above him who would have viewed him as a pretentious upstart."

With those thoughts, Brother Edward stopped writing to sharpen his quill which was in danger of leaving ink blots on his expensive parchment. His back seemed to ache perpetually these days so he stood and stretched it while he attended to his nib. When he had the point as he wanted, he resumed both his seat and his work. First he decided, "who then was this Theobald of Bec, now the Archbishop of Canterbury, who was such a patron of clever, ambitious, young men?"

Chapter 23

Theobald of Bec

Theobald had first entered the abbey and monastery of Bec in Normandy as a young man, where he became the Prior in 1127 and was then elected abbot in 1136 after which he had been chosen as Archbishop of Canterbury only a year later. Theobald had no important family connections to advance his career and few clerical allies so his election was probably influenced by the reputation of his Abbey which had already produced two archbishops of Canterbury, Lanfranc and Anselm.

Initially, his Archbishopric was to be overshadowed by the King's brother, Henry of Blois, bishop of Winchester, who had secured for himself the office of Papal Legate which gave him powers equal or even superior to those of the Archbishop.

"No point in being the King's brother if it did not get you advancement," thought Brother Edward.

Politically, Theobald was a cautious conformist, a highly competent administrator but not a great spiritual leader. To begin with he was generally obedient to King Stephen but that was a situation that was not going to last and his relationship with his King was to become turbulent, not helped by continual challenges to his authority from Stephen's younger brother, Bishop Henry who thought it was he who should be the Archbishop of Canterbury and not Theobald.

Theobald's actions in the coming years after his inauguration as Archbishop are inextricably intertwined with the history of Stephen's ascension to the throne, the Anarchy and all that followed it.

Even after the Battle of Lincoln, with Stephen held in captivity by Empress Matilda, Theobald did not immediately join her cause. Being a man of honour, he said that he would need to talk to Stephen, to whom he had given his oath of fealty, before switching sides. He consulted Stephen in person, then in prison at Bristol Castle, where he secured the captured King's permission to change allegiance. By an odd quirk of fate, his rival for the see of Canterbury, the King's brother, Bishop Henry, had already changed sides.

"So much for loyalty and brotherly love," thought Brother Edward. "Just another example of Stephen's lack of ruthlessness."

Theobald then travelled to Winchester for a Legatine Council called by Bishop Henry in an effort to depose his brother Stephen and crown Matilda as queen. The attempt failed and those gathered at Winchester then had to flee at the arrival of forces loyal to Stephen. This was when Matilda's chief supporter, her half-brother Robert, was captured. During their flight from Winchester Theobald and his fellow bishops were robbed of their horses and ecclesiastical vestments but somehow survived the ordeal.

During the negotiations which led to the exchange of King Stephen for Robert, Theobald took a leading part. Bishop Henry, as disloyal and two-faced as ever, changed sides yet again, held a second Legatine Council, this time in Westminster and reaffirmed Stephen as King. As Archbishop, it was Theobald's ceremonial duty to crown Stephen at Canterbury during the Christmas court held there. Being politically astute and probably scared for his life, Theobald carried out his duty. The ceremony of coronation was not a simple confirmation of a man as a king. It was the act of undergoing a coronation that made a man into a King, transformed him from a mere mortal to one appointed and approved by God to rule over his people. It was this ritual that made him legitimate, unassailable and protected him from any challenge.

"Theobald must have had more backbone than I have just given him credit for," Brother Edward thought as he went on to write the next part of Theobalds story:

In 1148 the Pope summoned the English bishops to the Council of Rheims but Stephen forbade all of them from attending other than three nominated by him personally. Theobald was not one of them. With a small retinue, all, including Theobald, dressed as poor monks, he made his way from London to the Kent coast. One of his party was a knight who had agreed to protect them as they travelled and another was Thomas of London.

When they arrived at the coast the weather was foul. The rain poured down and the wind howled.

"We must find a vessel to take us to France," Theobald told his dishevelled and miserable looking group, "and we must do it quickly. I fear the King will have sent soldiers to prevent our getting to France."

Easier said than done. Given the dreadful weather and the waves crashing on the shore it was going to be difficult to find anyone willing to risk either themselves or their boats on a crossing. "Whatever the risk," Theobald asserted, "I have to reach Rheims and the Pope as soon as possible. There must be someone who will be willing to take us.".

At the far end of the harbour they found what they were looking for but the sight of the transport on offer was not one to gladden their hearts. The boat itself did not look as if it would make it beyond the harbour mouth and the crew looked a scurrilous lot. The captain was a Saxon who looked no more trustworthy than did his craft. No matter the dangers he and his ship posed, they were their only chance of getting to France before the King's men caught up with them. A deal was struck.

"It may not be ideal," Theobald told his ragged followers, "but the Lord moves in mysterious ways and has sent us this ship to carry us to where we need to be. We will put our trust in Him, pray and come safely to our destination under His guiding hand. Now, let us board and be away from here." Brave words and well said but whether sufficient to the saving of their lives who knew.

As they left the shelter of the harbour wall, the boat rolled and wallowed, rose and fell as the sea tried to make its passage impossible. In all, there were now twelve bodies in a fishing boat with space only for a crew of four and no seating for their weary bones. They huddled in the bottom with the bilge water and the guts of long dead fish. They had not gone far before the knight added his stomach contents to the already putrid stew in the bottom of the boat. The foul smell of the knight's vomit soon made others sick. One of the monks emptied his stomach over the side, but the wind was so strong that it threw the contents back in his face. Could a long night forced to endure a monk's habit drenched with seawater and vomit be good for the health of any man?

Theobald seemed oblivious to both his travails and those of his sad group as he spent his time in prayers of a passionate intensity whilst those around him feared for their lives. As if things could get no worse, in the small hours of darkness they were struck by a huge wave beam on which swept over the boat in a great deluge of freezing saltwater. Theobald appeared not to notice even this, secure in his faith of the efficacy of his prayers.

Thomas's response to the conditions was of a more practical nature. Whilst Theobald prayed for deliverance, Thomas was trying to lend a hand to the sailors as they went about their business by throwing water back into the sea from the bottom of the boat using his hands to scoop the water over the side. A drop in the ocean one might say but better that doing nothing. When much of the water had been bailed out by Thomas and the sailors, he tried to help them haul down the sails. Thomas, despite his willingness to help, was no sailor and probably just got in the way of those who did know what they were doing but at least he was not cowering in the bottom of the boat awaiting a watery grave. Once the sails were down, the boat did not toss about quite so much but then neither did it make much headway so that their journey lasted even longer.

Theobald's prayers must have worked as at sometime during the morning the captain was able to run his craft aground on a shallow beach. Against all the odds they had reached France alive. The Archbishop was the first to step ashore where he sank to his knees to offer up a prayer for their deliverance. Thomas, ever the practical man, was counting the sailors, the clerics and the knight, to check that none had been lost overboard during the night. The crossing had taken more than a day and a night but must have seemed an eternity to those who undertook it.

It was during the ensuing council at Rheims that Thomas must have sensed real potential for his advancement in the Church. As a humble clerk of Theobald's court, he could hardly have been expected to speak in any of the great debates of the council but he made sure he was present at all the most important meetings and listened intently to all that was said. Although he did not speak at the grand occasions, he circulated among the various prelates and made new friends by virtue of his charm and, no doubt, his good looks. His future career as a great churchman and politician could be said to have started in earnest at Rheims in 1148. This was the same year that Empress Matilda returned to Normandy feeling that she had done all she could for her son and his cause by staying in England.

"This," Thomas must have thought, "is where I need and want to be, at the centre of power, mixing with men of influence. Men who can make the decisions that decide a nation's direction and destiny. I do not want to spend my life merely as a clerk." His naked ambition was going to drive him forward to greater things.

Whatever ambitions Thomas was harbouring, Stephen was furious when he heard that Theobald had disobeyed his orders and had attended the Pope's council at Rheims. This despite the fact that while he was there, Theobald had interceded with the Pope, who at that time was Eugenius III, on Stephen's behalf as initially, it had been the Pope's intention to excommunicate Stephen for forbidding the bishops' attendance. Theobald managed to persuade the Pope against this extreme course of action asking the Pope to allow the king to make amends for his behaviour. Stephen remained unimpressed. As punishment for attending at Reims despite his prohibition, he confiscated Theobald's property and forced him into exile in France.

"I have been told," Brother Edward surmised, "that Thomas had a memory like a book made of some imperishable and fire-proof parchment, inscribed with indelible ink. Everything that was set down in its pages stayed in them and did not fade or change. Thus, Thomas having witnessed all these events first-hand, must have stored the experiences away for recall and use at a later date. It was probably after this experience that Thomas would come to see Theobald's resistance as a shining example of an honest churchman's refusal to be bullied by a tyrant. Such resolute action, he later claimed, provided the precedent for his own sudden flight into exile."

Over the coming years, Thomas made himself more and more useful to Theobald who had, as we know, returned to England where he became attached to Matilda's side in the on-going civil war. Despite this change of sides by Theobald, Stephen had been forced to make some sort of peace with him because he wanted to have his son Eustace anointed as his successor and in England, only the Archbishop of Canterbury can anoint a king. Then, of course it was Theobald who had been a vital intermediary in the agreement to exchange the imprisoned Stephen for Matilda's half-brother Robert.

Like it or not, Theobald had found himself embroiled in the internecine politics of the time. Under less troubling circumstances Theobald's character and temperament might have kept him from the fray but the stalemate in the civil war gave him this unique opportunity. It obliged him to become as much a politician as a pastor. Although in many ways lynx-eyed and far-sighted, the archbishop lacked confidence as a negotiator and was a weak public speaker. Thomas, on the other hand had already conquered his childhood stammer and was a natural communicator. He made up in smooth-tongued oratory and quick footwork for what he still lacked in learning.

Be all that as it may, it was to be Theobald who would bring the two side together and thrash out the agreement which would lead to the final Treaty of Westminster which guaranteed Henry as Stephen's successor.

"There can be little doubt," Brother Edward thought to himself, "that this peace was successfully negotiated by Theobald. But there can also be little doubt that throughout the delicate discussions, Thomas was constantly by his side, rapidly emerging as an adept and determined fixer whom I have been told Theobald described as 'his first and only councillor'.

"I feel sure that the hand of Thomas must have been in there somewhere. Whilst it seems surprising that an archbishop would select Thomas as his spokesman, it is worth remembering that a religious vocation was unnecessary for the role. Theobald's clerks were not priests, even if the upper parts of their heads were shaved, or tonsured, to create a circular patch on the crown like those of the clergy and monks. When Thomas returned to London to visit his father or sisters and walked along Cheapside, he might easily have been confused with a priest."

Be that as it may, the agreement was reached in the summer of 1153 which effectively ended the Anarchy. Stephen announced the treaty in Winchester Cathedral and recognised

Henry, his nemesis, as his adopted son and successor, in return for which Henry would do homage to him. There was no mention of Matilda, now living peacefully in Normandy and leaving her son to get on with making himself the King she had fought so long and hard for him to be.

By the terms of the treaty Stephen promised to listen to Henry's advice but retained all his royal powers. In exchange for promises of the security of his lands, Stephen's remaining son, William, would do homage to Henry and renounce any claim he may have felt he had to the throne. Key royal castles would be held on Henry's behalf by guarantors, whilst in return Stephen would have access to Henry's castles. Importantly, the numerous hordes of much hated foreign mercenaries employed by Stephen would be demobilised and sent back to wherever they had come from.

Stephen and Henry sealed the treaty with a kiss of peace in the cathedral at Winchester.

When Stephen died suddenly in October 1154 Theobald was present at his deathbed. It was there that Stephen named the Archbishop as regent until Henry could take up the crown. During the six weeks before Henry arrived, the Archbishop had little difficulty in keeping the peace and after the new King's arrival, Theobald crowned both Henry and his wife, Eleanor of Aquitaine, at Westminster Abbey.

At the end of yet another long day at his writing desk, Brother Edward contemplated how his story was progressing. "I think that is the first part finished with," he thought. "Now the important part can begin. The tale of how Thomas of London and King Henry, the second of that name and our current ruler, came to meet and how that meeting was to change both of their lives."

Chapter 24

Thomas becomes an Archdeacon

The Law, the Church, and the King – three snakes slithering round each other as they climb the greasy pole.

After completing his morning rituals, instead of going straight to the scriptorium as he would usually do, Brother Edward shuffled through the cloisters to visit Prior Luc.

"Come in, come in Brother, no need to stand on ceremony," the Prior beckoned when he saw the elderly monk at his door, "sit yourself down and tell me what brings you to see me. Not bad news I hope."

"No Prior Luc, not bad news," came the reply, "but I thought I should update you on how I progress with the task you set me." He took a seat whilst he continued, "I have finished the first part of the story you wanted me to write and I wanted your blessing and authority to continue with the next part."

"But of course, Brother. The story must be completed. It is my ardent desire that it is you that should write it. None know better how it ends and the world should know the truth of it and how and why it came about. Now sit a while with me and share a glass of wine before you return to your labours."

Later, in the dimness of the scriptorium, lit only by a guttering candle, Brother Edward contemplated how he should construct his story so it might make full sense to any future reader. "The beginning is done and now I must relate those things that took place to bring my saga to its sad conclusion." Once again, he took up his quill and wrote:

We know that Thomas had become a confidant and favourite of Theobald the Archbishop of Canterbury. Sometime in 1154 Thomas's career was to take a rapid leap upwards and to some extent it was because of his arch enemy from his days at Merton

Priory, Roger of Pont L'Évêque. Archbishop Theobald had decided that Roger should become the Archdeacon of York which left the Archdeaconry of Canterbury vacant.

"Ah Thomas, come in and sit down." The Archbishop set aside the letter he had been reading. "I wanted to see you and impart what I feel is good news for your future career in my employ. Tell me," he continued, "what do you believe are the duties of a good Archdeacon?"

"Well Lord," Thomas began, feeling the possibility of advancement coming his way, "a good archdeacon should act as the right hand of his Archbishop. He would act as his deputy and representative during those times when the Archbishop himself may be absent from the See. Further, an efficient archdeacon would help to administer all of the vacant churches and prebends under the Archbishop's care and managing all of the business negotiations pertaining to the church lands in the Archbishop's See both secular and spiritual."

"A man with power to wield," Thomas thought but kept that to himself.

"A fair answer Thomas. As you may know, I have appointed Roger of Pont L'Évêque to be Archdeacon of York and thus the position of Archdeacon has become vacant in Canterbury and it is a position I believe you are ready to fill."

Thomas had already been trusted by Theobald to carry out important diplomatic missions on his behalf when in late 1149 he had been sent alone on a diplomatic mission to Rome. Here he was tasked with securing Theobald's appointment as resident Papal Legate in England and then on a second, even more important embassy to Rome, he secured the papal decree forbidding Eustace's coronation much to the chagrin of Stephen and the joy of Henry.

Now, the Archdeaconry of Canterbury was to be his. With an income of at least £100 a year, more even than Roger would receive in his new post at York, which no doubt annoyed Roger beyond belief. This would only have added piquancy to Thomas' appointment to Canterbury. Thomas's days as a just another clerk in the Archbishop's employ, although one much favoured, were over. He was being given the status and power he had long sought and craved. From this point on, Thomas's progress was going to be meteoric.

Brother Edward smiled to himself as he wrote this. "I expect the discomfiture of his old-time enemy, Roger of Pont L'Évêque, added to his feeling of elation. His income would now be roughly the same as the annual income of a baron. The archdeaconry was a far more significant position than its name suggests, giving Thomas both wealth and status and putting him alongside the likes bishops and abbots.

Chapter 25

Henry

When Brother Edward took up his quill the following day it was with a new sense of vigour, the background to his history, for that is what it was becoming, he had now written and he could take the story forward to its climactic ending. "It seems strange to me," he mused, "that the things of which I will now write I have lived through and more than that, I witnessed first-hand the terrible denouement to come.

"I have been a priest and celibate all my life so what would I know of families other than that of the Church? What I do know from observation is that I don't think anyone has a normal family and that King Henry, the second of that name, was possibly even less normal than most.

There exists a legend that his family comes from the Devil. For a man of God this is particularly disturbing. The legend goes thus:

One of Henry's ancestors, an early Count of Anjou known as Geoffrey Greymantle, fell in love with a mysterious woman of unknown origin. Her beguiling beauty drew the Count into a dangerous marriage and the couple had three children. Like now, life revolved around religion and regular worship and, so the story goes, the Count became concerned that his wife attended mass only rarely. Even when she did, she was restless in church and always left before Holy Communion took place. One day, the Count ordered some of his men to force her to stay during Communion but screaming wildly, she broke free and flew out of a window. The countess was never seen again.

She left behind her husband and their son, Fulk Nerr, also known as "Fulk the Black." Her son's notoriety and violent temper was seen as proof that his mother had surely been a child of the devil giving rise to them being known as 'the Devil's Brood'. Because of this legend, the heirs of Count Geoffrey

Greymantle were seen as a dangerous and ruthless family with ferocious tempers and became notorious for their violent, inter-familial disputes. From this heritage came our King.

Of course, it is a well-known fact that our current King Henry's parents never cared for each other. Theirs was a union of convenience agreed upon between their powerful fathers. Henry, the first of that name, had chosen Geoffrey to sire his grandchildren simply because his lands were strategically placed on the Norman frontiers and he needed the support of Geoffrey's father, his erstwhile enemy, Fulk of Anjou. As we have seen, he accordingly forced the highly reluctant Matilda to marry the fifteen-year-old Geoffrey. The pair disliked each other from the outset of their union and neither was inclined to pretend otherwise and so the scene was set for an extremely stormy and vexatious marriage. They were, however, finally prevailed upon by the formidable Henry, the first of that name, to do their duty and produce an heir to England. Dutifully, they had three sons and Henry, who is now our King, was the eldest of these and always the favourite of his adoring mother.

Henry's was to become a vast inheritance. Initially, from his father, he received the Counties of Anjou and Maine, the Duchy of Normandy and his claim to the Kingdom of England through his grandfather and mother. More was to come.

On the death of King Stephen in 1154 when Henry came to the English throne in accordance with the terms of the Treaty of Westminster, he was only 21. He had landed in England in December 1154 where he took oaths of loyalty from his barons. With him, he brought his wife Eleanor of Aquitaine and they were both crowned at Westminster Abbey by Theobald.

"This new King, although only a young man, had already achieved much in life," thought Brother Edward as he set about constructing the next part of his story, "I have heard him described him thus by Prior Luc who has seen the King in person:"

"He is of medium height, bordering on short but strongly built with a broad, square, lion-like face and possessed of immense dynamic energy and a formidable temper." As a younger man he had the red hair of his father but with the coming of age I am told it has become grey and although he appears in no danger of baldness, his head has been closely shaved. He has a spherical head in which his eyes are full, guileless, and dove-like when he is at peace but gleam like fire and grow bloodshot when his temper is aroused and in bursts of passion they flash like lightning, or so I have been told by one who has been unfortunate enough to see him in that state. He has spent so much time in the saddle that his legs have become bowed, he has a broad chest and a boxer's arms all of which announce him as a man strong, agile and bold. I am told that he seldom sits, unless riding a horse or eating and seems to be continually on the move other than when he be in council or in his books. It seems there is always bow, arrow, sword or spear in his hands."

Henry is also said to have a compassionate side to his character. I have heard tell that while crossing the Channel, he was accompanied by twenty-five ships. A great storm blew up and scattered the fleet so that most of them ended up wrecked on the rocks. Now these desperate sailors faced ruin but Henry ensured that they would be suitably recompensed for their losses. He found out the estimated loss of the disaster to each sailor and although he had no legal reason to do so, he reimbursed each one. The final cost to his personal treasury was considerable but this was an extraordinary act of kindness.

"I have never heard him speak," Brother Edward wrote, "but I have been told by someone who has, that his voice is harsh and cracked even to this day. Now, having described Henry, the second of that name's physical traits, I must write of what becomes of the twin subjects of my story:"

Henry came to the crown after 19 years of civil war and anarchy and immediately set about restoring law and order in his new kingdom. The country he inherited was littered with the illegal castles built during King Stephen's anarchic reign by out-of-control barons. Henry quickly made his presence felt. All the illegal castles were summarily demolished. Henceforth, only Henry would be permitted to build castles! As a King, he would be an autocrat and brook no arguments. Being a King was his trade. If the barons wanted forgiveness for past indiscretions and transgressions against the State then they would need to appeal to God, forgiveness was his trade and not the King's.

During Stephen's reign, many of the territories in Normandy and England had slipped out of his control and been lost to royal hegemony. With the death of Stephen, the Norman line of kings had come to an end and Henry, the second of that name, would begin a new ruling dynasty and stamp his own formidable style on it. Here was a man who did not care for magnificent clothing and was never still in one place. This was a new, young, dynamic King who was intelligent and had acquired an immense knowledge of both language and law. He must have scared the living daylights out of the barons over whom he now ruled.

Henry worked on the principal that, "if you do not have any fight in you, you might as well be dead," but he was also shrewd enough to understand that with the huge expanse of territory that he now controlled, even with his boundless energy, he could not do it all himself.

At the same time, Henry was only too well aware of what happens if the King does not keep a firm grip on the levers of power. He took very seriously his coronation oath to ensure justice and peace for the realm. He also knew that traditionally, only he, as King, could administer justice but if was to spend much of his time away from England he would need an efficient administrative and legal system that could operate in his absence. To achieve this end, he appointed Justices to travel the country in his name and whilst doing so to keep accurate records of everything they did and saw. This meant a better system of record keeping was also needed so he instituted an Exchequer which was effectively a system of governance at 'arm's length'. This would enable Henry to stay in touch with what was going on in his various provinces without having to be there in person.

Brother Edward was pondering this novel, new approach to ruling when another thought struck him. "Kings," he realised, "are expected to live off their Royal Lands and can only impose taxation in times of national crisis or national need such as a war. Henry however has never imposed a tax on us during his reign. Well, not so far. Where then was his income coming from given that so many Royal Lands had been lost or given away by Stephen during the Anarchy? This situation must have reduced Henry's income drastically. Now," thought Brother Edward, "that all gives more reason to the speed at which Henry set about recovering all those estates and titles given away or sold by his predecessor. In addition, Henry soon developed the habit of when a landowner died, he would, where possible, take their estates back into royal ownership so he could benefit from the revenues. Much less trouble than having to go to war and fight for it."

But what of Henry himself during this time? He had married Eleanor of Aquitaine two years before which had done nothing to endear him to Louis VII of France to whom she had previously been wed. She was more than 10 years older than the young English King but they were immediately attracted to each other. Perhaps their mutual love of power is what chiefly drew the two together although they do say that there was an immediate physical attraction. She was after all a woman of truly exceptional qualities, famous for her sparkling black eyes, intelligence and personality. She had a love of the sophisticated, courtly values of her ancestors, the counts of Poitou. Henry was a young, virile man, in his prime and with the likelihood of soon becoming the King of England.

Eleanor had been barely fifteen in 1137 when her father, William X, duke of Aquitaine and count of Poitou, died on a pilgrimage to the shrine of St James at Santiago de Compostela, leaving her as his sole heiress. That same year she had married the sixteen-year-old Louis shortly before he became King. But, as Louis grew older, he became more devout and ascetic and his passion for Eleanor waned. As the second son, he had been bred in the cloister with a life in the Church ahead of him. He had never thought to be King. For four years, rumours had been rife about the marriage. She, feisty and formidable, now turned thirty, had not borne him a son, raising doubts in his mind about her fecundity. In reality, and in view of future 'produce', this is more likely to have been his fault than hers. She had been overheard complaining of how her husband was more like a monk than a king.

Whatever their marital differences may have been, it did not stop Eleanor from accompanying Louis on Crusade to the Holy Land but by the time the couple reached Antioch the marriage was almost certainly over in everything but name. This was especially so after rumours became common knowledge that

Eleanor was having an affair with her uncle whilst in the Holy Land.

A church council at Beaugency annulled the marriage of Louis and Eleanor on the grounds of consanguinity, even though they had cohabited for almost sixteen years and she had already given him two healthy daughters. Since the couple were fourth cousins and related in a whole tangle of other ways within the prohibited degrees, the Church should have barred them from marrying in the first place or granted them a special dispensation. They had done neither.

Eleanor had demanded the annulment, and when it was granted it was Henry, the dashing young Count of Anjou who stepped in swiftly to make his claim on her. Hinting at a purely sexual motive, rumours quickly circulated that Eleanor had first cast lascivious eyes on Henry when he had come to Paris to do homage for Normandy. He was a handsome young man with status and power so why would she not be attracted to him? Louis was obviously not giving her whatever it was she felt in need of.

Whatever the reasons, by just eight short weeks later the teenage Henry had seduced Eleanor and married her. This was a move that shocked Europe. Henry was now the owner of more French land than the King of France himself. And his ambitions, spurred on by both his wife and mother, were only just beginning.

For the nineteen-year-old Henry, Eleanor's attraction may have lain more in the fact that she claimed descent from Charlemagne and was the sole heiress to an empire in south-west France rather than any simple, carnal desire.

Some rumours at the time even asserted that she had, at one time, been the mistress of Henry's father, Geoffrey. Be that as it may, it seems not to have deterred the 19-year-old Henry from making the match. There can be no doubt that Eleanor was a beauty who would have turned the head of any man especially a red-blooded Englishman, to say nothing of the lands that the young man would be able to claim as the lady's husband.

What she had not bargained for was just how quickly her new, young beau would be making demands for her to hand over her rights to the control of Aquitaine.

At this point, Brother Edward stopped to consider. "Would or could what I am about to write be thought of as treason? To tell the story I am embarked upon in a truthful and unbiased way, I will have to write things that may not be seen as such. The King about whom I am going to write is still with us. Whether he will ever read what I write is unclear but if he does and finds fault with it I may find myself a guest of the headsman."

For the sake of a lucid, historical account he would continue to write the facts as he honestly understood them and leave their interpretation to others, whatever the consequences. Although his conscience would be clear, still Brother Edward wrestled with the difficulty of bring the two most important threads of his tale together. "The lord does indeed work in an unknown fashion which we mortals are not always able to understand," he thought, "but to bring these two forces of nature together, Henry, King of England and Thomas of London, was surely a risk only the Lord would take."

Thomas had been an Archdeacon for some time before Henry's triumphal return to England but even that position had not been without its problems. There were rumours of double-dealing by the Archdeacon involving Church lands and the withholding of taxes and benefices all of which were to Thomas's financial advantage. At a later date these rumours would come back to haunt him.

Henry and Eleanor had remained in France while in England, Theobald assumed the regency in the King's absence. On 7 December, the couple returned and landed near Southampton. They were jointly crowned by the Archbishop at Westminster Abbey on the 19th of the same month. Thomas was there too: for nine years he had been Theobald's clerk and right-hand man, involved in the most delicate and thrilling of jousting matches involving Church and State but his star was rising.

Once again the contentious question of to whom did the Church owe its primary allegiance reared its ugly head and things between Theobald and the King became fraught. The two men spoke to each other in French. Henry never spoke English; that was the language of the peasants he ruled. They could have conversed in Latin had they wished as both were fluent in its use.

"Sire," Theobald pleaded with Henry, "we have been over and over this issue time and time again. Is it not enough that I have proved my loyalty and that of the Church in England to your King's majesty in many ways already? Was it not me who interceded with King Stephen and your mother the Empress at Wallingford to broker the treaty that gave you the crown in your own undisputed right? Yet, you still do not trust me. I owe you my allegiance in all things temporal but I must, in all faith, also serve my spiritual leader, the Holy Father in Rome. That is a situation I cannot alter."

Henry grew red in the face and Theobald knew that his King was not happy with him. Henry was a bully relying on threats and taunts. As we now know, Henry's voice was harsh and cracked from constantly barking out orders when on horseback.

"Never mind the fine words Archbishop. You are my subject and as such, you will obey me in all things. Let that be an end to it."

Theobald, ever the diplomat knew when to hold his tongue. He knew there were other ways to change the King's mind.

"You are, as always right my King. May I broach a different subject with you"?

"You may."

"Since your return from France I have noticed that some aspects of governance in the country need closer scrutiny possibly due to you trying to do everything yourself. I also observe that as yet, you have not appointed a Chancellor to oversee civil matters on your behalf through your new Chancellery. Would you not consider the appointment of someone to take that responsibility and burden from your shoulders?"

"You think I am not capable of governing my own realm Theobald?"

"The opposite Sire. I believe you need more time and freedom to be a more effective ruler. Yours is the responsibility of deciding which direction the country will take whilst it becomes someone else's responsibility to see those dictates carried out and enforced. Moreover," he continued, "a chancellor of the right quality could increase your revenues by making the most effective use of all the resources under your jurisdiction. Think of how much more you could do if your exchequer was filled to its full potential?"

Theobald knew that Henry would be desperate for money not only to run his army and civil service but to pay for his household and all that entailed. "Now I have him interested," Theobald thought to himself, "avarice is always an effective enticement to action."

Theobald was well aware that in England at this time much of the power still rested with the Barons who maintained their own castles and private armies. During the lawless years of the anarchy many had declared what amounted to independence and had built new castles without royal permission as bases from which their armies could harass rivals and friends alike. Stephen had conspicuously failed to resolve this problem.

"Imagine," Theobald continued, dangling the bait of untapped resources just waiting to be realised, "how much more the royal treasury would benefit from the revenue of all those castles built without your royal approval. Think of all the fines you could levy against those who built them." Theobald stopped here. He had made his point and planted the seed. Now he must let the King see the wisdom of his words for himself.

Henry was silent for a moment while he considered what the Archbishop had said. Then he spoke. "You are right, much of the country's economy is in ruins and I have no doubt that few expect me, a new and inexperienced King to adequately deal with the situation. However Lord Archbishop you can be rest assured that I will set about the task of kingship with energy and a degree of understanding with which my mother seemed not to have possessed. I have not been unaware that my mother, the Empress Matilda, has been derided on occasion for her arrogance in dealing with her subjects. Perhaps if she had been able to be more tolerant and reasonable in the way she dealt with the Londoners for instance, then they may not have been quite so quick to thwart her coronation attempt. I have no intention of making a similar mistake but the fact remains, I am the King and I will make the changes that I see fit to make."

From Theobald's viewpoint as Head of the Church in England, the Church were still unsure how to respond to their new monarch, for it was, as yet, unclear how this new monarch would respond to her. The Church had two chief concerns. First was, the worrying youth of the king and the second and more important was the well-known antipathy of the majority of his courtiers towards the Church's right to liberty. Theobald was responding to the new situation with the manoeuvres of a statesman rather than a priest. The king, he realized, needed to be influenced and influenced by someone other than his worldly courtiers.

Therefore, Theobald advised Henry to, "have a care to listen to the advice of your Barons but ensure you have enough loyal men doing your bidding to keep the country in check. In addition, I suggest you have someone on whom you could rely completely to give you trustworthy advice. Someone in whom you could confide and place your trust."

"Hmm, you could be right my Lord Archbishop and I have no doubt you have someone you would recommend for the position."

"Indeed Sire. You may already be aware of the man that, in my humble opinion, would be perfect for the job. He has, for some time been an important part of my household but your Lordship's needs are more important than mine. He is a valued member of my entourage whom I would be sad to lose but," here Theobald laid on a little more obsequiousness, "to have him serve you and the greater good of the realm would be a sacrifice happily made."

"Sometimes Theobald you are overly full of flattery. However, I am keen to know this man who will make me rich, curb my troublesome barons whilst at the same time, allow me more leisure time with my hawks and hounds?"

"Thomas of London is the man of whom I speak," answered the archbishop, "some call him Thomas Beckette. He is well learned in the law, reads, writes and speaks three languages. As a diplomat I have found him second to none and apart from these practical qualifications for the post he is full of charm and wit. I am also told that he is a tolerable huntsman."

"Was he not with you when you mediated the treaty with Stephen at Wallingford?"

"The very man Sire. It was at the siege of Crowmarsh that you would have first seen him when he acted as my emissary in many of the negotiations both there and those that followed."

"What you are saying is, at least in part, is that I owe my throne to him?"

The archbishop thought he might have gone too far and made too much of Thomas's virtues and was quick to respond. "You are King by heavenly right Sire. No man can claim any part of sitting you on the throne as its rightful owner other than the Almighty."

Henry considered and then spoke, "Let us have him in then and I will get his measure for myself."

Secretly, whatever honey Theobald had poured into Henry's ear, he foresaw the King as both a danger and potential evil to the Church. He had to admit to himself again that there were times, when in private, he had come to regret his role as Kingmaker at the end of the Anarchy. Therefore, the Archbishop, being fearful for the future, thought to put in place some defence against the evil which was felt might well be imminent. By placing his own man, Thomas, at the heart of the royal court he thought he might be able to steer the King into a more sympathetic attitude towards the Church and it seemed to too good an opportunity to miss. Thomas was, after all, Theobald's man.

Whether Theobald's assessment of Thomas was correct we will find out in due course. Suffice for now to say that Theobald was successful in introducing Thomas into the King's councils. Through Theobald's political astuteness Thomas had been brought to Henry's attention and with his natural charm and wit Thomas was about to climb to the top of the political tree.

During the King's Christmas celebrations held at Bermondsey Abbey immediately after Henry and Eleonor had been crowned at Westminster by Theobald, the Archbishop got his wish. Thomas, a middle-class Londoner, was nominated as Henry's Chancellor and was appointed to the post within a month of the coronation. Thomas found himself catapulted into the limelight as the King's Chancellor, one of the highest offices in the kingdom and a meteoric promotion for anyone, let alone a man of Thomas's relatively humble background. At a stroke he

125

had become Henry's confidant, with the right to attend all meetings of the King's Council whether invited or not. He had important financial and judicial duties to fulfil. He was suddenly chief custodian of the King's Seal besides being in charge of the royal scriptorium. It would be he and his clerks who would draft royal charters and decrees. In short, he had probably just become the second most powerful man in the country.

However, the first letter that Thomas is reputed to have found on his desk after arriving at court was from Arnulf of Lisieux, to whom Theobald had appealed for assistance in his efforts to secure Thomas' appointment. Arnulf, was a slippery courtier-bishop and for over four years had been the Henry's chief adviser in Normandy whilst the now King was still only the Count of Anjou and no one is said to have understood Henry's psychology better. This was despite the fact that Arnulf had accompanied Louis VII of France and Eleanor on the second crusade as a papal legate in charge of the Anglo-Norman contingent. Somehow, soon after his return, he had succeeded in ingratiating himself with Henry.

What Arnulf had written to Thomas was this:

'Friendship is a rare virtue and nowhere is it more rarely found than between those who are invited to give counsel to kings and to direct the affairs of kingdoms. To say nothing of other difficulties, ambition sits with a heavy weight upon their minds and as long as each fear to be outstripped by the vigilance of the other, envy springs up between them, which, before long, does not fail to become open hatred.'

Thomas would have done well to heed these words of caution it. "Be that as it may," Brother Edward thought, "whatever words of advice Thomas had been given, like many a talented and ambitious bureaucrat, he was eager to raise the status of both the office he held and his personal standing in it. The advice of Arnulf forgotten, it would be Thomas who would transform the Chancellorship into a great office of state rather than the mere clerical and administrative bureau that it was when he arrived."

"Here," Brother Edward noted, "I should mention a man who will play an important part in the story but much later. For now, it is sufficient to give him a name and explain in brief his duties and connection to the newly appointed Chancellor."

William FitzStephen was Thomas's personal household clerk and would serve Thomas for nearly ten years. When Thomas became Chancellor he gave his clerk William full authority to act in his name in all diocesan matters pertaining to the Archdeaconry of Canterbury. William was appointed as the subdeacon becoming Thomas's man-on-the-spot and made responsible for perusing all letters and petitions involving the diocese. More of William later.

Here, Brother Grim made an important observation in his writing which was this. "Henry was now twenty-one whilst Thomas was just two days short of his thirty-fourth birthday. What was unusual, given the differences in their social backgrounds, was just how quickly the two men became close friends. This new state of affairs was not to Eleonor's liking and she made her feelings plain to her husband."

"That man," she said of Thomas, "is nothing but a common trader's son. I do not know why you even allow him in the house never mind spend time carousing with him. It is beneath your royal dignity to associate so closely with him. He is a middle-class upstart and nothing more. Personally, I cannot stand the man, and if it were possible, your mother dislikes him even more than I do. He's a social climber of the worst sort kind and nothing good is going to come of your friendship with him."

Henry's response to these words of complaint were unambiguous. "In that case wife both you and my mother should stay out of the way when he is around. He is a fine fellow and I enjoy his company and the wisdom of his words. Anyway, he always manages to make me laugh.

"I have been told," Brother Edward recalled, "that the King would often call at the Chancellor's house at dinner time, arriving, bow in hand, directly from hunting. Ofttimes he would even ride his horse straight into the Chancellor's Hall. Sometimes it was merely to take a drink and after a quick talk with Thomas he would leave. At other times he might stay to eat. He had been seen to vault over the tables to sit down beside his new friend while those around made space for him. Such was their rapport that Thomas could one day be able to say that he "knew the King inside out." It would seem to some that never were two men more of one mind or better friends.

127

"I forget where I heard it," Brother Edward continued, "but I heard tell that they when they had finished a day's business, they would play together like boys of the same age. It is well known that the King's favourite recreation was and still is, hunting. This was a passion that Thomas shared ever since his holidays with Richard de L'Aigle in his youth so whenever possible they would enjoy each other's company at the chase. It is common knowledge that the King is a man of boundless energy, rarely sitting down except at meals or when in the saddle. This ability, allied to Thomas's mental capacities and aptitude for hard work meant they made a formidable team."

During the 19 years of Stephen's reign the crown had suffered many losses to both the Barons and the Church. When Henry began his reign, he was, as we have seen, determined to reverse those losses.

Henry knew that he had to rebuild his control of the territories that his grandfather, Henry, the first of that name, had once governed. In this regard he may well have been influenced by his mother, Matilda, who had always had a strong sense of ancestral rights and privileges. It was a quest that Henry was passionate to pursue. To reinforce his position as King he began to use his heraldic design on all his charters and documents; a wax seal made with his signet ring with either a leopard or a lion engraved on it. The majority of his people could not read but would recognise the picture and know that it was the King's will and commandment in the document.

"Thomas," he told his new Chancellor, "an idea not coupled with action will never get any bigger than the brain it occupied. It is my intention to reintroduce the ancestral customs of my grandfather; King Henry, the first of that name, and you are going to help me do it. The secret to getting things done is, as I have said, to act. I will let nothing stand in my way even if I have to go back on some of the concessions I made as part of my gaining the crown. Which, as we both know was mine by right anyway. Those transgressions against Royal Charters and lands in Stephen's time will be reversed, whoever or whatever may have been the cause of them."

Thomas spoke in the softer, more measured tones that he had adopted and continued to use as a strategy to overcome his

128

stammer and answered, "Sire, you have given me the powers needed and I will not hesitate to use them to help you achieve your aims. I am yours to command."

Like his new friend and benefactor, the King, Thomas also began as he meant to go on. The country they had inherited had just suffered from almost two decades of war. The anarchy that had been rife, the illegal castles many of the barons had built, the mercenary armies they had hired, all that was going to stop. There would be no more building or hiring outside the law.

Thomas was as good as his word. He rode non-stop around the country both with the King and alone, where he drafted or witnessed a flurry of charters from places as far apart as London, and Burton-on-Trent in Staffordshire. These charters restored lands or castles to their rightful owners, particularly to the King which, in reality, was the main purpose of the exercise. Thomas was fulfilling Theobald's promise.

Henry and Thomas were wasting no time in dealing ruthlessly with the mess, mayhem and ruin left by the disastrous previous reign and civil wars. Barons who had illegally built castles during Stephen's reign were given short shrift and their castles razed to the ground or sequestered to the King's estates. Over a hundred illegally built castles were demolished as soon as Thomas became Chancellor. The privy purse began to fill and with it, Thomas's status grew in the King's eyes.

As early as 1157, Thomas re-introduced the Laws of Scutage through which Henry's subjects were reminded that they must, by Law, equip themselves and their entourage for military service. As an alternative to providing the required men, a baron could pay a levy to the King in their place. This was Scutage. In effect a tax, which although it relieved the Barons of the need to provide men, it could prove to be an expensive alternative. It was an extremely unpopular move by Thomas after the lax years of the Anarchy which many Barons had enjoyed.

Scutage went hand in hand with one of Henry's earliest proclamations, probably drafted by Thomas's hand, in which a time limit was set for the departure from England of Stephen's hated Flemish mercenaries. Of course, with the monies raised by Scutage, Henry in an act of supreme hypocrisy, could hire his own mercenaries to fight his battles for him.

In the meanwhile, Thomas had set about levying the money needed to finance the king's campaign against his brother Geoffrey in Anjou. By now wars were increasingly being fought by professional soldiers and Henry had thought it wise to hire an army of mercenaries locally in Anjou rather than summoning the feudal host in England and transporting it across the Channel.

While raising more than enough money to pay for Henry's troops, Thomas had caused outraged protests from the Barons and the Church, including from Theobald himself, who petitioned for exemption but to his extreme chagrin, was refused.

Thomas, as chancellor had harnessed his formidable strength of purpose to the carrying out of the king's policies including the one to curb the power and jurisdiction of the Church.

Theobald was understandably upset by Thomas' actions.

"Thomas, you disappoint me. You seem to have shown undue severity towards the persons and interests of Church. When I recommended you to the King I little expected you to so quickly forget your loyalty to me and the cause which I serve. You appear to have forgotten to whom you owe your rapid rise in status."

"Lord archbishop," Thomas replied, "your patronage is not forgotten, merely superseded. I now serve the King and it is to him that my first duty must lie."

"I am afraid Thomas that that is a weak excuse. Your first duty is to God and those who do his work and not to temporal powers. I urge you to remember this in the future. Kings come and go but God and the Church remain."

Like his grandfather Henry, the second of that name, has a restless spirit which is always looking for a fresh challenge. To this day, he is never idle, working as need requires or his mood dictates, sometimes late into the night. He is like a human chariot dragging all after him, he still mounts his horse at daybreak, comes back in the evening after a hard day's riding and then exhausts his companions by keeping them on their feet until midnight. What is surprising is that Thomas, although older, could keep pace with him. If and when Henry went abroad while Thomas was Chancellor, then Thomas would go with him and the two were seldom apart.

Where the two men differed was in some aspects of their character and the way they got things done. Thomas relied on charisma and his quicksilver oratory to get his own way whereas Henry's chief way of getting things done was his temper, which would flare up in seconds. The King's favourite expletive, the one to which Thomas would become most accustomed, was 'by God's eyes', or, when he was especially roused, 'by God's eyes and throat' or even, 'by God's eyes and testicles'. Henry shunned the use of the shorter Anglo-Saxon oaths about bodily parts and functions common in the vulgar language of his peasant subjects.

Thomas' relationship to Henry must have, at times, seemed like the stories told in the bible of Joseph and the Pharaoh in Egypt. Thomas was strenuous in aiding the king in his policy of gathering all power into the hands of the monarchy, even when that policy went against claims of the Church which, of course, continually brought Thomas into conflict with his benefactor Theobald.

"One must wonder," ruminated Brother Edward, "whether Thomas, older than Henry by 13 years and celibate, may well have felt a kind of elder-brother affection for his King. There can be no doubt that Thomas must have fallen for Henry's talents and charm. At the same time, he must also have enjoyed the satisfaction of moving in a rank of society to which he had not been born. Who can tell what the King's true attitude to this older man really was but the efficiency and intelligence of Thomas must have come as some relief to him surrounded as he was by mostly illiterate and at times hostile barons and churchmen?"

Whatever the relationship between these two men, the King has a notorious temper that can explode at any moment and Thomas must always have been aware of the shaky ground on which he stood. The other side of this is that the King apparently also has a wicked sense of humour whereby he likes to tease and undermine his courtiers and remind them who is the person in control.

This is borne out by a story told by William FitzStephen, he who was mentioned earlier, who tells the story of Thomas and the king riding together through the streets of London. It was a cold day when the King noticed an old man coming towards them, poor and clad in a thin and ragged coat. "Do you see that man? How poor he is, how frail, and how scantily clad! Would it not be an act of charity to give him a thick warm cloak?"

Thomas agreed and the King replied: "You shall have the credit for this act of charity" and then attempted to strip his Chancellor of his new scarlet and grey cloak. After a brief struggle Thomas reluctantly allowed the king to overcome him. The King then later told his attendants what had happened and they all had a good laugh at Thomas's expense. What happened to the beggar who got Thomas' cloak no-one knows but I cannot imagine what a beggar would do with such a fine cloak lined with the fur of pure unspotted white stoats. If he tried to sell it any potential buyers would assume that he had stolen it in which case the beggar would most likely be locked up, maimed or hanged by the sheriff. Not much of a gift really.

It must strike one as strange that Thomas knowing Henry as he did and being a man of keen intellect, would do what he could to avoid incurring the King's wrath. He knew only too well that Henry could not and would not tolerate disloyalty or breach of trust. Once his enmity was stirred, Henry would never forgive and forget. It only makes what happens in the not-too-distant future all the more surprising. Entering into confrontation with a child of the Angevin 'Devil's Brood' was never going to be a sensible idea.

Chapter 26

The Embassy to Louis in Paris

Thomas had now been Chancellor for three years and during that time had welcomed ambassadors from across Europe wishing to pay their respects to a King who was clearly going to be one of the future arbiters of events in Europe. His training in the arts of diplomacy and negotiation under the tutelage of Archbishop Theobald were not going to be wasted. He welcomed envoys from the German emperor, Frederick Barbarossa, and from the Moorish king of Valencia and Murcia as well as the King of Norway. He lavished on them everything they needed for their stay in England. Welcoming the Germans, Thomas gave them a sumptuous gift of gold coins and four prize gyrfalcons.

Be that as it may, Henry was still at loggerheads with his main rival, Louis of France over the perennially disputed frontier territories of the Vexin which as we all know are those lands bordering Normandy and France. The County of Vexin had been a part of France but when the Norseman, Rollo had invaded the territory, Charles, the one known as 'the Simple', had agreed a treaty with the invader dividing the Vexin between France and the new kingdom of Normandy. Two hundred years later and the county of Vexin was a heavily contested border between the Angevin King Henry, the second of that name, and the Capetian King Louis in France. Its importance lay in its close proximity to Paris and the location of the route to the coastal cities of Normandy.

This dispute over the Vexin was set to continue interminably and at first, any diplomacy with France went slowly but a breakthrough came in the spring of 1158. Louis and his second wife, Constance of Castile, remember his first wife was now married to Henry, had a daughter whom they christened Margaret.

Henry called for his trusted advisor and friend, the Chancellor. "I see an opportunity here Thomas. Much as my grandfather used my mother the Empress Matilda as a pawn in the game of power I see an opportunity to do the same. What if we offer our cousin Louis of France our son Henry in a marriage to his new daughter?"

"Though she be barely out of the cradle Lord and your son not quite four I see it as a worthy match with much to recommend it to both sides. If, of course terms can be agreed but as there are only two forces that unite men, either fear or self-interest, I see no obstacle to a satisfactory outcome. Louis may not fear you but his self-interest will sway his judgement in the matter."

Henry nodded. "Good. First I must debate the matter with my Barons but they will, of course, agree with whatever I tell them to agree to." After debating the proposed betrothal with his Barons, who as he had predicted, gave their approval to the plan, Henry gave his chancellor instructions to arrange everything.

"The plan is agreed Thomas. You will go to France with my full authority to forge this dynastic alliance through the betrothal of my son and heir, the Young Henry, to the Princess Margaret. This match will be on the clear understanding that her dowry will be the lands of the Vexin. I have great faith in your abilities Thomas. I think of a true and skillful diplomat as one who can tell you to go to hell in such a way that you actually look forward to the trip. You have those skills in abundance."

"Thank you for those words my Lord. I will not let you down."

"I know Thomas, I know."

Thomas was elated and for his part, meant to spare no expense in demonstrating to the French all the luxury and ostentation that the Angevin empire could afford. This embassy was to be a display of splendour and opulence worthy of his King, a man who ruled territories stretching a thousand miles from the far north of England to the far south of Aquitaine. His thinking was that if people saw how he the Chancellor travelled, then how much greater must be the King whom he served?

Thomas told his servants and officials, "I want nothing spared that money can buy. We will show this French King that we the English and Angevins know how to conduct an embassy." Soon, all was hustle and bustle in preparation for the journey to Paris. Thomas planned to take over 200 mounted followers in his retinue. These would include his knights, clerks, stewards, servants, esquires and young pages, all to be fitted out in costly new clothing, each according to his rank.

Thomas himself was to be no exception. He was determined to travel in style, equipping himself with twenty-four changes of clothes. Most of these would be worn no more than once or twice and then he was going to give them away as either presents to Louis's councillors or gifts to the poor.

In the event, few of his possessions were to escape his extraordinary exhibition of philanthropy, neither his rare furs, rich silks and expensive cloaks, nor his tapestries, carpets and bed-hangings, all of which he had taken with him. He gave with lavish abundance to the point of recklessness. Not only did he take all his most expensive clothes to impress his hosts but for his own recreation he also took several packs of hunting dogs, together with falcons and some of the exotic birds from his mews and aviaries.

Soon, there was a mountain of baggage needed to transport all that would be necessary for such a huge expedition. Thomas, using all his organisational skills, allocated each of his household departments its own wagons. Each wagon was to be drawn by five horses, each comparable in size and strength to a warhorse. In addition, each horse had its own groom wearing a brand-new tunic walking alongside it whilst each wagon had its own driver and guard also garbed in new livery.

The wagons were laden with clothes, furniture, cushions, bed linen, food and drink as well as kitchen equipment and two were carrying the finest English beer. To each wagon was chained a great mastiff, as strong as a lion or a bear and fierce enough to frighten away would be thieves or vagabonds.

There was more. Behind these wagons would come twelve packhorses, once again, each with its own groom but to add to the spectacle, each horse had a monkey on its back. How that must have enthralled the onlookers as the caravan passed. Many would never have seen a monkey before. "Indeed," thought Brother Edward, "I have only ever seen pictures of these creatures. Never one in real life." The packhorses bore bundles containing the most valuable items: the ornaments and vestments of Thomas's chapel, his rare books and manuscripts, his gold and silver plate, money, vases, bowls, goblets, flagons, basins, saltcellars, spoons and plates.

This cavalcade wound its way through the countryside and every time it approached a French village or castle, it would form itself into a procession to impress and amaze the onlookers, to whom free English beer would be distributed. First walked the footmen, around 250 of them in groups of six or more, filling the width of the road and singing as they went. Behind them were Thomas's hunting dogs and greyhounds on leashes and chains and led by their keepers. Then came the wagons, covered with hides to protect the luggage, followed by the packhorses, now being ridden by their grooms.

As he wrote, Brother Edward thought, "I can just imagine the surprised and curious villagers running from their houses to see what the approaching noise was all about. Rural peasants and gentry alike would never have seen anything like it, they would be clamouring to find out to whom this spectacular parade belonged."

To match his talents as a power broker, Thomas had always had a theatrical streak which he used to the full on his journey through the French countryside. In his parade, he was keeping the best until the last. Little did the onlookers know as they watched this extravaganza trundle past that the main attraction was still to come. A short distance behind the main column came the esquires leading their chargers and carrying the shields of their knights; then came their young pages; then the falconers, each with a hawk on his glove; after them the clerks, stewards and lesser functionaries of Thomas's household riding two by two. Last of all, surrounded by a phalanx of his house knights came the Chancellor himself. How he must have revelled in the wonderment of his audience.

Thomas had another trick up his sleeve which he knew would impress the French King and his courtiers.

136

In the past, it has been the custom of the Capetian kings to offer unstinting hospitality to their guests and as Thomas approached to within some thirty miles of Paris, Louis issued a proclamation forbidding the sale of any victuals whatsoever to the Chancellor or his servants during their stay since he would provide them. Thomas was determined to upstage his hosts and sent his purveyors ahead in disguise and using false names. They were given orders to go to all the markets and fairs in the vicinity of Paris. There, on his instructions, they bought up such a supply of bread, meat, fish and wine that when he arrived at his lodgings at the Temple, he found it stocked with three days' provisions for 1,000 men. Thereafter, Thomas showered every imaginable courtesy upon his hosts. Each member of the French court, from the grandest aristocrat to the humblest serving-man, received a token of his wealth and generosity. Knowing no bounds, his generous liberality included gifts to all the masters and students in the 'schools' where he had once been a student. Such was his desire to make an unforgettable impact he even included the landlords and creditors of all the English students then resident in the city.

Thomas returned and reported his achievements to Henry.

"I think Lord King that you will be pleased with the outcome of my embassy, at least I hope you are," Thomas said. "King Louis has confirmed his promise of the betrothal of his daughter Margaret to the young prince Henry. The expenditure has been huge but the reward will be even greater."

"Well done Thomas. The betrothal is a bonus. More importantly I think with the terms of this dynastic treaty you have beguiled Louis into believing that this rapprochement with we Angevins will increase his security."

"Indeed Lord. I have secured a written undertaking that as her dowry, the lands and castles of the whole of the Norman Vexin will be restored to you on the day of his daughter's wedding to your son. In return however, Margaret is to receive a settlement of £2,000, the revenues of the cities of Lincoln and Avranches and lands sufficient to support 500 knights in England and Normandy. I have also received confirmation of your ancestral claim, as Count of Anjou, to be the hereditary High Steward of

France. This is a strategy that should prepare the way for your annexation of Brittany in the not-too-distant future."

"What a friend and confidant you are Thomas. Your efforts and services will not be forgotten." The avaricious side of Henry now showed, "the promised castles. When will I get those," he wanted to know?

Thomas must have thought, "is there no pleasing this man" but of course, kept that thought to himself. "As soon as the couple are married, the castles will become yours. In the meanwhile, they have been placed under the guardianship of the Knights Templar," was what the Chancellor replied.

Not everyone was as pleased with Thomas as was the King. Many Barons and nobles resented this London upstart and his closeness to the King. Theobald certainly thought that the lavish lifestyle his protege was indulging in was not quite what he had in mind when he had recommended him to Henry. He being particularly upset by the taxes his erstwhile clerk had levied to pay for the foreign embassies, albeit in the name of the King, some of which hit the largest churches very heavily and indeed, Theobald himself had suffered from a heavy Scutage demand which Thomas refused to reduce.

Wherever he went, the Chancellor always travelled in style, always spent coin lavishly, but whose coin was it? That was a question waiting to be answered when things eventually turned sour between the King and his Chancellor.

Chapter 27

Thomas the warrior

The two men sat on a bench in the cloister gardens enjoying wine from a stone flagon.

"Let me pour you another cup Brother Edward. It has been a good vintage this year and the Master Cellarer has done an excellent job in getting the best from our crop of grapes."

"Indeed, Prior Luc," the other replied, "a decent vintage indeed. Mind you, probably too good as it encourages one to over-indulge and leads to regret in the morning."

"I cannot imagine that ever being the case with a man as worthy as yourself." Prior Luc smiled as he looked at the bent frame of his older companion.

"I think you flatter me. In my younger days I have to admit to a liking for both the grape and the grain but now an occasional cup in good company suffices for my needs."

"How then goes the work Brother," the Prior asked changing the subject.

"I think tolerably well thank you. I have reached the part of the story that I believe will probably come as a surprise to many who read it."

"And which part would that be?"

"The part when Thomas of London has become not only the King's Chancellor but also a warrior who leads men into battle whilst dressed in full armour and carrying a sword. That incarnation of Thomas of London is often overlooked. People much prefer to see him as a man of God, not of war but that aspect of his story merely makes the ending all the more bizarre.

"I have since discovered from my reading," Brother Edward continued, "that there was a notable English precedent for there being a warrior-chancellor. Early in the reign of Henry, the first of that name, his chancellor, Waldric, who also loved hunting and falconry as did our Thomas, had put on chainmail and fought at the battle of Tinchebrai. It was he who personally took the King's brother, Robert Curthose, prisoner. Nor while at the Council of Rheims with Theobald in 1148 could Thomas have failed to notice the fabled Albero von Montreuil, Archbishop of Trier, seated in a place of honour by the side of Pope Eugenius despite having led knights bravely into battle in Italy and northern Germany earlier in his career."

"All that reading you must do Brother," the Prior said, "little surprise your eyes are failing."

At a great council of the Barons beginning in 1157, Henry announced a summer campaign to crush the most powerful of the northern Welsh princes, Owain of Gwynedd. Wales had been pacified up to a point by Henry's grandfather after which several of the local princes had done him homage. Little of this authority had survived the anarchy of Stephen's reign, especially in the north of the country and the new Henry was determined to change that situation.

Owain had taken the lead in harassing the English settlers that had been 'planted' there after the earlier conquest in William, known as, the Conqueror's time. That was almost 100 years ago and it was once again time to teach the unruly Welsh a lesson. Thomas strongly supported this declaration of war but recognised it as a risky venture. The Welsh were a savage race who knew how to fight and more importantly knew their wild and rugged country much better than any invader.

Surprisingly, Thomas consulted soothsayers for advice on the most propitious moment to attack, not something that his old employer Theobald would have approved of. On this suspect and flimsy advice, Henry and Thomas ordered the feudal host to muster south of Chester within two weeks. From there it was to march along the coast of the Dee estuary while a fleet quietly shadowed it offshore and carried its provisions and equipment.

Never mind his warlike attitude to the Welsh, Thomas had for ever been criticised for his love of blood sports by his long-time colleague John of Salisbury. John had been secretary to Archbishop Theobald for seven years and while at Canterbury had become acquainted with Thomas, who became one of the significant influences in John's life. During his time at Canterbury, John went on many missions to the Papal See and it was probably on one of these that he made the acquaintance of Nicholas Breakspear. This was the same Nicholas that had preceded Thomas as a pupil at Merton Priory School. In 1154 Nicholas became Pope Adrian IV and the following year John visited him, remaining with him at Benevento for several months.

Despite his friendship with Thomas, it did not stop John from pointing out to his friend that both the Church and Archbishop Theobald frowned on his love of hunting almost as much as it frowned on warfare. He argued that far from being the sport of kings or gentlemen, it undermined human reason as powerfully as madness or intoxication and debased human nature. It merely encouraged men to kill one another as well as beasts or fowl. Thomas ignored his friend's well-meant words of advice and continued to hunt and go to war.

Henry's campaign against Owain got off to a bad start when the Welsh trapped him in a clever ambush. Just when it looked as though victory was in the grasp of the Welsh, a relieving force of English soldiers arrived and Henry won the day. It was as close a shave as Henry would ever want to experience. Having won the victory, he began advancing deeper into Snowdonia and the Owain faction decided to sue for peace before its situation became worse and in August their leaders came to Henry's camp under a safe-conduct. Here, they handed over hostages, including Owain's son, as a gesture of good faith. Prince Owain then did homage to the King for his lands in Gwynedd, satisfying Henry's demands for overlordship.

Thomas was obviously in favour of war but his desire to be true warrior was going to be a little longer in coming. Thomas, on this occasion, was not able to march very far with the royal army before Henry decided his chancellor was more use elsewhere.

"I understand your frustration Thomas but I need your skills where you can do most good. While I'm in the field I need to know that the business of the country is in good hands. Yours. When I am finished with the Welsh there will be plenty of treaties and new charters to write." Henry, as we have seen, was soon receiving Owain's homage and Thomas and his clerks were kept busy handling the paperwork in Chester.

141

Two years later, however, Thomas found himself where he wanted to be; in the vanguard of an army, fearlessly leading his own contingent of knights into battle. The flashpoint and opportunity Thomas had longed for was Aquitaine, where Henry, to his wife's delight, at last meant to attempt to enforce her ancestral claim to possession of the city and county of Toulouse. Eleanor was one of the main driving forces behind this new campaign across the Channel.

She had first raised the matter with Henry some years before when she told Henry, "You know as well as I do that Toulouse rightly belongs to me. I am the Duchess of Aquitaine so the overlordship of Toulouse has always been mine. Just because Raymond of Languedoc has moved in to claim it does not mean it is his. How long are you going to stand by and see your wife denied what is rightly hers?"

Now he told her bluntly, "it is not, as you know full well, that simple. Raymond is married to King Louis' sister Constance, who also happens to be the widow of the usurper Stephen's son Eustace. With Louis as his ally and no fewer than three young sons by Constance available to succeed him, Raymond feels in a strong position to hold us Angevins at bay for ever."

Her reply was equally blunt. "If you don't act now, Henry, the opportunity to regain my lost territory will be fast slipping away. For me, it must be a case of now or never to reclaim my rightful inheritance." Eleanor knew that Henry's ambition and greed for more territory would outweigh any misgivings he might have and the situation would not be ignored.

Henry now set out to enforce Eleanor's rights as Duchess of Aquitaine to the overlordship of the county of Toulouse. The prize would be an empire which extended from the borders of Scotland to the shores of the Mediterranean. How could he resist the challenge and such a prize? Apart from any claims his wife might have, Henry knew full well that the city of Toulouse controlled all the trade routes and links into Spain and the Mediterranean. Once in English hands, Henry would control even more of France and that would really annoy Louis.

Now Thomas would have his opportunity to become a true warrior and not merely the pusher of a pen when he and his King embarked on this ambitious, perhaps overambitious, expedition. The battle for Toulouse.

Henry chose to lead only an elite cohort of around 1,500 knights across the Channel on the first stage of their long journey south and to place a greater reliance on the mercenaries he would be able to hire closer to the seat of the action. The feudal hosts of Normandy, Anjou and Aquitaine supplied further reinforcements, which, when everyone assembled at Poitiers at midsummer 1159, made up a combined army perhaps amounting to over 4,500 knights with some 10,000 supporting troops. These would have needed more than 1,500 wagons for their tents and equipment and another 600 for their supplies of food and barrels of beer. All these things, Thomas arranged.

A very considerable army was assembled at Poitiers at midsummer in 1159, despite the danger that Louis himself might join the opponents of Henry's claim. Louis's sister was, after all, married to Raymond, now calling himself Count of Toulouse and was denying that he was a vassal of Aquitaine and therefore, of Eleonor.

Now this, made things complicated for Henry. Not only had he sworn an oath of loyalty to Louis, but the person of the French King as ultimate lord of these lands was particularly sacred. If Louis was on the battlefield, Henry would have the unwelcome dilemma of either breaking his feudal oath by attacking Louis, or simply withdrawing and leaving the field to the French king and his allies without a blow being struck. More importantly, without the prize of Toulouse which was the whole point of the expedition.

Before unleashing his forces, Henry met Louis at Tours, urging him to advise his brother-in-law Raymond to surrender peacefully while he still had the chance. He then took a detour to Blaye on the Gironde estuary, some thirty miles north of Bordeaux, to make a pact with Raymond's bitter rival, the Count of Barcelona. When these moves failed to impress Raymond in any way, Henry, flanked by Thomas, his warrior Chancellor, led his troops at a leisurely pace through Périgord in the direction of Quercy, a county famous for its rolling countryside and fertile soil. This was an area traditionally part of the Duchy of Aquitaine and therefore under the authority of Eleanor. As well as Toulouse and to add insult to injury, this area too had been impertinently claimed by Raymond.

As they set out, Henry told Thomas, "I mean to overawe this upstart Count. I will show him that I have more than sufficient forces to annihilate him whenever he chooses to meet me. He will rue the day he decided to make an enemy of me."

After halting briefly at the town of Périgueux to replenish with fresh provisions, Henry marched south to besiege the ancient walled citadel at Cahors.

An old Roman fortress set on a rocky height overlooking a wide bend in the River Lot as it meandered slowly down through Quercy towards the Garonne, Cahors had once been defended by its towering barbican and encircling walls. From the scouts he had sent ahead, Henry knew that these walls had fallen badly into disrepair and as a consequence, the citizens opened their gates to him without a fight. Unwilling to waste time and giving Raymond more time to gather his forces, the King continued at speed south towards Toulouse. By the second week of July he had pitched his camp outside the southern walls of Toulouse, possibly near the Porte Montoulieu about 500 yards east of the Château Narbonnais.

With Henry keen to make the expedition a speedy success, Thomas continued to throw himself into his new military duties with his customary enthusiasm. He had hand-picked a force of 700 knights from his own household and these men were already among Henry's elite troops. Thomas was determined to lead them in person.

But, while the army waited for its orders, King Louis arrived to parley with the opposing parties where he proposed acting as an impartial umpire. Raymond was having none of it and denounced Henry as the aggressor and appealed to his brother-in-law to save him. Henry was now in a cleft stick and had to make a difficult choice. Should he retreat in ignominy or should he attack the city? Even had Henry's army been able to penetrate the city, there were chains at every crossroads, catapults stationed on the tops of the towers guarding the narrow, cobbled streets, the Château Narbonnais, to which Louis had retreated, was a notoriously difficult target. A formidable fortress, it was integrated into the walls of the city, further protected by massive earthen ramparts. Henry faced a stark dilemma and not just whether he should or even could attack and take a well defended city but should he break his vows and attack his feudal overlord now in the city.

For the first time in their relationship, a serious quarrel between Thomas and Henry broke out. It happened at a council of war attended by all Henry's barons and captains at which he laid out his dilemma in no uncertain terms.

"Should I attempt to take the city by storm, or should I watch and wait to see if Louis will withdraw? If I risk an attack and storm the city, our army could incur huge losses, only to end up saddled with my overlord as a prisoner. Remember, Louis still has no male heir and my treaty with him, which as we all know was only recently concluded, would be in grave danger. I have to consider my dynasty's succession to the French throne which will be through my young son's future bride Margaret who, again as we are also all to well aware, is Louis's infant daughter. All this needs to be considered. Is the moment to turn this new-found amity with France upside down?" Henry wanted to know what he should do.

The barons veered strongly towards the side of caution but Thomas, forgetting to whom he was speaking, all but accused them of cowardice.

"You are deceiving the King only to save your own skins." The barons were horrified at this slight to their knightly prowess and attempted to shout Thomas down. Notwithstanding their shouts of protest, Thomas went on, "Louis has forfeited his rights as a feudal overlord by openly supporting our King's enemies. By standing against him here," he insisted, "the king of France has abdicated his position as our King Henry's feudal overlord. I vote and advise that the attack should go ahead. Think also of the effects on our own soldiers of their idling away time in the blistering summer sun."

Thomas's words were to no avail. Henry sided with the barons, and when Thomas still stood his ground, believing his arguments were valid, the king ordered him to be silent. Cracks were beginning to show in the closeness between the two men. Apart from the change in the atmosphere between the two men,

Thomas had succeeded in making enemies of those whom he had insulted with his strong words.

Then, when Louis' reinforcements arrived from France, the matter was put beyond all doubt. Determined not to waste any more time and in the hope of tempting Louis to leave his lair Henry ordered his army to decamp from around Toulouse. This they did and began besieging other castles and towns in the vicinity of the city, razing them to the ground and laying waste the countryside around about. Then fate struck a second blow to his hopes of success when his army became ravaged by dysentery and malaria. Now, he had no choice and in late September, he retreated first to Cahors and from there back to Normandy. His main force might have gone but he had left garrisons in several of the hill-top towns he had captured in Quercy. What rankled most for Henry was that Louis, for once, had successfully outwitted and outmanoeuvred him, judging correctly that, for all his weaponry, his rival, Henry, would not dare to attack his feudal overlord.

When the withdrawal had reached Cahors, emergency repairs were need to the walls after which Henry entrusted the citadel to Thomas before moving on to Normandy. Whatever repairs had been made to the walls, there was no question that the town would remain difficult to defend. This made it a 'poisoned cup' for whoever was unlucky enough to be given the job.

Henry, ever one to hold a grudge, took the opportunity the defence of Cahors offered to make his erstwhile friend suffer for daring to argue with him at Toulouse. Just to add to what would amount to a punishment duty and still smarting from his Chancellor's outspoken objections in the council of war, the king added another twist of the knife.

"You have asked me to give you the money you need to pay your troops and to buy provisions. That is not going to happen. They are your soldiers and are therefore your responsibility so you will have to pay their costs. However, I am prepared to lend you the money you need and you can repay it at a later date."

Thomas had little choice but to acquiesce. At the same time, Henry assigned overall command of his other Quercy garrisons to his disgraced former standard-bearer, Henry of Essex, he who had dropped the King's standard in a Welsh ambush during

Henry's campaign into Wales of 1157. Allowing the King's standard to fall on the battlefield was verging on treason and not easily forgiven. These two appointments only served as a strong reminder and reinforcement of the idea that he meant these tasks to be more of a punishment than a privilege. When asked to take on these commands all the other barons had found excuses as to why they could not undertake the task, however honoured they might feel that the King had thought them worthy.

By now, these towns and castles were all that Henry had to show for his punitive expedition down into Toulouse. This had been at huge expense and he made it clear that he did not expect to lose any of them. Thomas was left under no illusion as to what was expected of him.

Of course, whatever the politics and motivation had been for Henry giving him the task, Thomas relished the opportunity to prove himself capable of it. He felt that luck was, once again, on his side. He had been given the chance to prove once and for all that he was a warrior of the highest calibre and would show his detractors that he was equal if not better than them at everything he did. "I might be considered a low-born Londoner by many but I have more talent and ambition in my little finger than most of them will ever have." Thomas was never short on self-belief.

In his zeal to make Cahors secure, he took stupendous personal risks. In order to take three nearby heavily fortified castles, Thomas, wearing full armour, suddenly led his 700 knights out of the citadel and riding at the head of his troops successfully stormed and captured the three castles. Then, without adequate protection to his rear he galloped after his opponents to the far side of the Garonne. For all the thrilling action, his bravery was risky in the extreme. The reality was that he had risked leading his best troops straight into an enemy ambush and ultimate slaughter. His desperate urge to win his spurs and prove his mettle in a decisive battle just illustrated his inexperience in the practical art of warfare. When one of his household knights berated him for taking such risks with not only his own life but with those of his men, he merely replied, "faint heart never won the day." The same aversion to sensible caution had almost cost him his life as a teenager when he fell into a millstream while out hawking with Richer de l'Aigle. Once again, it seems that even as a warrior he was a newcomer aspiring to be an insider.

Thomas stayed in the south and did not re-join Henry in Normandy until the county of Quercy had been fully secured. Now, another difficult challenge awaited him. As he crossed the Norman frontier, he discovered to his horror that fighting had resumed between Louis and Henry in the Vexin and that French troops had invaded Normandy. In retaliation Henry had invaded France, razing the town of Beauvais to the ground before laying siege to the castle of Guerberoi and levelling it. He had then attacked Count Simon of Evreux, forcing him to abandon his castles at Rochefort, Epernon and Montfort, which effectively sliced the French royal demesne in two, giving the Angevins control of the main road between Paris and Orléans.

As soon as Thomas reappeared, Henry sent him and his troops to join in the fighting. In reality and being the experienced campaigner he was, Henry could not seriously have expected to hold such an exposed position for long. A series of sharp frosts were already announcing the arrival of a particularly cold winter so he was determined to take as much territory as he could before a truce was agreed. To help achieve this Thomas was assigned 1,200 mercenaries to supplement his own troop of knights plus around 4,000 others hired to serve them and attend to their horses. As in Quercy, the costs of so large a body of men quickly grew, since each knight required £3 per day for the keep of his men and horses. Once again, Thomas had to borrow heavily, this time from a Jewish moneylender on Henry's guarantee. As before, he had little choice, but these obligations, together amounting to 1,000 silver marks, were to be a serious liability. That debt was never repaid and Henry would never forget it.

Quite what Thomas's men did during the Vexin campaign is not clear since the records from that time have been lost. "Which is a bit of a shame," thought Brother Edward. "But I know that on at least one occasion Thomas repeated the recklessness of Cahors. Riding at a gallop at the head of his men towards the enemy he Engaged Engelram of Trie, a famous French knight, in single combat. Thomas succeeded in knocking his opponent off his horse and claimed his charger as a prize."

With his adrenalin high and his concentration closing out everything but a desire for victory, it might have seemed to Thomas as if warfare was becoming his true vocation. A temporary truce had been arranged during the winter but expired as spring returned and a peaceful solution to the conflict was looked for between the two warring Kings. Exploiting his cordial relationship with Louis, Thomas led the negotiations on Henry's side.

"So, Thomas," Henry asked, "what have you been able to agree with your friend Louis?" Thomas detected a slight sneer when Henry used the word 'friend'.

"I believe I have been able to secure terms which, in the circumstances, are extremely favourable to you my Lord. King Louis has confirmed that all your conquests in Quercy will remain yours in return for which you agree to the withdrawal of all your forces of occupation from France. Further, I have convinced him to return the lands of the old Norman Vexin to you which is really what you have always wanted. Louis will hold back only Gisors and some other strategically important castles. These coveted castles are to be held in trust until his daughter Margaret's wedding day, when they will revert to you my Lord as the final element of her dowry settlement. As neutral guarantors of the peace agreement King Louis summoned to his presence three leading Knights Templar who are already familiar figures to you in London, Richard of Hastings, Osto of St-Omer and Robert de Pirou and swore them on oath to hold the castles until after the wedding. I hope you; my Lord find these terms agreeable?"

"I do Thomas. You have done well, as I expected you would. Theobald was not wrong when he recommended you as a useful negotiator."

Thomas had salvaged the dynastic alliance on which he had spent so much time and effort during his embassy to Paris. Louis did not expect his daughter Margaret, who was still barely two, to be married for another ten years or more. Henry, on the other hand and whatever he might have told Thomas at the time, would never be content with any settlement that did not give him everything he wanted. He wanted the castles now. He was not prepared to wait for the marriage to happen before the return of the castles he thought should be his. Henry was ever impatient with any delay in the fulfilment of his wishes and breaking agreements when it suited him was not something that troubled his conscience.

Now twenty-seven and supremely confident of his abilities, Henry intended to strike and to win even if it meant using underhand methods. Nothing could be allowed to stand in his way. When Constance of Castile died suddenly in September 1160 he got the excuse he needed to take action. Louis announced within a fortnight of Constance's death that he would take a third wife, Adela of Blois-Champagne, dead King Stephen's niece. There was method to Louis' decision. He was determined to father a son and heir as soon as possible, so had chosen a bride from a family able to trace its descent from William the Conqueror and so stake a claim, however flimsy, to the kingdom of England. The inference and possible consequences of this marriage inflamed Henry. Provoked beyond reason, Henry decided to take matters into his own hands.

When he heard of the King's plans Thomas felt it was important to advise him of Canon law as it currently stood. "My Lord," he told Henry, "I would not be doing my duty if I failed to bring to your attention the Church's law as it now stands. That law strictly forbids the weddings of children under twelve."

"Well, you are the expert, find a way around the law. Create one if necessary. I will have this marriage between my son and Louis' daughter take place as soon as possible, whatever the Church says."

Somehow a clandestine licence for the wedding to go ahead was quickly extorted from papal representatives. Whether this was arranged by Henry or Thomas, no-one is quite sure.

On 2 November, the young prince Henry married Margaret in Normandy, where she had conveniently been living for the past two years as Henry's ward and where she would continue to live until she reached the age of twelve. Not quite a prisoner but close enough. As a consequence of the hastily arranged marriage, the Templars, according to their oaths, were honour bound to hand over the castles in their care to a triumphant Henry. Louis, on the other hand was furious. He accused Henry of fraud and the

Templars of bare-faced treachery. Louis was not going to take this piece of blatant trickery lying down.

Assisted by his new wife's relatives, he crossed the frontier and harried Touraine, but Henry retaliated and stormed the castle of Chaumont on the Loire. It was a stalemate in which neither monarch achieved very much but probably felt better for their mutual shows of force.

Thomas, meanwhile, had come safely through his baptism of arms on the battlefields of Quercy and Normandy. Thanks to him, Henry's territorial gains in Quercy had been secured, while from the peace settlement he had negotiated with Louis the King had recovered the whole of the Norman Vexin, as he had long been trying to do. Whether all these things had been achieved by methods fair or foul is open to interpretation and depended on which side of the argument one stood..

For all the gains Henry had made, the original aim of the campaign had not been achieved. Henry would gradually allow Eleanor's claim to outright possession of the lands occupied by Count Raymond to fall into abeyance. He replaced this claim instead by a more nebulous demand for homage which reinforced the point that, where his empire was concerned, he would always put his interests ahead of Eleanor's. This understandably did little to make the relationship between the King and his wife a harmonious one.

Another result of the Toulouse campaign as far as our story goes was a cooling in the friendship between Henry and Thomas, even if the Chancellor was hardly to blame for what had gone wrong. Although Thomas still retained much of his old influence, he was after all still the Chancellor but found that after their heated disagreement before the gates of Toulouse, Henry would deploy many of the same controlling tactics against him as he used against everyone else. Outwardly it appeared that his reputation had recovered and it would seem to the world as if all was still well. He was still given a place of honour at Prince Henry's wedding and was still sufficiently high in the King's favour that the boy would now be placed in his household to be educated with the other sons of the leading barons who served as pages there.

The behaviour and seeming lack of moral scruples displayed by Thomas at the gates of Toulouse may have persuaded Henry of his Chancellor's lack of any true religious zeal, thus presenting the King with a possible opportunity in the future.

Chapter 28

Thomas the Archbishop

Brother Edward began a new part of his story which had now reached a pivotal point.

"King Henry," he wrote, "seldom makes mistakes and even if he does, no-one dares to tell him he has. His friendship with Thomas no longer had the closeness of previous years but they still had a strong working relationship and Henry trusted Thomas's judgement in most things and he was still sure of his Chancellor's loyalty towards him."

Thomas, on the other hand, had soon realised that he was always going to be the lesser partner in an unequal friendship. The business of the beggar and the cloak had made that clear as had his being given the punishment task of defending Cahors after the withdrawal from Toulouse.

The two men were different in many ways but so are lots of friends. Thomas certainly enjoyed the high life, and was hugely hedonistic in many regards, furnishing his home lavishly, socialising hard and sailing to France on his own ships. He liked extravagant clothes and his public shows of wealth was clearly demonstrated during his embassy to Paris. Thomas was known to give with prodigality and always acted with panache.

Henry, conversely, disliked show and ostentation. He rarely wore new or even clean clothes. He disliked spending his money unless he had to, which was usually when he could not find someone else's to spend.

Thomas's behaviour differed from Henry's in one particular regard. From all that we know of Thomas, he always took being chaste seriously. It is no secret that the King did not. Perhaps, this should have warned Henry that perhaps his Chancellor was not without a measure of piety albeit well hidden.

Henry was about to make the biggest mistake of his life.

By 1162, Thomas had been Henry's Chancellor for almost seven years but that was about to change. Archbishop Theobald died in 1161 leaving the post of Archbishop of Canterbury vacant. Henry, with the help of Thomas had already succeeded in restoring the power of the monarchy and central government over the nobles after the Anarchy. Now, he would turn his attention to the church which he felt still had much more power than it had done during the reign of his grandfather, Henry, the first of that name. He was determined to do to the church what he had done to his nobles and who better to help him in this endeavour than Thomas? In Thomas, he saw a man who would be an ideal ally at the highest echelons of the church, who would have no qualms in wearing the robes but in reality would be doing his, that is to say Henry's business.

The See of Canterbury had remained vacant for almost a year before Henry proposed that Thomas should fill the vacancy. This should hardly have come as a surprise to Thomas but for Henry, it was not simply a case, as some would have seen it, of the King promoting a friend.

Henry's reason for wanting Thomas as Archbishop in Theobald's place was a pragmatic decision. Henry was only interested in the results and consequences of actions that he thought benefited him. In his later years, Theobald had become a particularly nagging thorn in Henry's side and was certainly slowing down, if not stopping altogether, the King's efforts to curtail some of the Church's powers. Henry deeply resented the independence of the Church which had its own legal system and whose loyalty to God and the Pope came before its loyalty to the Crown.

Henry gave Thomas the good news. "I have decided that you are to be the next Archbishop of Canterbury."

Thomas said nothing.

"Why the glum face Thomas? This position will afford you untold wealth and power, the things you have always craved. Do not pretend that it is not so."

Thomas had, by now, learned to understand the king's character as well as the wickedness and rapacity of his officials. He knew that if he were to accept the post offered to him, he would lose either the favour of God or that of the King.

From a very young age Thomas had, had a strong Christian faith instilled in him by his mother as well as spending all that time at Merton Priory where his beliefs were no doubt strengthened at the hands of his monk tutors. True he may have been thought by some contemporaries to be a man of pleasure-seeking bent, enthused by hawking and hunting and ostentatious shows of opulence but was only a veneer hiding a much deeper, more profound religiosity? For he could not, when it came to the crux of the matter, in all conscience obey God at the same time as obeying the King nor on the other hand, he realised, give precedence to the laws of the Church without making an enemy of the King.

Therefore, he answered, "My lord, I am flattered that you think me worthy of the position but I am happy to remain as your Chancellor. I am in reality but a clerk whilst to be an Archbishop I would need to be an ordained priest and I have no calling for that life. I am, as ever, flattered that you think so highly of me but an Archbishop is not something I want to be. I beg you my Prince, do not do this."

Thomas should have known better than to argue with Henry never mind attempt to disobey what was obviously a command. He had tried that before and it had brought him only trouble. He would have done well to remember his humiliation during the council of war at Toulouse. Henry ruled by force and fear. To survive as long as he had in the febrile service of Henry, Thomas had proved himself to be shrewd and disciplined as chancellor. He should have known Henry well enough by this time in their relationship, it could no longer be called a friendship, to be aware of the limitations of his position. In plain terms, that meant doing nothing which might offend the king.

It is not good enough for Henry to win. He has to be seen by all to do so. As a king appointed by God he has free rein to be wilful, autocratic and capricious. He is a ruler with an innate appreciation of his awesome powers which he is quite prepared to use when it suits him. He has always been able to regularly cut his courtiers and officials down to size by ambushing them and sometimes, reducing them to jelly when the mood takes him.

When he was a younger man Henry still had to prove himself to those around him while he was creating a direction for himself.

At that time, there can be no doubt that he found Thomas useful, amusing and companionable, thus indulging him and treating him as a favourite, He was also well aware that such advantages could always be withdrawn. Perhaps now was the time for Henry to give a sharp tug on his chancellor's reins.

But now, the King's face was stony. "You misunderstand me Lord Chancellor. I am not asking you to be the Archbishop of Canterbury, I am telling you that, that is what you are going to be. Do not forget your place and dare to refuse my wishes. You should know by now that I make a much better friend than an enemy. My opinion of power and authority is that I'm all for it. Ninety-five out of every hundred people in my empire need to be told what to do and in this instance, that includes you. So, prepare yourself to be my next Archbishop, which is exactly who you are going to be, like it or not. The ultimate power and authority within my realm rests with and flows from, me. The matter is settled, we will not discuss it further.

Henry's plan to promote Thomas was obviously an attempt to increase his direct power over the Church through the back door. In the same way that Theobald had insinuated Thomas into Henry's court, Henry was going try the same strategy with Thomas and the Church. He wanted his man on the inside. Perhaps he should have considered more carefully how Theobald's plan to infiltrate his court had backfired in that far from being the church's man, Thomas had become Henry's man.

In the scriptorium, Brother Edward laid aside his quill whilst he considered how to best continue his story. He took stock of the situation. Henry and Thomas had drifted apart, if indeed they had ever been as close as many assumed they had. Henry was determined to reassert what he perceived as his rights over the Church and he would enlist the proven skills of Thomas to aid him in doing so. To say the least, Thomas was reticent. He had a way of life that suited him with the money and power to do as he liked as long as he kept on the right side of a vindictive King. The fly in that particular ointment was Henry's wish to make him Archbishop of Canterbury. Thomas knew it was a circle he could not square so he would have to go along with Henry's plan whether he liked it or not.

"That just about sums it up and makes it clear in my mind but I must enquire of Prior Luc as to whether he can find me a copy of William FitzStephen's book that he has written concerning the life of Thomas. He too was present at the end. I know Prior Luc has many contacts with other learned men who may know of the whereabouts of such a valuable resource." Brother Edward picked up his quill and began to write again:

It was not just Thomas who was unhappy with Henry's wish to appoint him as archbishop. Indeed, there were quite possibly more against it than in favour of it. Many of the existing prelates were fully set against it for a multitude of reasons not the least being that, as Thomas himself had pointed out, he was not an ordained priest. An archdeacon he might have been but that did not make him a cleric and even then he had been accused many times of abusing that position for his own gain. The majority of churchmen were against his elevation to the highest place in the English Church whether the King wanted it or not. Apart from which, it was ultimately a decision for the Pope in Rome to make and not Henry's. Which, of course was, all part of the reason for Henry wanting Thomas at the top of the organisation he wanted to change.

On a theological basis the Church's list of objections to Thomas was a long one, not the least being his venial sins. "Many times," they said, "and in many places he did wrong on the king's behalf. He is also very materialistic, loving as he does expensive food, wine and clothes. His critics also feared that as Thomas, so they thought, was a close friend of the King, he would not be an independent leader of the church and as such would not put the needs of the Church first." They were not blind to the schemes the King might be capable of.

There were, however, those who thought Thomas had some redeeming qualities and that he might not be as bad as his public persona suggested. Guernes of Pont-Sainte-Maxence had been reported as saying "Proud he may have been during the day but he used to make amends privately to God at night." Others thought that the main difference between Thomas and the King and his other courtiers was that despite his well-known worldly vanities Thomas was recognised as being chaste in body and healthy in soul. This would have stood out as an impressive achievement in royal palaces, where whores crowded around the gatehouses and fornication was considered normal behaviour. It has been said that Henry actively encouraged Thomas to join in the debauchery but with no success. Thomas refused these overtures saying, "I am a chaste man who hates indecency and depravity". It may be an undeniable fact that Thomas was hungry for power but perhaps not at the price of his soul.

Even though some had spoken up for him, the thought of Thomas as their Archbishop angered most of the leading churchmen. They stressed again, that Thomas had never been a priest and that when he fought against the French during the Toulouse campaign he had earned a reputation as a cruel military commander. It was claimed that he destroyed cities and towns, put manors to the torch without pity and deprived many of all their possessions. How many deaths had Thomas been accountable for? One of the bishops who opposed his appointment was Gilbert Foliot of Hereford. He himself was a complex figure, he was an ascetic and known for his pious life but may secretly have thought that the Archbishopric should have been his. To further Henry's wishes, in a highly unusual but not completely unheard-of procedure, Thomas became a priest on 2 June, and on 3 June, against his wishes, he was consecrated Archbishop.

Whereas Henry had the confidence of a born aristocrat, the manners of a schoolyard bully and the stomach of an ox he was always anxious and insecure by temperament. Never able to manage stress well, he suffered from a digestive ailment which, I am told, began to trigger intermittent bouts of increasingly painful and debilitating stomach problems. Severe mental strain linked to overwork would cause it to flare up, leading to short but agonizing periods of pain making the King even more unpredictable than ever. Remember, by now, Henry was not only dealing with the problems he perceived within the Church but also with those caused by warring, rebellious sons and a difficult, manipulative wife. It is little wonder that he looked for an ally and mistakenly thought Thomas would be that man.

158

Chapter 29

War between Thomas and Henry

Consider, if Thomas's friendship with Henry was indeed shallower and less sincere than we have been led to believe, is it then possible that he was always less in thrall to the royal personage than appears to have been the case? Is it the case that he was always going to be his own man? Thomas had always been close to his mother as a child and whatever he may have been outwardly, had he always been privately extremely devout> Someone who prayed several times a day. Was this a hint of the man he was soon to become and one that Henry had overlooked completely?

When Thomas had at first refused the post of Archbishop, he had warned Henry that he knew the King's plans for the Church and that if he were the Archbishop, he must, in good faith, oppose them. He again begged Henry not to make him Archbishop.

If Henry had been able to foresee the future or to realise what troubles he had just unleashed for himself he may not have been quite so hasty in his actions.

Brother Edward thought deeply about reasons and a possible explanation for what next happened to Thomas. "We must take, as always, the gospels as a source of enlightenment for the things that happen in life which we do not readily understand and in this case, the Book of Acts gives us our answer. After being forced into a role he had neither sought nor wanted, Thomas had what could be called his "Road to Damascus" moment. He could no longer deny his conscience. "

It seemed to Brother Edward that when Thomas became Archbishop, "he threw off the layman and became the complete Archbishop. Thomas had been a member of Theobald's household for many years, a place of ecclesiastical excellence and high learning, much of which must have been absorbed by a man with an enquiring mind such as Thomas. Even though Thomas was not in holy orders, Henry may have underestimated the influence of this early experience and been blinded by the wish to have his confidante controlling the Church. Perhaps," Brother Edward thought, "that the possibility that Thomas's early exposure by both his mother and Theobald to devoutness went much deeper and had been overlooked. Were the trappings of secular power merely a veneer to hide the real man? Did he realise on becoming Archbishop an underlying spiritual vocation which had, until now, been kept repressed by the over-riding ambition for worldly things? Greed, it is such a mean, small-minded vice. As if money matters at all? True, it matters to many people, especially those who do not have it but only to those who have nothing of real value in their lives. Had Thomas found his true calling?

Thomas was well aware that in the eyes of many respected churchmen he did not deserve to be Archbishop. He was, as we have seen, thought too worldly and too much the King's friend to be trusted with such a position. His response to these criticisms surprised everyone, even those who thought they knew him well. His self-esteem wounded, Thomas set out to prove to the world that he was going to become the best of all possible Archbishops. From the very beginning it would seem that Thomas would go out of his way to defy Henry and his plans for the Church.

While Henry was still in France, Thomas showed that now he had been made Archbishop against his wishes he meant to make himself independent of royal control and did this by resigning as Chancellor without consulting the King. Thomas gave his reason for taking this action as a conflict of interests, maintaining that he would not be able to serve both the King and the Church equally at the same time. Of course, this took away the whole reason for the King appointing him to the position in the first place. This was not the situation Henry had envisaged and this was only the start.

On a personal level, after being appointed as Archbishop, Thomas began to show a greater concern for the poor than had previously been the case. Every morning, he ordered that his staff should bring thirteen poor people to his home and after washing their feet he would personally serve them a meal. When the meal was over, he give each one of them four silver pennies. One of Thomas's first acts was to double his predecessor Theobald's expenditure on the poor as well as sending food and clothing to the homes of the sick. Gone were his expensive clothes. Instead, he now wore a simple monastic habit and as a penance for previous sins he slept on a cold, stone floor.

This was a changed man. Gone was his customary splendour of clothing and furnishings. These were aspects of the man that had so worried his contemporaries when he was the archdeacon. His blatant misuse of that position for his own gain whilst neglecting the duties that went with it troubled them greatly. One particular annoyance had been Thomas's heavy-handed approach to the Church when the bishops had complained about the heavy rates of Scutage being levied on them. Perhaps most serious of all, in the eyes of many churchmen, was his ignoring of Theobald's summons to visit him when he lay dying, the man who had been the first to give him support and favour despite his low-born status. Up to the point where the King had appointed him Archbishop of Canterbury there was little doubt that in public affairs he had been Henry's man.

This sudden and dramatic change in Thomas puzzled Brother Edward. "I shall seek guidance on this matter from a wiser mind than my own," he decided.

"What brings you to me this morning Brother?" Prior Luc asked. "Come in and share a cup of wine with me while we talk."

"A vexatious problem to which I have no creditable answer and without the answer, the story will be somehow incomplete." Brother Edward then elucidated his concerns about the seemingly inexplicable volte face in Thomas's behaviour and asked the question of his Prior, "what caused it?"

"A conundrum indeed Brother. As you have said, the only plausible answer and the one which we, as men of God, must put our faith in, is that like the blessed Saint Paul, Thomas was shown his truth path by the Lord. You need look no further than that for your answer."

Even though he was a man of the Church, Brother Edward was not entirely convinced by his Prior's explanation but it relieved him of further responsibility for any deeper thought on the matter and thus the onus of finding an answer had been removed from his frail shoulders. If Prior Luc said that Thomas had been spoken to by the Almighty then that was good enough for him. He need look no further for an explanation. Miracles did happen. Anyway, Prior Luc always served the best wine in the priory so the visit had been doubly successful. Now it was time to eat and then he would return to his work in the scriptorium.

All during his mid-day meal, Brother Edward continued to ponder the question he had asked his prior. Could he believe that the only reason for Thomas's new-found austerity of conduct could truly have come about by divine intervention only? Was it not the case that when told by Henry of his intention to make him archbishop, Thomas's immediate reaction had been to say an emphatic 'no'? Even given the cooling of the relationship between the two, Thomas must have been aware of what Henry had in mind for the Church and if care of the Church was being placed in his hands then the two must fall out.

The more Brother Edward thought about it, the more he thought that there may have been an even more simple answer than the intervention of a higher being. Thomas had always been supremely ambitious but at the same time, had always been in thrall to whoever was his direct superior whether that was Theobald or then Henry. Was the giving up of a few creature comforts a price worth paying to give him real power and independence? As Archbishop of Canterbury, only the Pope would be in a position to question his actions and decisions and he was many miles away in Rome. Even the doubting bishops would be subservient to Thomas's will. In some ways, Thomas as Archbishop would be on an equal footing with the King. Looking further to the future, might not a diligent Archbishop fighting a King to protect the Church not, one day, be considered worthy of being a Pope?

The clash of the two men was not long in coming. The crux of the matter was fundamental. For Henry, the status quo between Church and State was out of balance. Henry believed that he, representing the State, should always be superior to the Church. Diametrically opposed to that thought was Thomas's view that the superiority of Church over State was to him a fact

162

which allowed for no discussion and hence forward, for him, would never be in any doubt.

To reinforce his position and that of the Church, Thomas set about recovering lands he maintained had been stolen during the Anarchy by the Barons. He was, after all only following what Henry had told him to do as Chancellor but with a major difference. Any lands and revenues he now recovered were going to go to the Church and not into Henry's treasury. Thomas's actions in this had been endorsed by Pope Alexander III at a general council held in Tours in 1163 which Thomas had attended and during which had made a formal complaint of the infringements by the laity on the rights and immunities of the Church. Henry was not pleased with this development. This was not how things were supposed to work.

Thomas soon came into conflict with a certain Roger of Clare, Earl of Hertford. Thomas insisted that some of the manors in Kent should come under the ownership of the See of Canterbury. Roger disagreed and refused to give them up. When Thomas sent a messenger to Roger with a letter asking for a meeting, Roger responded by forcing the messenger to eat the letter. Thomas was not impressed by this turn of events and as a matter of policy set out to excommunicate all those who dared to oppose him.

Here, Brother Edward paused in his writing for a moment's reflection. "To think, that at the time this was going on, I was the rector at Saltwood, one of the manors under scrutiny and from where I would later move to Cambridge. Perhaps if things had been different I would not be sitting here writing this."

Henry must have felt that Thomas was being as obstructive as possible in his animosity towards him, even to the extent of meddling in the marriage plans of Henry's youngest brother William FitzEmpress. This particular problem arose when William wanted to marry Isabel de Warenne.

Heiress, **Isabel de Warenne**, Countess of Surrey and Warenne had been married to King Stephen's youngest son, William of Blois. He had died while returning from campaigning in Toulouse, thus leaving Isabel a wealthy young widow, and a highly desirable marriage prize. Though recently widowed, Isabel would have been well aware that she was expected to remarry. The fact that she held the mighty earldom of Surrey would have made settling her future even more pressing. The earl of Warenne, her father, had contributed knights and men from his own lands to the armies of both King Stephen and Henry. Henry would naturally have expected this to continue but Isabel could not be expected to lead men into battle. Which is why she needed a husband and a that husband had to be someone loyal to King Henry. His brother William would fit the requirements ideally.

William FitzEmpress therefore sought a dispensation to marry Isabel. Because of their complicated heritage and a previous marriage, they would need a dispensation from 'affinity'. Isabel's degree of affinity was counted from her as a widow through her deceased husband William of Blois, who was a double second cousin of William. The men's maternal grandmothers were siblings and FitzEmpress' maternal grandfather was the sibling of Blois' paternal grandmother. A tangled web. Such dispensations were usually granted without difficulty of fuss. In this case however, the dispensation was refused by Thomas on the grounds of consanguinity. This objection appeared to Henry to be petty in that it was not due to a blood relationship between Isabel and William but between William and Isabel's first husband, William of Blois because they were second cousins. The outcome was that shortly after the marriage was disallowed on the orders of Thomas, William died, his friends saying of a broken heart after being disappointed in his desire to marry Isabel. He was only 27, a relatively young man. Just something else to sour relations between the King and his Archbishop which was to come back and haunt Thomas much later.

Henry now had an archbishop who was being much more difficult and stubborn than Theobald had ever been and relations between the Crown and the Church were deteriorating rapidly. Henry could never and would never forgive anyone or anything he thought disloyal and Thomas now definitely in that category and on that sobering thought, Brother Edward dusted his manuscript and went in search of his supper.

After his supper Brother Edward returned to his perch in the scriptorium and though weary, continued with his writing by the

164

light of a guttering candle. Little wonder his eyesight was failing him. Picking up his quill, he wrote:

By 1163 Thomas had been archbishop for almost two years when Henry returned from Normandy after a long spell in his French territories. He came with a determination to make the changes he planned to the status of the Church. He wanted to revert to the situation between Church and State as it had been during his grandfather Henry's time when the King had, had strict control over the church. This meant him going against the trend of Gregorian Reform which had spread from Italy to France and then to Henry's domains across the Channel and onto England with ideas of free elections to clerical posts, the inviolability of church property, the freedom of appeal to Rome, and clerical immunity from lay tribunals. Henry was having none of it. He saw it as his duty to protect the traditional rights of his royal government in regard to the Church.

One of the first things Henry was told when he got back from Normandy was that while he had been away, there had been a dramatic increase in serious crime. The king's officials claimed that over a hundred murderers had escaped their proper punishment because they had claimed their right to be tried in Church courts. To make it worse, not all of those that had sought the privilege of a trial in a Church court were exclusively clergymen. The definition of who was a clergyman was loose and any man who had been trained by the church, whether for the priesthood or not, could choose to be tried by a Church court. This meant that clerks and even a Church employee who had merely been taught to read and write by the Church had a right to a Church court trial. This was obviously to an offender's advantage, as Church courts could not impose punishments that caused blood to be spilt so, physical retribution such as execution or mutilation were not going to happen. If a priest committed a murder, the worst that could happen to him was that he would be defrocked. There were plenty of examples of clergy found guilty of murder or robbery who only received 'spiritual' punishments, such as suspension from office or banishment from the altar.

A serious clash between Church and State was now inevitable. Henry made it clear that he was going to extend the jurisdiction of secular courts to English Churchmen. Thomas made it equally clear that it was not going to happen while he was Archbishop. The battle lines had been drawn.

Chapter 30

Clarendon and exile beckon

After his late night, Brother Edward had slept well and was early in the scriptorium, eager to write the next part of his story. He began:

Perhaps it was the fact of his being low-born that ate away at Thomas throughout his life. He had been born with an urge to excel, proud and unbending. Whatever task he took on, he would carry it out to the utmost of his abilities.

Therefore, once Henry had appointed him Archbishop of Canterbury, Thomas took it as his responsibility to protect the interests of the English Church against the plans of a man he knew to be ruthless. At this time, Thomas knew full well that the Holy Father, Alexander III, was in exile in France and dependent on the charity of the French Church and Kings like Henry in England and Louis in France. Now, Henry was putting into action his desire to extend his control over the English Church by revising the 'customs of his grandfather' or 'customs of the realm.'

Thomas was standing in his path and was well aware of Henry's way of getting things done. As an example of what he was up against, he remembered that Henry had once ordered Winchester to, "hold free and fair elections but be sure to elect my man Robert to the post". Not very subtle.

Now, as Archbishop, Thomas fully committed himself to the observance of Canon Law, the Law of the Church, giving clergymen the right to be tried in an ecclesiastical court which was, as we know, often more lenient than that of the State. Although this would be the primary cause of the rift between the two men it was not the only one. Henry had other grievances with his new Archbishop.

1163 was to be a year of confrontation between two powerful men who both thought they were right. There were to be arguments, re-visiting of old sleights and new issues to be fought over.

The first of these were the actions Thomas took to recover lands lost to his archdiocese. Much of it had been seized by local lords in Stephen's reign, and there were still important castles which had not been given back. He had recently returned from a great Church council at Tours, at which edicts against those who took property from the Church had been proclaimed; and he now demanded the restitution of four castles in Kent from their occupiers. To do this he used a spurious royal writ, and no longer being Chancellor, he technically had no authority to use. These rights gave him the power to have any alienated lands restored. No such writ had been granted, only the King could do that and Thomas's high-handedness caused many complaints to the King from those whose lands Thomas was reacquiring for the Church by this using what amounted to a subterfuge or even, a fraud. Thomas was flexing his muscles at the King's expense and as far as Henry was concerned this was something he could not allow to go on.

Thomas appeared intent on angering Henry by making full use of his powers as Archbishop. Thomas excommunicated a tenant-in-chief for resisting his attempt to install a priest in a church were the tenant claimed it was his right to name the appointee and not Thomas's. This was a risky thing to do as a tenant-in-chief held his lands directly from the King as opposed to holding them from another nobleman. This type of tenure was one which denoted great honour and by his high-handed action, Thomas was issuing a direct challenge to the King's authority. Thomas had to give way on the matter after Henry made it clear that the custom of England was that no tenant-in-chief could be excommunicated without royal permission.

Chapter 31

Woodstock

Then, at the beginning of July 1163 Henry summoned a Grand Council of Bishops, Barons and other magnates to his hunting lodge at Woodstock among whom was Thomas. The prime purpose for the Council was for Henry to be able to receive, in front of and witnessed by his vassals, Malcolm, King of the Scots, Rhys Prince of South Wales, Owain of the north and five important persons from Wales, when they paid homage to the King and his son, Young Henry. With these acts of homage, Henry had now become the titular overlord of the whole of this island.

More importantly and germane to the falling out between Henry and Thomas was that it was at this council that Henry attempted to have Sheriff's Aid, a custom which at that time prevailed in England, paid not directly to the sheriffs as was currently done, but into his royal treasury. The custom was that two shillings for each hide of land held by a landowner was paid to the sheriffs who guarded the counties. Henry was quick to see that if the two shillings from each of those hides were lumped into a single whole they would form a huge amount and it was this money that he wished to have for his own use and income. Thomas, as the son of a former sheriff of London and the secretary to another for just over two years before entering Theobald's service, knew only too well the likely impact of stripping the sheriffs of their only legitimate source of funds. Knowing the King as he did, Thomas was also well aware that once monies were paid into the treasury they were then unlikely to be disbursed to the Sheriffs.

Of course, prior to his appointment as Archbishop of Canterbury, Thomas, in his position as Chancellor, would have known intimately what rights the king had or did not have to raise taxes, and in what circumstances.

This led to vociferous disagreement by Thomas to Henry's proposal which he made with forthrightness but also with some modesty, remembering to whom he was speaking.

"This aid has always been a free will offering, neither compulsory nor a duty, to the sheriffs and cannot be compelled and making it a compulsory payment to the treasury amounts to a tax. If your sheriffs act peacefully and in a restrained manner towards our people, then the aid will be gladly paid, as is the custom. If, however, we feel they have not done their duty, we will not be under obligation to pay, and neither legally will they be able to be enforce payment by the landowners. I tell you now that if this is made a tax, not a penny will be paid from my estates or church lands," Thomas stated. "I find it surprising that an attempt is being made by the King to extort money from landowners, such as the Barons here present and the Church and it will not be popular. The customs relating to these payments of Sherriff's Aid have long been held," he added.

As can be imagined, the King was furious with his Archbishop's reply. "By the eyes of God," he said, "this 'aid' will be recorded as the King's revenue. Nor is it your right to contradict me in this matter. You will submit to my will or face the consequences."

Lacking any moderation in his speech, Thomas was not still finished and retorted, "by the eyes on which you have sworn I say again on this question, never from my land, whilst I am alive, will anything be given other than by free will." This was a complete volte face by Thomas as it was exactly the kind of scheme which as Chancellor he would have implemented himself on behalf of the King. Now it seemed as if he was determined to set himself up as an antagonist to the King.

Henry was wise enough to see that those assembled had been swayed by Thomas's words and reluctantly accepted that he was not, on this occasion, going to get his own way. On the one hand he had all the authority and power of a man appointed by God. He could if he so wished, have had Thomas's tongue ripped out for daring to disagree with him. On the other hand, he was wise and experienced enough to know that now was not the time for such a show of his capabilities. There would be another day for the evening of scores.

Still the feud raged on. Clarembald, a monk appointed Abbott, by command of the King, to St Augustine's Abbey in Canterbury in 1163 decided to side with the King. After his appointment, Clarembald refused to make a profession of obedience to Thomas, claiming that the abbey was exempt from oversight by the Archbishop and that swearing obedience to him would compromise the Abbey's independence. Unsurprisingly, Henry backed him in this, perhaps wishing that Thomas would follow the Abbott's example and do as he was told by the man who promoted him. Then Henry took a step that he knew would irritate Thomas even further by seeking the Papal Legateship for Roger of Pont L'Évêque, Archbishop of York and Thomas's bête noire of old, rather than for Thomas who felt the position should have been his. As the Papal Legate Roger would be the personal representative of the Pope in England and thereby empowered to deal with all matters of the Catholic faith and for the settlement of ecclesiastical business. He would, in effect, outrank Thomas which was a situation that Henry knew full well would peeve Thomas enormously.

Chapter 32

Westminster

As the end of the year approached, the two men were no nearer a compromise in their positions and in October Henry summoned the ecclesiastical hierarchy to a council in Westminster. The issue of what to do with 'criminous clerks', members of the clergy who had been accused of committing a serious secular crime but were tried in ecclesiastical courts by "benefit of clergy" being the main item on his agenda. This was centred around the question that had long been a bone of contention between the King and the Church. Henry was determined that this problem was going to be dealt with and that this time, he would get his way. As long ago as 1158 the King had complained that in his view, which was the one that counted, archdeacons and deans were coercing more from people than he was receiving in revenue and that many of these payments were being illegally obtained by these so called criminous clerks. Put simply, Henry made various complaints about how the church was governed, not just their attitude to criminous clerks but also the fact that appeals were being made above his head directly to the Pope.

Elsewhere in Europe however, the issue of criminous clerks had never become a major bone of contention between Church and State. Could the only reason for its becoming a major issue in England be because of the personalities involved? This was, at its core, a quarrel between Thomas and Henry and need never have reached the stage it did. It was going to be as vicious as any quarrel between erstwhile close friends could be.

Thomas held to his belief that all clergy, whether only in minor orders or not, were not to be dealt with by secular powers. "Only the ecclesiastical hierarchy can judge them for crimes, even those that are secular in nature," was his position on the question.

Thomas's stance remained that priests, if in an ecclesiastical court were found guilty of serious crimes even such as rape or murder, could not be then handed over to the secular authority. Because, he maintained, they had already been punished, usually by being deprived of their holy orders and the principle was that 'God did not permit a second punishment for the same offence'. To plead 'benefit of clergy' was to claim exemption from all secular authority that is to say, from the King's authority. Henry was intent on changing that situation. There can be no doubt that when he had made Thomas both Chancellor and Archbishop, Henry had thought to resolve this conflict, and to bring about the full restoration of the crown's authority. He had never expected Thomas to fight him over the issue.

Henry told the assembled bishops, "this position deprives me of the ability to govern effectively, and also undermines law and order in England. Furthermore," he added, "the laws and customs of England support this view, and Theobald of Bec, your previous archbishop, had admitted in 1154, to the Papacy, that the English custom was to allow secular courts to try clerks accused of crimes. I am told that as many as one person in five of the male population in England is protected by these ecclesiastical rules which means I have no control over one fifth of the people I rule. This cannot and will not continue." Henry then demanded that the English bishops now upheld what he considered to be those established customs of England regarding matters such as excommunication, criminous clerks and appeals to Rome.

To begin with, the bishops disagreed with the king, who then asked them if they would agree merely to observe the ancient customs of England in principle, without being required to take an oath or the clerks making any record of their agreement. The bishops, much to Henry's fury, remained steadfastly behind Thomas and led by him as their Archbishop initially refused to agree to Henry's demands. Then, however, the next day, the Bishops did agree to swear a partial and conditional oath to Henry but refused to agree to observe any of the customs if they conflicted with Canon law. To their oath, they had attached the caveat "saving their order" thus still not giving Henry the full support he wanted or expected and giving the bishops an escape route when making the oath. Henry stormed off saying that this was, "poisonous sophistry".

Thomas had not finished and added, "my Lord, I am not unmindful of the favours which, not you alone, but God, who dispenses all things, has condescended to confer on me through you. Wherefore, far be it from me to show myself ungrateful or to act contrary to your will in anything, only so long as it accords with the will of God."

These words were barely out of his mouth when Henry cut him short. "I neither need nor want a sermon. Are you not the son of one of my villeins? Answer me yes or no."

"In truth," replied Thomas, stung by the jibe against his middle-class ancestry, "I am not sprung from royal ancestors, but neither was St Peter, the prince of the Apostles, to whom the Lord deigned to give the keys of the Kingdom of Heaven and the primacy of the whole Church."

"True," responded the King "but he died for his Lord."

'And I,' answered Thomas, "will die for my Lord when the time comes. I trust and rely only in God, for cursed is the man that puts his hope in man."

"Perhaps," Brother Edward thought as he considered what next to write, "That Thomas spoke in the heat of the moment and we have no reason to believe he was making a serious threat against the King or indeed predicting and courting martyrdom. As far as Thomas was concerned at this point in time, he still believed that he could win."

After a few moments, Thomas had calmed down and added more soberly, "I can only answer, as I did before, that I am ready to please and honour you," then adding what would become his perpetual answer, "saving my order."

Now Henry could be in no doubt that his Archbishop had become his adversary and out of spite, removed his son and heir, Young Henry, from Thomas's household where he had been since he was small boy. The young prince had formed a strong attachment to Thomas and is reputed to have said that "Thomas showed him more fatherly love in a day than his father did for his entire life". By removing his son from Thomas's sphere of influence Henry was giving a sure sign that his friendship with the Archbishop was well and truly over. While he was at it,

Henry confiscated all the honours that he had formerly given to Thomas like his benefice of the church at Oxford, gifted to him by Theobald.

This was effectively a dismissal of Thomas from royal favour.

Over the next year, both sides tried to gain advantages over the other by striving with diplomatic efforts to secure allies. Arnulf of Lisieux, he who had left Thomas a cautionary letter about the vagaries of politics, changed sides and began to advise and support the King rather than the Archbishop. He then acted as Henry's envoy to the other Bishops and attempted to persuade them to Henry's cause. Both sides petitioned the Papacy, and Thomas also sent diplomatic envoys and letters to King Louis in France and to the Holy Roman Emperor in Germany hoping to gain their support. The Pope declined to take sides and urged moderation on both factions. Thomas being well aware of what incurring Henry's wrath might entail should he push him too far, began to make provision for possible safe places of refuge across the Channel if he should need to go into exile.

In late October Henry ordered Thomas to meet him at a rendezvous outside Northampton, close beside Derngate. In a display of royal power Henry refused Thomas entry to the town on the pretext that it was already full with his own courtiers and their servants and there was no room for the Archbishop and his retinue. When they did meet, at first it is said that they could not even approach each other with ease as both rode stallions that reared and pranced until they were forced to change mounts. Once new horses had been found, they took themselves away from a crowd that had gathered to watch. When they were alone, Henry berated Thomas for his ingratitude, using arguments he would repeat again and again over the next few years saying, "Have I not raised you from a poor and lowly station to the pinnacle of rank and honour? How comes it that so many benefits, so many proofs of my love for you, well known to all, have been so erased from your mind that you are now not only ungrateful but obstruct me in everything?"

Chapter 33

Clarendon

In the face of at what he saw as Thomas's public betrayal at Westminster, Henry still rankled and was more determined than ever to bring his recalcitrant Archbishop to heel. He called a great council at his royal hunting lodge at Clarendon in Wiltshire which Thomas was ordered to attend.

When Thomas arrived at Clarendon, his worst fears were realized just as he had suspected he they would be when he read the details of those customs for which Henry expected his approval. Just as the Church had recently produced an authoritative written version of its own laws, which laid out the extent of Papal influence in the realm and the degree to which Church members were subservient to the crown and English legal custom. Henry was set on doing the same for secular legislation. Henry had deceived Thomas and instead of asking him to agree to the vague concept of ancient customs he had gone to the trouble of having them written out on manuscript. The King was demanding an unconditional assent by the Church to all traditional royal rights which previously had only been oral tradition. Now, they were written out and they were henceforth to be known as the Constitutions of Clarendon. These 16 articles asserted the king's right to punish criminous clerks, forbade excommunication of royal officials and appeals to Rome, and gave the king the revenues of vacant sees and the power to influence episcopal elections. Henry was justified in saying that these rights had been exercised by his grandfather Henry, the first of that name, but Thomas was also justified in maintaining that they contravened Church law. Thomas saw he sixteen Constitutions as an intention to curb clerical independence and weaken the connection of the English church with Rome.

Thomas knew that if he accepted Henry's new document there would be no room for manoeuvre. In any case he was sure that Henry had slipped in, if not new clauses, at least interpretations of the ancient customs favourable to the royal government. "These written customs," Thomas averred, "are pernicious innovations, contrary to canon law, and I refuse to assent to them." This was not just plain obstinacy but a recognition by Thomas of the significance of the King's demands with a huge amount at stake for whichever of the two men lost the argument.

In a battle of wills such as this was becoming, it is ultimately the personalities of the protagonists that will count. Henry's strength lay in his determination to have his way as the anointed King. His word was law. His weakness on the other hand lay in his susceptibility to violent anger, which was a serious problem in moments of crisis and this was fuelled by his feeling that Thomas had betrayed him.

Thomas, on the other hand, acted with cool deliberation, all his diplomatic negotiating skills being brought to bear. He argued with a calculating and steely resolve to inflict as much damage as he could on the King. His principal weapon, which he was ready to unleash without the least warning, and without any attempt at negotiation was excommunication, an ecclesiastical censure depriving a person of the rights of Church membership. This was a feared outcome for anyone being thus punished, perhaps worse than being physically executed and that included Henry. Someone thus punished would become like the living dead, outside society and God's mercy. Thomas's weakness was his steadfast, inflexible refusal to compromise in any way.

For Thomas the so-called Constitutions and the 16 articles they contained simply represented a blatant attempt by Henry to exert state control over the Church in England. During the turmoil of the Anarchy the Church had been able to extend its sphere of influence and Henry was intent on reversing that trend. The majority of the Constitutions were simply a restatement of English custom and practice to which Thomas had no complaint, but severe controversy erupted over two clauses which made clerics accused of a crime, answerable to the legal authority of crown courts rather than ecclesiastical courts and prevented appeals to the church in Rome without royal permission.

As we have seen, the question of what to do about criminous clerks had been on-going for months with arguments back and forth between the Church and the State. The problem was brought to a head by the case of Philip de Brois, a canon of Bedford who was acquitted in the court of the Bishop of Lincoln of the charge of murdering a knight.

This outcome of the trial proved unacceptable to the Sheriff of Bedford who attempted to re-open the case in the Royal court and was furiously abused by Bishop Philip for his efforts. Henry, of course, took the side of his Sheriff and angrily insisted on justice being done in his courts on firstly, the charge of homicide and then on an additional charge of contempt so that a more fitting punishment for these crimes could be seen to be done. Thomas attempted to resolve the situation by banishing Philip but the King's and his faction remained extremely unhappy. The whole affair merely highlighted the woeful inadequacy of Canon law in punishing robbers and murderers.

Henry's way of solving the impasse had as we know, on the surface, been a simple one.

"Once a cleric or someone protected by Canon law had been found guilty by the church of such serious crimes in the ecclesiastical courts they should be deprived of the protection of the Church," he said, "and then be handed over to the secular authorities for punishment."

However much of a neat and innocuous compromise it might have appeared on the face of it, it contained the central implication that a man handed over to criminal law was no longer a clerk. This undermined the whole basis of clerical immunity. Thomas and his Bishops would have none of it and so the argument had dragged on with neither side prepared to give way on the matter. Now, at Clarendon, Henry was making another attempt at getting his proposal past Thomas and the Bishops.

Henry's legal team had drawn up a closely and cleverly worded document which was a deliberate attempt to fool the Bishops into committing to something they had not previously agreed. For three days, the Bishops refused to sign as Henry ranted and railed at them.

Henry cajoled the Bishops, telling them, "On the analogy of the oath of fealty which they all swore to the King on taking up office, to obey him "in life and limb and earthly honour saving their order", they would swear to observe the royal customs "saving their order": in other words, anything in the Constitutions contrary to Canon law was excluded from their consent.

To this, Thomas replied, "I have been over and over the precedents for clerical immunity. What I now say is that the Lord King's proposals are an innovation. To our minds innovation must be seen as pernicious, an offence against the established order of society as ordained by God. These are not things we can put our name to."

Then after endless cajoling and argument and to everyone's shock, Thomas told the bishops that he had reconsidered and decided that they had no choice but to accede to the King's demands. Why he changed his mind, to this day no-one knows but he and all the bishops reluctantly signed the document.

Thomas then immediately sought the Pope's absolution from the oath he had just sworn to uphold the King's written customs. Pope Alexander was all too aware that this would constitute open defiance of Henry which might, in turn, lead to the loss of his support which Alexander saw as crucial to his remaining Pope. Currently, Alexander was engaged in an on-going feud between himself and the person he and others considered to be an antipope calling himself Victor IV. This was an embarrassing schism in the Church caused initially by internal politics in Rome. Both men considered themselves to be the legitimate Pope but both were supported by different monarchs ruling in Europe at the time. If Alexander wanted to hold on to his papal crown, he was well aware that he could not afford to have Henry switch his allegiance to his rival and so refused to give Thomas absolution.

After this rejection by the Pope, Thomas told the bishops, "it is the Lord's will that I committed this perjury by submitting for the present to take a false oath. I will do penance for it hereafter as I chose." That was to be not long in coming.

Within days, in yet another twist to the plot and with a deliberate piece of theatre, Thomas donned the garb of a penitent, imposed a fast upon himself and publicly repented of his oath to uphold the Constitutions. Brother Edward thought he knew what Thomas's defence for his change of stance may well have been.

179

"was it likely that the Archbishop thought he was defending the rights of the Church, in all its parts against evil customs and the violence and injustice of secular power? Most of the bishops probably agreed with him but few were prepared to go against the wishes of the King and recant their oaths."

Henry was incandescent with rage. This, in his eyes, was the ultimate act of treachery, something he could and would not tolerate. He was determined to exact revenge on Thomas for what he perceived as a personal act of treachery against him. His first course of action was an attempt to forestall Thomas's request for absolution by getting the Constitutions ratified by the Pope, but the Pope, not wishing to lose the support of either party, prevaricated and stalemate was resumed.

Brother Edward could not help thinking to himself that by his actions at Clarendon, "Thomas had not only managed to make a fool of himself but had made an implacable enemy of the King." Henry would now be out to take revenge on Thomas any way he could for the debacle at Clarendon.

The council at Clarendon had ended untidily and Henry was looking for an opportunity to humiliate his former friend and he did this with ruthless determination. Thomas, during his time as Chancellor, had made many enemies at court when he had been aiding Henry in the recovery of lost and stolen Royal lands. Now many of these enemies were amongst the King's chief advisers, all equally intent on getting their own back on the former Chancellor.

Then, a few months after the meeting at Clarendon, Henry saw his chance for revenge with what was, in reality, a trivial matter.

Chapter 34

September 1164

One of Thomas's vassals, John the Marshal from Kent, had a case before the Archbishop's court regarding land tenure. However, among the customs recorded by Henry, or more probably written on his instructions, was a clause allowing a vassal who claimed failure in obtaining what they thought was justice in the court of their immediate lord to have the case transferred to the royal court. With royal support being inferred, John the Marshal swore in front of two witnesses that the Archbishop had not given him justice.

John the Marshal was relying on a clause of the 'ancestral customs' which made the property rights of the higher clergy subject to judicial review in the royal courts. Thus, he obtained a writ summoning Thomas to appear before the King and his judges on 14 September. When the case came up, Thomas said he was too ill to answer the summons and failed to appear. Instead, he sent four knights with letters from himself and the sheriff of Kent. In the letters he pointed out the transgressions committed by John the Marshal and his failure to satisfy the archiepiscopal court of his case. The court ignored both the knights and the letters.

This was just the excuse Henry was looking for. He was determined to bring the quarrel to where he could control it in person. He ruled that since Thomas had neither answered the summons in person nor sent what he had considered to be a valid excuse, he had insulted the King. John the Marshal was granted a fresh writ, ordering Thomas to appear again at a great council at Northampton and there, before all the Barons, Bishops and great men of the realm, Thomas was to be put on trial. Henry wanted him humiliated in public.

Thomas, in the meanwhile, made overtures to Henry for a meeting in an attempt to resolve the situation man to man but to no avail. Even when Thomas attempted to meet the king at his palace at Woodstock, where the King was known to spend time with his mistress, Rosamund Clifford, the park gates were shut firmly in his face.

By now, Thomas must have realised that the King was intent on his destruction. He was in no doubt about the lengths Henry was capable of going to when he did not get his own way and was actively making enquiries into possible escape routes into exile. He listened carefully to his friend John of Canterbury, who a month or so earlier had identified the Cistercian abbey of Pontigny in northern Burgundy a possible place of refuge should it become necessary.

"I advise you," John told his friend, "to establish a closer friendship with the Abbot of Pontigny, preferably in person if, you are able to get to France in the near future. You could use the pretext of pursuing your case to obtain a licence to leave the country. If that is not possible for whatever reason at least contact the abbot by letter. The abbey is ready to serve you even in temporal affairs if it should be necessary". John added a confidential postscript he marked as for Thomas's eyes alone, "I have chosen Pontigny as my own place of exile, when I am no longer able to bear the torments of our torturer."

Feeling trapped and with nowhere to run, Thomas by the beginning of August, had decided to take John's advice. Before dawn one morning he rode out from his manor of Aldington, near Hythe in Kent. He took with him Herbert of Bosham and a few trusted companions to Romney, where he hired a ship and attempted to cross the Channel. The vessel was under the command of Adam of Charing, a well-known figure in Kent who, when the vessel was some way out to sea, decided to turn back to the English shore. He gave Thomas the excuse that the wind was in the wrong direction for the voyage but in reality it was obvious that he feared the King's reprisals should he be caught in aiding the Archbishop to escape the King. A second attempt was made to escape but was no more successful than the first and Thomas had no choice other than to retrace his steps to his palace in Canterbury. When he got there, he found it almost deserted as most of his clerks had returned to their own homes as soon as they discovered that their Archbishop had fled.

In a farcical twist, the King's bailiffs arrived at the palace the next day, declaring that they had heard of the Archbishop's flight and had come to confiscate his goods on orders of the King. When Thomas appeared to greet them, they had no option but to withdraw in confusion. Adam of Charing was not quite so lucky and despite not actually taking Thomas all the way to France, was given a huge fine of 100 silver marks for his role in the attempted escape.

When he heard of Thomas's efforts to abscond, Henry was furious. What he feared most, was that Thomas would go straight to Pope Alexander with his complaints and that as a result, England would be placed under an interdict. This would mean that the people of England would be unable to hear mass, take the sacraments, bury their dead or baptise their children. The effect on the country would have been catastrophic.

To make matter worse for himself, Thomas's attempted flight had contravened the clause of the 'ancestral customs' that required any Bishop who wished to leave the country first to obtain a licence from the King, this time, Henry chose to step back from taking immediate action. Instead, he summoned Thomas to return to Woodstock, where he entertained him for several days in a display of studied politeness. His only reference to the escape attempt was to enquire sarcastically, "So, my Lord Archbishop, you wish to leave my kingdom: I suppose you think it not large enough to hold both of us?"

In attempting to flee the country without royal permission, Thomas had merely added to his troubles. He now had no possibility of avoiding a trial in the Royal court in the matter of John the Marshal's confiscated land but had also added a possible insult to the King by his attempted flight to France.

Chapter 35

Northampton

Thomas arrived at Northampton with a large retinue. With him were at least 40 clerks, chaplains, monks and a military escort of knights. When he arrived, he was told once again that there were no lodgings for him in the town so he took up residence at the Cluniac priory of Saint Andrew.

When the trial took place, all the Bishops, Earls and Barons of the Kingdom were present, including Roger of Pont L'Évêque, Archbishop of York, the most senior clergyman in England after the Archbishop of Canterbury and also Thomas's implacable enemy. At the time of the trial at Northampton, the court was in mourning for the death of the King's youngest brother, William, who had allegedly pined to death at Rouen as the result of Thomas's refusal to license his wedding to the widowed Isabel de Warenne. This loss had focused Henry's growing animosity towards his Archbishop. William had been a favourite of both the King and his inner circle. They could never forgive Thomas for what they saw as an action equated to the poisoning of the younger brother. Another of Henry's brothers, Hamelin, was at the trial and spoke in support of Henry. Hamelin and Thomas engaged in an unsavoury war of words when Hamelin defended Henry's dignity and called Thomas a traitor to his face. Hamelin's denunciation of Thomas was no doubt motivated by the injury he perceived as being caused to the royal family by Thomas's interference in William's desire to marry Isabel de Warenne. Thomas's position was under threat and old scores were being settled.

When charged firstly with contempt of court for disobeying the King's writ on 14 September in the case of John the Marshal, Thomas replied, "the Royal courts have no jurisdiction over actions I took in pursuance of my Holy office as Archbishop."

That notwithstanding, the court found Thomas guilty of perjury by having ignored the original summons and under pressure from the Bishops he accepted the sentence of confiscation of all his non-landed property pending the pleasure of the king. Surprisingly despite this judgement, the original dispute over John the Marshal's lands was decided in the Archbishop's favour.

Without warning, Henry now moved direction and brought fresh charges of embezzlement and false accounting against Thomas. For this, Thomas was totally unprepared. Henry's men at the Exchequer, who just happened to include John the Marshal, had already worked out which fiefs or vacant bishoprics had been granted to Thomas and for which he was therefore legally accountable. As Chancellor, Thomas had been expected to make fixed annual payments to the Exchequer, but not necessarily to file detailed accounts. Thomas was unable to produce any official receipts for his deposits into the Exchequer and any copies of the warrants for expenditure he claimed he had made on Henry's behalf. Thomas insisted that he had declared his annual accounts verbally and informally to Henry and secured, in return, a verbal discharge. Now it appeared that formal, written confirmation of his authority for his financial transactions was needed. Henry had set a cunning trap into which Thomas had blindly walked.

Thomas was asked to account for around £300 for the castles of Eye and Berkhamsted to which he replied, "I protest that I have received no warning of these charges and have been summoned only to answer to matters arising from the suit of John the Marshal. Furthermore," he added, "I was freed from any outstanding debts relating to my Chancellorship when I was appointed Archbishop." In an attempt to pacify Henry, he continued, "I can recall spending that sum and a great deal more on building repairs at these castles and at the palace of Westminster and that the refurbishment of Westminster Hall alone had been especially costly."

Thomas's words were falling on deaf ears. The King had already decided to deny that he had either authorised the expenditure or exonerated Thomas from these debts. It was his word against Thomas's and there was no doubt with whom the court would decide. Still trying to appease Henry, Thomas insisted that he would not allow a dispute over money to undermine their relationship and to this end, he found three sureties to guarantee reimbursement of the disputed sums. The court was adjourned for the night and Thomas returned to his lodgings but no-one dared to visit him, such was the atmosphere of foreboding that Henry had created. Who would risk having any association with the accused Archbishop for fear that they would fall prey to the King's anger?

In the morning, a Friday, Henry went back on the attack. This time claiming the sum of 500 silver marks had been borrowed from him by Thomas during the Toulouse campaign of 1159. Thomas protested again that his writ of summons had not mentioned charges like these, but he was willing to answer them. He conceded that he had borrowed the money but again claimed that it had been written off. This, Henry strenuously denied. Thomas was, of course, unable to offer any written evidence to support his claim that he was no longer liable for the debt. No surprise that a verdict was given in the King's favour. In this game of cat and mouse Henry demanded sureties for the money. Thomas nonchalantly replied, "my Lord King, my assets will be more than sufficient to meet the demand but I will need a little time to raise the cash." Henry then replied angrily, "since I have already confiscated the bulk of your wealth, you must find sureties immediately or go to prison."

Although Thomas found the needed sureties they proved of little use to him. Henry was not after Thomas for money, he wanted to humiliate and destroy his onetime friend once and for all. At this point, Henry required Thomas to account for all the other revenues which had passed through his hands during his time as both Chancellor and Archbishop. Since the sums involved had been vast, the result of another judgement against him would be bankruptcy. Now the penalties could be life imprisonment or sequestration of the lands of the Archbishopric. If that happened, much of the property belonging to the Church of Canterbury would fall into Henry's hands. Thomas asked for time to consider his response and the court was adjourned while he took counsel.

186

Sunday was meant to be a day of rest, but Becket spent it at the priory in earnest, worried meetings with his clerks. The Archbishop did not leave the priory all day. The psychological and emotional pressure was mounting just as Henry had planned it would. As dusk fell, the strain became unbearable and, later that night, Thomas's stomach problem flared up in a highly aggravated form. Herbert of Bosham, his close friend says, "he was struck by an illness that is called a colic, his loins were shaking with cold and pain. It was necessary to keep his pillows warm and replace them regularly."

When Monday morning came he was unable to ride to the castle and Henry and the barons suspected a subterfuge. Considering this alleged sickness to be a lie, some of the leading barons were dispatched to investigate the claim. Meanwhile, a rumour was spreading that Henry had been overheard swearing that, "if he does not yield, I will have him executed or thrown into a dungeon to rot." One of the Barons told Henry, "King William, your great grandfather, who conquered England, knew how to tame his clerics. He would have had this man castrated and thrown into a pit,"

All this may well have just been rumour but the story reached the ears of Thomas's clerks and then, no doubt, to those of Thomas himself.

Tuesday brought no better news. Bishops appeared at the priory to say that Henry had set his mind to trying Thomas as a traitor and that he would do it today. They wanted him to resign or submit unconditionally to the king. Thomas had no intention of doing that, he asked them, "why are so few of you guided by principle or love of the Church? Is it that some of you act simply out of ambition or fear?" Even if they were set against him, he was their spiritual leader. If they allowed him to be defeated, they and the Church would go down with him.

Thomas was not going without a fight and began the day at morning mass saying, "Princes sit and speak against me; but thy servant, Lord, is occupied in thy statutes."

Instead of being cowed by the pressure being put on him by Henry, Thomas had decided that his best form of defence would be attack. Once again he was a warrior fighting for his life. Those gathered in the hall were shocked at the sight of Thomas arriving at the court, with his archepiscopal cross in his own hands. When walking into the great hall, he was confronted by Roger of Pont l'Évêque also carrying his cross. It looked like the two would come to blows until Hilary of Chichester accused Thomas of being the progenitor of the trouble.

"You started all this when you ordered we Bishops to follow your lead at Clarendon and then changed your mind. Now you are ordering us to go against our promise to the king," he shouted at him.

Thomas's answer was unequivocal, "whatever happened at Clarendon and whatever mistakes I may have made there, the disputed customs were afterwards condemned as 'obnoxious' by the Holy Father. If we lapsed at Clarendon, if the flesh was weak, we must take heart again and with the strength of the Holy Spirit fight the old enemy who hopes that those who stand will fall, and those who have fallen will not get up again."

So powerful was his cross as a symbol of Thomas's position and power that for the rest of the trial Henry refused to meet with him face to face fearing that Thomas might excommunicate him. The atmosphere had become so toxic that Archbishop and King stayed in their separate rooms as the Bishops and Barons shuffled between them with messages and counter offers in the hope of a solution.

When the trial began and the charges were read out to him, Thomas continued to state that he was not prepared to hear them saying that "you have no rights to judge me", but the verdict would not be long in coming.

After much coming and going, Thomas was still seated and holding his cross when the barons and knights came down the stairs for the final time. The King remained alone upstairs as if not wanting to be part of the final act. When the doors were opened again, the Earls appeared to deliver it and as they entered the lower chamber, Thomas refused to rise and sat grim-faced. There followed a brief moment of confusion and argument as to who should read out the verdict but earl Robert de Beaumont accepted the task and tried to do his best with reading out the sentence regardless of Thomas's protestations of their legality.

In the face of Thomas's protestations, the nervous earl stumbled over his lines and from his chair, Thomas interrupted him shouting, "I forbid you or anyone else here present to judge me." De Beaumont hesitated giving Thomas the opportunity to leap his feet, brandishing his cross above his head shouting, "these proceedings are out of order, because in the case for which I have been summoned here, my opponent, John the Marshal, has not appeared, and therefore no sentence can be passed. It is not for you to judge your Archbishop for a crime! Such as I am, I am your father, and you are magnates of the household, lay powers, secular persons. I refuse to hear your judgement."

At the same time, he threatened to suspend all those bishops "who had, had the temerity to pass judgement on their own Archbishop."

Chaos broke out and cries of "perjurer" and "traitor" rang out from the assembled Barons. Some called out that the treason was clear and that Thomas must hear the sentence. Thomas was having none of it and walked towards the door, carrying his cross. Walking through the Great Hall he heard Ranulf de Broc, the royal whoremaster, and Hamelin, the king's brother, who had earlier spoken against him, joining in the chorus. Rounding on them, he shouted back, "If only I were a knight and not an Archbishop, my own fist would give you the lie.'

"I have tried to find a source telling me exactly what the sentence passed on Thomas was but can find none," surmised Brother Edward, as he neared the end of this part of his story, "but I think it likely that Thomas was almost certainly condemned to life imprisonment."

Once out into the castle-yard Thomas quickly mounted his horse, scooping up Herbert of Bosham into the saddle behind him but found that the gates of the outer bailey were locked. The porter was absent from his post but a bunch of keys was hanging from the wall. Fortunately, one fitted the gates and the Archbishop, closely followed by the rest of his clerks, made their escape through the town. As they rode back to the priory, Thomas veered wildly from side to side. He was still carrying his cross and with Herbert behind him, he could scarcely control his horse.

That evening, after his flight from the castle, Thomas sent three of the Bishops with a message to Henry asking for a surety of safe-conduct for his journey back to Canterbury. The ominous reply came by return that the King would not make a decision until the following day. Although Thomas had heard that he was not to be molested within the precincts of Northampton, he was fearing in earnest for his life and that the risk of arrest elsewhere was high. He decided the time had come to put John of Salisbury's escape plan into immediate effect.

Chapter 36

Escape to France

Brother Edward enjoyed a good night's sleep and once he had attended to the early morning rituals of his priory and then broken his fast, he was back on his cushion in the scriptorium. Picking up his quill he began the account of Thomas's flight from England in his effort to avoid the wrath of a vengeful King. Brother Edward continued writing thus:

After supper at the priory, besides the loyal Herbert of Bosham, only three trusted servants were let into the secret escape plan. One was his personal servant, Roger de Bray whilst the other two were Gilbertine lay-brethren. These two brothers he took as guides as most of the priories associated with their order were in Lincolnshire and on the eastern side of the country so they would have a good knowledge of the roads and byways. Herbert was instructed to leave separately and make for Canterbury with all possible haste and once there, gather as much cash and silver plate as he could find. Having done that, he should then travel on to St Bertin's monastery at St-Omer in France for a rendezvous with Thomas who would get there as soon as he could.

To allay any suspicions at the castle, Thomas had made no secret of his intention of spending the night in the priory chapel in vigil and prayer. Here he would await the King's decision as to whether he would be given permission to return to Canterbury or not. A bed was made up for him behind the high altar by the monks who later reported seeing him sleeping there as they passed by to sing their night offices.

The little group of fugitives led by Thomas left an hour before dawn in pitch darkness and during a torrential rainstorm, which he hoped would cover the sound of the horses' hooves. Thomas rode out of the priory with only his three chosen companions as an escort. He was thinly disguised as a lay brother and using the alias of Brother Christian. They had mounted themselves on borrowed chargers and made their escape through the north gate of the town which they knew to be unguarded. Early the next morning Henry of Winchester called at the priory to ask the archbishop's chamberlain how Thomas was, only to receive the jocular reply, "He is doing rather well since he left late last night in a hurry and no one knows where he has gone." When this was reported to the King, his sinister reply was, "We've not finished with this wretched fellow yet."

"I wonder," mused Brother Edward to himself as he was writing, "what were the emotions running through Thomas's mind? They must have been a heady mixture of fear and excitement as he and his men rode hard through the night hoping to outrun any pursuers."

Quite rightly, Thomas guessed that once his flight was discovered Henry would send his soldiers southwards on the assumption that their quarry would be heading for Canterbury and the Kent coast. Instead, he initially headed east riding hard for Grantham where the small party stopped for a few hours' sleep before riding north for the last 25 miles to their intended destination of Lincoln. Once they reached Lincoln, they went into hiding and stayed with a fuller known as James, a friend of one of his guides.

Fortunately, this man James lived close by the river Witham and was thus able to arrange for a boat to take Thomas and his men south eastwards towards Boston and then through the fens of Norfolk. During their river journey and thanks to the local knowledge of the two lay brothers in the group, they were able to stay in Gilbertine priories along the way. To make themselves inconspicuous, he and his companions travelled only by night, hiding themselves away by day.

Whether Henry's men did pursue Thomas or not we cannot be certain but it is a possibility that Henry had decided that his Archbishop putting himself in self-imposed exile might be the best place for him. After all, Archbishops in exile were no novelty. Fifty years earlier, Archbishop Anselm had gone into exile twice during his quarrel with Henry's grandfather, King Henry, the first of that name. The current Henry was hopeful that an appeal to the Pope might result in an outcome favourable to himself in his dispute with the errant Thomas. In this, Henry was well aware that Pope Alexander would be keen to keep Henry's support in the on-going wrangle over who was actually the Pope; Alexander or the man he thought an imposter. Paschal III, who had just become the second Antipope of Alexander's pontificate, was being supported by the Holy Roman Emperor, Frederick Barbarossa, it being Frederick's imperial army that had made Paschal's enthronement as Pope possible and Alexander III to become a fugitive. Henry and Louis of France supported Alexander's claim to the Papal throne which Alexander knew was only a conditional support and depended on him keeping the two monarchs on his side.

From the time that Thomas had made his escape from the castle at Northampton, almost three weeks had passed. Three weeks of hiding and keeping on the move. Dressed in miserable clothes and at the mercy of freezing weather it had not been a happy time. Always a fear in the back of his mind of being caught by Henry's soldiers and being hauled back to an unpleasant audience with the King. Enduring three weeks of hardship and suffering were as nothing when compared to the possibility of spending the rest of his life rotting away in a dungeon, or worse.

Using a chaplain called Gilbert, whom he had recruited at the Gilbertine priory of Chicksands in Bedfordshire to guide him on the last and most dangerous part of his journey, Thomas headed south and finally arrived at Eastry in Kent. This was a manor belonging to the see of Canterbury and was only a short distance from the archiepiscopal port at Sandwich. Somehow Thomas had managed to slip through the net that Henry had spread to catch him.

A small skiff had been found and with it a man prepared to take the party across the Channel. Arrangements were quickly made and in the very early morning of 2 November 1164 Thomas left the shores of England.

Their vessel was so small that they could take no luggage other than the clothes in which they stood. If Thomas thought that his journey with Theobald all those years before had been fraught, he was about to find out just how bad it really could be trying to cross the Channel in the depths of winter. With hardly any seaboard, they were soon awash with freezing water and dreading an imminent capsize but providence and prayers must have been on their side. At dusk they landed on the shingle shore of Oye, only four miles from the town of Gravelines but by now they were in a parlous state. They were afraid, freezing cold and much weakened by the effects of seasickness having been tossed and buffeted by the waves for endless hours. The Channel in November was an unwelcoming place to be but they had arrived in France and so, in theory at least, were safe from the clutches of Henry.

When he left the small boat, Thomas collapsed exhausted on the shingle beach unable to take another step. Somehow and from somewhere, one of his companions managed to find a swaybacked nag which he hired for a penny. For a bridle it had only a rope made of straw around its neck. With Thomas hoisted on its back they managed to reach Gravelines an hour or two after nightfall. Fortune was indeed favouring the brave.

The rumours of his escape had quickly spread, including across the Channel, into France and into Louis' territory. By now, everyone knew it was likely that he had either landed somewhere along the coast or was shortly about to do so. Henry was sure to have his spies in France on the lookout for his absconding Archbishop. Thomas soon discovered that his 'disguise' was totally unconvincing and that keeping himself out of the public gaze was going to be a wise decision. Whatever he might be wearing, his demeanour would soon give him away and the lie to his not being the poor monk he was trying to portray.

In one instance, at a wayside inn, when he sat down to eat a simple meal of bread and cheese he quickly betrayed himself by his speech and polished accent and the party quickly moved on. He could not, it would seem, hide his refinement, innate air of authority or his sophisticated manners to say nothing of his unusual height.

In defiance of the risks, Thomas was keen to make the rendezvous with Herbert of Bosham at St Omer as soon as he could, so throwing caution to the winds, he travelled in the daytime in the vain hope that his miserable disguise would protect him from discovery. It failed almost immediately when he passed a young knight with a falcon on his wrist. A lifelong expert in falconry Thomas was famous for being able to spot a prize gyrfalcon at twenty paces. He took only a quick sidelong glance of appreciation at the stranger's fine bird for the knight to see instantly through the thin disguise. To Thomas's horror, the young man called out, "Either that's the Archbishop of Canterbury or his double!" To which Thomas gave the weak answer, "Do you honestly believe that the Archbishop of Canterbury travels in this style," and hurried on before any more was said.

They were now in the territory of Henry's cousin, Count Philip of Flanders, so had to be especially careful to not be taken up by Philip's soldiers who may well have been on the lookout for the small band of fugitives as a favour to their lord's cousin. The weather was miserable, rain and hail continued to beat down on them, the road thick with mud and potholes hampered their every step but eventually they reached the environs of St-Omer. Not wishing to take any unnecessary risks, Thomas sent one of his guides ahead to make sure it was safe to enter the town. On the guide's return the news he brought was not good. As soon as he realised that Thomas had escaped, Henry had dispatched a deputation to the Pope at Sens to plead for Thomas's deposition or suspension. They had crossed the Channel on the same day as Thomas but presumably in a good deal more comfort. The deputation was led by Gilbert Foliot, Roger of Pont l'Évêque and Hilary of Chichester, all sworn enemies of the Archbishop. As if this was not bad enough, to make matters worse they were, at this very moment, staying in the castle at St-Omer.

On hearing these tidings, Thomas made the decision to stay hidden a while longer and made his way to the Cistercian abbey of Clairmarais, three miles north-east of the town. Once there, he concealed himself even deeper into the surrounding marshes and moved once again across the marshes in a rowing boat to a hermitage called Oldminster which belonged to St Bertin's Abbey. Here he was safely surrounded by water and was able to stay out of sight for three days. As soon as he thought it was safe, he retraced his steps to St-Omer, where he gave thanks for his narrow escape and recovered his spirits at St Bertin's Abbey. He was given a hero's welcome by Abbot Godescal and his monks who saw Thomas as a valiant protector of the Church's rights.

As they had agreed at Northampton, Herbert of Bosham was waiting to greet his Archbishop. When the two men met, Herbert was shocked at the sight of the gaunt, blistered, unshaven, stooping figure who greeted him; how changed from the man who only a short while before had confronted the King and his bishops at Northampton. He gave Thomas the unwelcome news that he had only managed to find a little over 66 pounds in cash at Canterbury and a few silver vases that might raise a little more when needed. This was far less than Thomas had been hoping for.

During his short stay at St Bertin's, Thomas was to find out just how precarious his position had become.

Whilst on his way home from a pilgrimage to Santiago de Compostela, Richard de Lucy, who owed Thomas his homage, came to visit him and begged him, "in the name of friendship to return to England and submit to Henry's will." Thomas of course refused which led to an angry scene.

De Lucy declared, "then, from henceforward I will forever be your sworn enemy."

To which Thomas answered, "You are my vassal and may not say such things to me."

"In that case, I will take back my homage," Richard responded.

Thomas instantly rebounded with "It was not meant as a loan."

Richard had effectively declared war on Thomas by siding with Henry. Yet another ally had deserted his camp and Thomas knew that for the time being at least, France would have to be his home. With little or no money or assets to call on to support himself he would be forced to place himself at the mercy of the Pope and King Louis and hope that one, or both, would give him shelter from Henry for as long as it took for the situation he found himself in to be resolved.

Chapter 37

The Exile Years

Thomas may have managed to get himself to France but his troubles were not yet over. Both he and Henry were stubborn men with huge amounts of personal pride at stake. Thomas refused to back down without being proved right in his views while Henry on the other hand claimed that his Archbishop was in France of his own volition and he had never forced him to go there. Thomas had seen Henry at close hand during the years as his Chancellor and for good reason did not trust him to keep his word about anything. Conversely, Henry quite simply felt that he had been betrayed by Thomas whom he had thought of as loyal and trusted friend and therefore owed him nothing. Neither man would give in.

They were like two small boys, each blaming the other and refusing to be wrong. "Were they novices," thought Brother Edward, "I would give them both a sound thrashing and tell them not to be so childish. When one was a King and the other an Archbishop, one would expect that they could come to a reasonable accord as grown men on their own."

Then, both men decided independently to do the same thing. As soon as they possibly could, they would present their cases to the Pope in Sens, each asking him to make a judgement in their favour.

After leaving the castle at St Omer, Henry's envoys divided themselves into two groups. The main party rode directly to Sens for an audience with the pope. Henry, knowing that Alexander needed his support to remain as Pope, thought that his envoys would make quick work of Thomas's appeal. Thomas, however, had already sent Herbert of Bosham to Sens where he arrived a few hours after Henry's envoys. There, Herbert met Alexander in private and again laid out the archbishop's version of the quarrel to which the Pope listened intently and sympathetically, occasionally nodding in understanding.

While that first group interceded with the Pope, the Earl of Arundel, with the second group sought a meeting with King Louis at Compiègne, fifty miles north-east of Paris. When they arrived, they handed him a letter from Henry explaining how Thomas, now described disparagingly as "formerly the Archbishop of Canterbury", had "fled from the kingdom like a felon". Henry wanted the French king, his feudal overlord, to help him by not giving Thomas refuge or aid.

The envoys, on Henry's instructions, urged Louis to expel the Archbishop from his territories. "Thomas," they told him, "is one of your most determined enemies, a man who has, in the past, planned your death and been responsible for subjecting much of your lands to the will of the Angevins. When you were at Toulouse it was Thomas of Canterbury who urged our King to assault the city and take you prisoner."

Louis calmly replied that, "if a man had served me as well as Thomas has Henry then I would always be grateful to him."

To the chagrin of Henry's envoys, Louis kept asking, "but who precisely has deposed Thomas if he were no longer to be styled Archbishop?" The envoys failed to answer the question adequately but instead, appealed to Louis to write to Pope Alexander on Henry's behalf. This he refused to do and instead, wrote in Thomas's favour. Louis was keen to annoy Henry but without doing enough to provoke him into a new war. It is conceivable that Louis still felt the wound of Henry marrying Eleanor, his ex-wife and then producing multiple sons with her. More likely was the possibility that the French King was still sulking over Henry's getting the better of him over his daughter's marriage and the recovery of the disputed Vexin lands and castles rather than any goodwill towards Thomas.

After the envoys had left Louis with nothing to show for their efforts, Herbert of Bosham, who was not far behind them, arrived to give Louis Thomas's side of the story. At the same time, he asked the King to give Thomas safe-conduct for any onward journeys through France. Louis, ever a pious man, had always liked Thomas and was shocked at what he considered as unwarranted, bad treatment towards him.

Unlike Henry, Thomas was to put his appeal to the Pope in person and using his gift for theatrical drama, arrived at Sens on a great white charger lent to him by Miles of Thérouanne, an Englishman by birth. On his arrival, he threw himself at the Pontiff's feet, spread out his copy of the Constitutions of Clarendon and bemoaned his failure to protect the English church. Still more theatrically, he gave his episcopal ring to Alexander as a sign of his of resignation from the archbishopric.

As he handed over his ring, Thomas made an emotional speech to the Pope. "Recognizing my appointment to be uncanonical," he said, "and fearing lest the outcome turn out even worse for me, indeed seeing my powers unequal to the burden and afraid lest I lead to ruin the flock to whom I have been given in whatever way as pastor, I resign into your hands, father, the archiepiscopate of Canterbury." Thomas is said to have wept as he finished this confession and the Pope and all those present, were also said to have been brought to tears.

Alexander immediately returned the ring and much to the disquiet of some of his advisers, promised that Thomas would not be removed as Archbishop. These advisors were mostly of the opinion that Thomas's resignation should have been accepted and that would have been the end of the whole sorry affair. In the face of this opposition, Thomas had not only kept his episcopal ring but succeeded in obtaining a formal condemnation of the Constitutions of Clarendon from Alexander. Henry's envoys had been forced to leave Sens empty handed. Despite their spending three days distributing gifts and offering bribes in an effort to sway opinions, they had little choice but to abandon their task and return home to England. Henry must have been beside himself with rage when he heard that his envoys had achieved nothing.

The Pope and his cardinals had been immensely moved by Thomas's resignation. His despair was understandable, but it left them in a precarious quandary. What now? The easy choice, the feint-hearted choice, was to agree with Thomas, to accept his resignation and let him leave the field of battle. A new Archbishop could be appointed, one who would be less caustic as far as Henry was concerned, perhaps more suave in negotiation. Although, given Thomas's successes with diplomatic missions in the past, that would be difficult, if not impossible. Of course, with Thomas gone, it would be far more likely that a truce between the English State and the Church could be arranged. That was the easy solution, to let Thomas fall on his sword in despair.

Wiser thoughts than this, however, were in the minds of the Papal Council. If Thomas were allowed to surrendered now, it would be sending an unwanted message to all the princes and bishops of Europe. If Thomas, who had risked riches and honour and even his life in defence of the Church's liberty, could be deprived of his office by the Church herself, it would set a dismal precedent for all other ecclesiastics who were trying to resist the encroachments of their own sovereigns.

If Thomas fell, could not all bishops fall? If that were the case, then never in future would anyone dare to stand up to the will of a ruler, and so the prestige of the Catholic Church would totter and the Pope's authority would perish. "It is better then," they advised, "that he be reinstated even if unwilling and that assistance be given to him in every way. He fights for us all"

However, although he had kept Thomas as Archbishop of Canterbury, the Pope had forbidden his return to England until the dispute with Henry had been settled. Henry had asked the Pope, through the envoys he had dispatched to Sens, that Thomas be ordered back to England. Obviously, that did not happen but nor was Henry, on the other hand, ordered to desist with his accusations and attempts to have his Archbishop censured.

Instead, Thomas was instructed to leave the abbey at St Bertin's and to go and live in seclusion with just a few friends and companions at the abbey of Pontigny under the protection of the Cistercian monks there. Here Alexander hoped Thomas would learn to live without the affluence and luxury that he had enjoyed for the last ten years of his life.

While at Pontigny, Thomas tried to make up for the lost time which he had spent on more frivolous pursuits and threw himself into rigorous study. At first he asked the Abbot to allow him to eat meat, which is against the Rule of the Cistercian order, but as time went on he accustomed himself to the coarse vegetarian diet of the monks. He even took to some of the extreme ascetic practices that the saints of old were reputed to have lived by.

Although it was still winter, he immersed himself in the river that flowed by the monastery and stayed there until even the deepest parts of his bones were numbed.

There may well have been more to Alexander's ploy of sending Thomas to live with the Cistercians than simply offering him safe refuge. It might well have been that the Pope thought that in exile among the Cistercians, the exiled Archbishop would encounter unaccustomed hardship and frugality. This in turn would give him ample time to consider the advantages of a reconciliation with Henry and a return to an easier way of life. Failing that, he was likely to find himself in exile with all its attendant drawbacks for a very long time.

When he first arrived at the monastery at Pontingy one of the monks, known as Ailred and a monarchist through and through, told the General Chapter that, "we Cistercians should not shelter the Archbishop of Canterbury but should send him back to obey his King."

A Cistercian Abbott, Isaac of Stella, who although in a French monastery, happened to be an Englishman and he, unsurprisingly took the opposite view. "The Archbishop is fighting to protect the rights of the Church and it must be our duty to protect him in return." Isaac's point of view was the one that prevailed and Thomas was allowed to stay at Pontingy

The abbey of Pontigny is in a densely forested area of northern Burgundy and was founded in 1114 by Hugh of Mâcon. It is only twelve miles to the north-east of Auxerre, where Thomas had studied canon and civil law as a clerk in Theobald's household so was an area he already knew quite well. He would remain there for almost two years. In keeping with the Cistercian desires for self-sufficiency, it is an isolated spot where they could worship God and shield themselves from the cares of everyday life. Their dress was and still is of the simplest kind: habits of unbleached wool, vestments of the plainest white fustian or unembroidered linen. No precious metal is allowed except a few silver vessels such as chalices or incense boats for use at the Eucharist. Wall paintings, carvings or other decorations are forbidden, the windows are of the simplest shapes and filled with clear glass and no high towers were to be erected. Within a week, the exiles had found small, individual cells amongst the Abbey buildings.

Once at Pontigny, Thomas set about arming himself with all the books and information he thought he might need to better his education but also to carry on the fight against Henry. He made sure he laid hands on all the books he could find on Canon and Civil law. A wastrel he might have been as a young student in Paris but now he would make up for it. Thomas knew better than anyone that Henry liked nothing better than to spend his time in private reading or trying to unravel some difficult question with a group of his clerks. For the King, it was school every day, with constant meetings with the most learned thinkers and discussions on intellectual issues. Thomas had no intention of being second best when it came to learning or more importantly, not being knowledgeable enough in an argument about the law.

He made it clear to those around him, despite the Pope's earnest desire for a settlement between the two, that he had no intention of abandoning the charges that had been made against him. His thinking was that if Pope Alexander could govern the Roman Church from the sanctuary of Sens, then why could he not govern the English Church from Pontigny?

As soon as he had made himself comfortable in his new surroundings Thomas issued expostulatory letters to Henry and the Bishops who had opposed him. He then proceeded to excommunicate all violators of the prerogatives of the Church and included in the attack the principal officers of the Crown. Far from trying to reach an agreement with Henry he was adding fuel to the fire. However, his stay at Pontingy was not going to be as long as he thought.

Henry did not enjoy being bested. When his envoys returned empty-handed after their interview with the Pope, he was furious that Alexander had allowed Thomas take up residence at Pontigny. He was soon telling people, "I am close to renouncing this Pope and his treacherous cardinals. Perhaps I should give his rival, Paschall, the benefit of my support. In the meanwhile, I shall take reprisals against all those who have any connection with Thomas of Canterbury. I will make them all suffer."

On Christmas Day he took all the lands and revenues of the Church of Canterbury into his own hands. The very next day,

Boxing Day, he issued yet another order, "I want all of Thomas of Canterbury's relatives, servants and their families, sent into exile with immediate effect. I do not care whether they be men, women or children, they are all to go. I also want included anyone else who is known to have harboured or assisted him during his flight from Northampton." Still Henry was not finished. "All incomes owed to his clerks or family members are to be withheld. I want all of them reduced to penury."

These orders resulted in more that 400 of Thomas's friends, family and servants being exiled. While he was at it, he forbade any of those he had exiled to make an appeal to the Pope over the decision. Henry was applying financial and familial pressure to demonstrate the reality of the threats he had made at Clarendon and Northampton. An unfortunate consequence of this was that with no money or assets, Thomas was thrown further into the sphere of King Louis who was only too happy to offer his old friend refuge and protection.

Then Henry turned his ire towards the Pope and decreed that, "all revenues due to Alexander are to be frozen and kept by me in my treasury. There will be no appeals or visits to the Papal Curia without my express permission and from now on, anyone found bringing letters into England from the Pope or the Archbishop will be hanged or mutilated and then cast adrift in an open boat without oars by the sheriffs." Henry meant business.

In a characteristically concerned but obviously not insincere letter to Thomas describing the political and diplomatic scene, Arnulf of Lisieux offered the archbishop both a harsh reality check and a shrewd insight into Henry's psychology. Arnulf knew that however much Henry would like to outmanoeuvre Louis or the Pope in his efforts to rid himself of the problem of Thomas, he would manage to stay cool and rational. Arnulf, having had a close association with the English King for over twenty years, was in an ideal position to know.

In his letter, he advised Thomas that, "you are dealing with a man whose cunning frightens distant people, whose power overawes his neighbours and whose sternness terrifies his subjects. Above all, he will never yield to pressure, least of all to force. If you wish to recover your position as Archbishop, you will have to offer a solution that the King believes is really his own. You must keep in mind that in and around his vast territories he has neither superior who can frighten him nor subject who can resist him. Whatever does not yield to him, he considers unlawful. I urge you to settle this quarrel while you can and now is the opportune moment to do it. Henry needs to be in Wales where Prince Owain of Gwynedd is in revolt again. I believe that to avoid a possible war on two fronts and to buy time before marching into Wales, Henry will be willing to trade a reconciliation with you in the hope of achieving an Anglo-French peace." Arnulf concluded his letter by saying, "this split between you will become a problem for the whole duration of your exile if you do not adjust your position to include these things of which I have advised you. I would predict that however loyal or committed to your cause your supporters appear now, before long, they will simply tire or melt away."

It seemed strange to brother Edward that a man like Henry, who was rarely headstrong or impetuous in war or politics, a man who could be patient and relatively humble if approached in the right way, could call forth rage and resentment in an instant and become impossible to placate once inflamed. This was the man who would foam at the mouth, roll on the ground and chew straw when enraged. Thomas should have known better than to make an enemy of him.

Thomas was to remain at Pontigny for the next two years during which time he and Henry traded assault and counter assault on each other's positions. In 1166 Thomas excommunicated Henry's principal counsellors. Henry responded by applying pressure to the Cistercian Order's general convocation protesting at the aid the Cistercian monastery of Pontigny had given to Thomas and threatening to expel the Order from his lands. Although they did not explicitly expel Thomas from Pontigny the Cistercians appealed to his better nature and Thomas threw himself, once again, on King Louis' mercy. At Louis' recommendation, Thomas moved to the abbey of Columbe in Sens and spent the following four years of his exile there. These four years continued in much the same vein with the two men refusing to come to any accord and a form of stalemate ensued, each trying unsuccessfully to gain a decisive advantage over the other.

At one point, Alexander had written to both the belligerents urging them to refrain from further escalation of the dispute. In his letter to Henry, he stressed that he had forbidden the Archbishop from escalating the dispute whilst in writing to Thomas he said that he had begged the King to restore Thomas to Canterbury.

During these four long years of dispute, Papal Legates travelled to and fro between the parties trying to bring about a negotiated conclusion. Thomas continued with his strategy of excommunications against those of Henry's supporters who remained loyal to the King's position whilst Henry continued to insist that there could be no reconciliation until Thomas agreed to the Constitutions of Clarendon. All appeals from the Pope to either of them fell on deaf ears.

Somehow, in 1169, Papal Legates managed to arrange a face-to-face meeting between Henry and Thomas at Montmirail. The meeting did not result in the breakthrough that had been hoped for which was hardly surprising given that Thomas distrusted the King and was, in turn, by now, hated by him. Rather than placate Thomas, Henry had rubbed salt into the wound by adding new clauses to the Constitutions before the meeting. If Thomas had, had a problem with agreeing to the originals, he was surely not going to agree to any new ones being added.

Henry finally caused Thomas to snap through a snub to both his personal pride and prestige of his office. On 24 May 1170, he had his son, Henry the Younger, crowned at Canterbury by the Archbishop of York, Roger of Pont L'Évêque, Thomas's long-time adversary. This was a flagrant disregard of papal prohibition and of the immemorial custom and right that only the Archbishop of Canterbury could crown a king. Thomas, followed by the Pope, proceeded to excommunicate all those responsible.

Now, Henry, fearing that England would be placed under interdict was forced in June into a meeting with Thomas at Fréteval in an effort to limit the damage caused by the crowning of his son. Here, in a compromise which neatly ignored the original cause of the dispute, it was finally agreed that Thomas should return to Canterbury and receive back all the possessions of his see and re-crown Henry the Younger in a second ceremony. Neither party withdrew from their position regarding the Constitutions of Clarendon, which on this occasion were diplomatically, not mentioned.

However, when the formal act of reconciliation took place, all went well until Thomas attended Mass with the King in the hope of receiving the Kiss of Peace during the service. To avoid the issue and thus breaking his vow never to give Thomas a Kiss of Peace, Henry ordered that a requiem Mass should be said, in which the Kiss of Peace is not exchanged. Thomas now openly demanded this symbolic act of the King but Henry remained resolute and refused. A few days later they parted at Chaumont-en-Vexin. Henry expressed his good wishes to his Archbishop for his safe return to England. Thomas replied, "My lord, something tells me that I take leave of you now, never to see you again in this life."

In anger Henry asked, "Do you think me a liar and that I would go back on my word?"

Despite a swift denial from Thomas that he meant no such thing, his response failed to placate Henry. In a fit of pique Henry, having promised to escort Thomas to England, changed his mind and wrote a curt letter to say that matters of state, in the guise of a French foray across his frontiers in the Auvergne, would keep him in France. Thomas was to return to England without the King as had been the original plan.

Thomas was, to say the least, not pleased. He complained bitterly to the Archbishop of Rouen about the situation, "what price any agreements made between the King and me? He said he would be here himself but all he sends is a short letter. What about the money he promised me to pay my creditors before I return to England? What about the Kiss of Peace? Can I believe anything this King tells me? His word is just what a diplomat's should be: as clear as glass and as unstable as water."

He must have made a convincing argument because Rotrou, the Archbishop, gave him £300 to tide him over.

Some of this money, probably much to the chagrin of Rotrou, he immediately spent on having a good stock of French wine shipped over to England to await his arrival. Some of his old habits, despite his supposedly frugal lifestyle in exile, had not deserted him completely. Unfortunately, although Henry allowed the consignment to pass safely through his territories on the French side of the Channel, as soon as it arrived at Pevensey, it was confiscated by Thomas's enemies.

Other than the luxury of his wine, perhaps the most valuable luggage that Thomas took with him to England was his private library saying that, "I want to be buried in Canterbury and I want my books to be close to me." Did he have a premonition of impending doom?

In the town, while they waited to cross the Channel, lodgings were found for the attendant throng of clerks. All the baggage, including the carts loaded with books and the horses which they were to take with them had arrived at the port. Ships had been commissioned with one vessel being reserved solely for Thomas and his most trusted companions.

While he awaited at Wissant for the ship that was to take him across the Channel, he strolled along the beach enjoying the peace and solitude. Here, Milo, the Dean of Boulogne, came to warn him that the English coasts were being closely watched Ranulf de Broc's men and that he should take extreme care when he arrived. Milo's informants told him that the de Brocs were intending to apprehend Thomas as soon as he stepped onto English soil, search his baggage and seize any Papal decrees they found. "They are even threatening to cut off your head if you dare to step foot ashore," Milo warned Thomas.

"Nothing will stop me from making this journey," he retorted. "My flock have waited long years for my return and I will not disappoint them." Thomas must have been heartened by the arrival from Canterbury of Robert, the sacrist of the Cathedral who had brought with him that potent symbol of the Archbishop's power, his much-prized cross. The helmsman of the ship that had carried Robert to Wissant brought confirmation of that which Milo had intimated to Thomas during their walk along the beach. "If I were you," he told Herbert of Bosham, "I would stay here. There are a lot of knights just waiting for you and the Archbishop to arrive and their intentions are not friendly."

Herbert passed this latest piece of news to Thomas who merely reiterated his intention to return to Canterbury come what may.

On the night of 1st December in the year of 1170 Thomas and his party went aboard their ship and set out for England. There was a decent breeze blowing and although the original destination was Dover, in view of the recent intelligence about the welcoming committee there, they diverted to Sandwich. The journey took a little over 12 hours.

Not only was Sandwich a safer place because of the de Broc ruffians in Dover but it was the property of the Church and had been since it had been given to it by Canute in recompense for the sacking of Canterbury by his Viking countrymen more than a century before.

Sandwich afforded a fine anchorage, big enough to accommodate a small armada and as Thomas's ship turned into the harbour it mingled with other vessels in his fleet. To distinguish his from the other boats around him and not wanting to waste the opportunity for some drama, Thomas gave the order, "raise my cross on the prow so the people can see who and where I am."

The tide was out when they arrived so the boats were unable to tie up at the quay but instead, ground to a halt on the mud-flats. People from the town and there were many there to see their Archbishop arrive, waded out through the mud to carry their illustrious visitor and his party to the dry land so they would not have to get their feet wet. Once ashore, Thomas decided to stay the night in the town and was given lodgings in a large house not many yards from the quayside.

He was not long in the house before Ranulf de Broc, having heard that Thomas had eluded him at Dover, arrived with his knights. They were looking for Thomas, all wore armour and swords under their cloaks and were obviously in the mood for a fight. One of the Archbishop's men, John of Oxford, confronted them asking, "What do you think you are doing? Are you mad," he shouted, "the Archbishop is under the King's protection? If you bear a message from the Young King then if you surrender your weapons I will let you pass."

This they did and were allowed into the presence of the Archbishop who did not bother to rise in greeting. These people were beneath him and he wanted them to know it. "We are suspicious of any French clerks you have brought with you without a proper passport issued by the Crown. We intend to receive from any such person an oath of loyalty to King Henry as we have every right to do under the Constitution of 1169. Any person here without such authority is an illegal immigrant."

"I will vouch for everyone in my party," Thomas told them and anyway, "such an oath is only required of spies and I have no intention of allowing any of my clerks to swear such an oath."

The knights insisted that Thomas withdraw his excommunications against the bishops and royal servants but he told them quite calmly that, "nothing can be done at the moment and when I reach my Cathedral at Canterbury I will consider the matter further. Now I bid you good night for I must rest." The knights were not happy but muttering curses and threats they retrieved their weapons, mounted their horses and made their way back to Dover.

The next day Thomas and his cortege left Sandwich through the Canterbury gate and preceded by Alexander Llewelyn his crossbearer, set off on the 12 mile journey to the city. Along the way, he was received with tumultuous acclaim by the huge crowds that lined the road. As he left Sandwich and set out through the villages and hamlets of Kent, bells rang, organs sounded, psalms, hymns and spiritual songs were sung, parishioners processed with their crosses before them, monks knelt in prayer as he passed. In some places the peasants strew the road with garments and chanted, "blessed is he that cometh in the name of the Lord." He made his way slowly through Ash and then Wingham, one of his great manors, now returned to him. Then it was on through Littlebourne, another returned manor and lastly over the brow of Saint Martin's Hill. From here he could look down on the Cathedral and City that he had not seen for more than six years.

Thomas returned to Canterbury on December 2, three days before his fiftieth birthday.

When he arrived at Canterbury, he was received as a liberator. Clad once again in his silk robes rather than the garb of a Cistercian monk and riding in style on one of the three fine horses he had brought as gifts for the Young King, the Archbishop beheld his city and cathedral dressed as if for a major festival. When he reached the city, he rode through it until he reached the

Christchurch gates of the Cathedral. Here he dismounted and in solemn humility, walked barefoot through the precincts to the great western portal as became his status as Archbishop. Here he stopped and prostrated himself for a short while after which he arose and walked the length of his Cathedral again prostrating himself before the high altar. After some time, he made his way to his archiepiscopal throne where he greeted every monk with a Kiss of Peace and then preached a sermon in the Chapter House. He was being greeted with far greater enthusiasm than had ever awaited the King. When Henry was told of Thomas's tumultuous welcome he was furious. The citizens of Canterbury had never greeted him in such a fine manner. They wore their best Sunday clothes and held a great banquet for their primate, whilst all the while, organ music and the chanting of the Christ Church monks filled the cathedral and the Archbishop's palace resounded with the fanfares of trumpets.

This reaction by the citizens of Canterbury to the return of their Archbishop was hardly surprising given that during his absence, Canterbury had been effectively under siege from the ruffian Ranulf de Broc who, despite Henry's orders to the contrary, was still stripping the diocese and the city of its lands and wealth. The local population were hoping that Thomas would liberate them from the extortion and cruel regime of the de Brocs. They were not to be disappointed. On Christmas Day, Thomas used his sermon to excommunicate de Broc and others in his party, saying, "I have returned only to lift the yoke of servitude from Canterbury."

Unfortunately, it was not all plain sailing for Thomas on his return. The three Bishops that had officiated at the Young Henry's coronation and had then been excommunicated by Thomas sailed for the King's court in Normandy but not without first stirring up trouble at home. Seeking to put their despised rival at a disadvantage, they sent their ally Geoffrey Ridel to the Young King with the slanderous, inflammatory message that Thomas was plotting to depose him. In answer to this they suggested that Young Henry should declare Thomas of Canterbury "a public enemy to the King and the kingdom".

Be that as it may, shortly after his triumphant return to England, Thomas set out from Canterbury to visit the Young

King, not knowing of the by intercession of Geoffrey Ridel and journeyed to London. His intention was to see the Young Henry, make any peace with him that needed to be made, assure the young man of his loyalty to him and present him with his gift of the three fine horses.

As he approached London, Thomas's small group, he had only five others with him and not the army the King would later be told about, were swamped by huge crowds. When they were met by group of poor scholars and clerics of London churches he scattered largess amongst them. Reaching Southwark, he stopped at the house of the Bishop of Winchester and it was while he was there that messengers arrived from Young Henry. These messengers gave him an order from the Young King. "You are forbidden to set foot in any of the King's strongholds, towns, boroughs or castles. If you do", they warned him, "you will have reason to regret it."

Whether influenced by the poison poured into his ears by Geoffrey Ridel or his inborn fear of incurring his father's wrath, Young Henry would not allow Thomas an audience.

It was at this time that the news was brought to Thomas at Southwark that the ship bringing his wine from France had been intercepted by Ranulf de Broc who had slashed the rigging, stolen the anchors, murdered some of the crew and put the rest in the prison at Pevensey. To his credit, when the Young King heard of this, he ordered restitution be made by Ranulf de Broc to Thomas for the loss of both the ship and the wine.

With a heavy heart, Thomas returned to Canterbury taking his three fine, Flanders horses with him.

After their negotiations at Fréteval, there can be little doubt Henry expected that in return for the concessions he had made, Thomas would similarly moderate his stance in their argument about the Church's, rights. If that was Henry's expectation of his Archbishop then he was about to be sadly disabused of the thought. Thomas did little to calm the troubled waters which still obviously existed in the relationship between the two men. Before even leaving France, Thomas had sent letters ahead immediately excommunicating his old ecclesiastical enemies, including the Archbishop of York and the bishops who had crowned the Young Henry as well as any royal servants he believed remained hostile to him. These were not the actions of a man looking for a peaceful life, especially knowing that Henry could not be trusted and was almost certainly plotting to go back on his word sooner rather than later. Thomas seemed almost to be goading Henry into further action and retribution.

Even without the threats being made by de Broc and his cronies, life was not going to be easy for Thomas. Even Henry the Young King had refused to meet the man he had once claimed had treated him better than his own father. Thomas's position was now delicate. He needed to recover his authority in England but at the same time, avoid becoming a yes-man of the King. True, he had been allowed to come home but under the surface, nothing much had changed. Henry had refused to give him the Kiss of Peace which would have signified an end to all animosity between the two and in view of that, Thomas quite rightly could not trust Henry to keep his word about anything.

Brother Edward knew first-hand from Gilbert Foliot what happened next. As he sat to write the next piece of the story, he remembered the day in 1174 when, through chance, he had met the Bishop who then related to him the details of his meeting with the King in Normandy.

The three excommunicated bishops, Jocelin of Salisbury, Roger of York and Gilbert Foliot of London, immediately left for Normandy after their excommunications were pronounced in order to set their grievances before the King, who was at his Christmas court. When they reached the King at Bur-le-Roi, a hunting-lodge near Bayeux, they were at once shown into his presence by, of all people, Ranulf de Broc, the terror of Canterbury.

When they began to complain about Thomas's treatment of them, they added a little more fuel to the fire when they told Henry that Thomas had been careering about the kingdom at the head of a strong force of armed men and planned to depose the Young Henry.

When the bishops had finished their tale of woe, Henry was understandably furious..

"Can it be true?" Henry wanted to know, "that, that man has maintained his excommunications against you three, despite the peace I made with him?"

"I swear my Lord," answered Roger of York, "it is true. There are many others who have been censured by him and he has excommunicated everyone who was at the coronation of the Young King and anyone who consented to it."

"By God's eyes," exploded the king, using his favourite oath, "I myself consented to it: it was my idea. Has he excommunicated me as well? A man who has eaten my bread," he raged, "who came to my court poor and I have raised him high, now he draws up his heel to kick me in the teeth! He has shamed my kin, shamed my realm: the grief goes to my heart, and no one has avenged me! What miserable drones and traitors have I nourished and promoted in my realms, who let their lord be treated with such shameful contempt by a low-born clerk. Is there not even a single one who is willing to avenge me of the wrongs I have suffered?"

Roger of York could say nothing in answer to this tirade but must have inwardly thought that the King would no longer allow Thomas of Canterbury to treat him, the ruler of an empire, with this level of disrespect. Ranulf De Broc, who was standing in the background by a door, seemed pleased to see the king so furious and decided that it afforded him an ideal opportunity and the excuse he needed to wreak vengeance on Thomas whilst at the same time placing him in high regard by his King. He could avenge his excommunication pronounced on Christmas day, the loss of income from controlling the city and the money he'd had to pay as restitution for the intercepted wine cargo. Revenge would be sweet.

Unfortunately for Thomas, it would seem that not all the King's men were miserable, cowardly drones after all. From all the evidence I have been able to gather during the years since, Ranulf de Broc would seem to have been chief instigator of what was to come next in Thomas's life, and that the actual murderers had been stirred up to their action by Ranulf. However, at the same time I have also found evidence that tells me Roger, the Archbishop of York and a lifelong enemy of Thomas, also had a hand in it.

After the King's rant, Roger left the room and was heard to say, "Thomas of Canterbury is troubling the whole kingdom. If the man were dead then peace would be restored." In a further damming act, he went further and gave each of Ranulf's four knights 60 marks to cover their travel costs. These four were Hugh de Morville, William de Tracy, Reginald fitzUrse and Richard le Breto.

Soon, the four knights set off from Bur-le-Roi and made haste to the Channel. There can be little doubt that they were acting on a huge hint from Roger and specific orders from Ranulf de Broc especially as the first place they made for after landing in England was Ranulf's castle at Saltwood. The castle lies on one of the few small hills on the marshes near the town of Hythe, a simple square keep, built of local stone. It is surrounded by a curtain wall which encloses the bailey with its stables, storehouses and all those other amenities needed for a garrison. Although the castle is part of the Canterbury fief it had been appropriated by the de Brocs, probably with the King's acquiescence, as soon as Thomas had gone into exile. To a great extent, the power of the de Brocs depended on the continued absence of the Archbishop; preferably, permanently.

Separately, Henry sent men to guard the English ports, in case Thomas should make yet another attempt to escape back across the channel and there once again, seek the protection of his friend and protector, Louis of France. Effectively, Henry had Thomas surrounded. In the meanwhile, he ordered emissaries to be dispatched to Thomas in Canterbury and the Pope in Rome to demand the withdrawal of the excommunications that had so angered him. By the time Henry's messengers reached their destinations, it would be too late.

Chapter 38

Edward's Story

Brother Edward took up a new sheet of vellum and began to write.

My story is nearing its conclusion and now I must recount the rest from personal knowledge and experience. The last I wrote was of the four knights leaving the King in Normandy, probably at the urging of Ranulf de Broc, to ride to Canterbury and confront the vilified Archbishop. Little did I know that soon I would be meeting them in person but I get ahead of myself.

It would have been late in the year of 1170 that I heard through a fellow brother who had travelled to us from London that Thomas of Canterbury, our Archbishop, was to return from exile. At this news, I determined to seek permission from the Prior to travel to Canterbury in an effort to seek an audience with the Archbishop, or at least to see the man in person. The Prior at that time was Prior Luc s predecessor, a brother called Edwin.

I told him of my desire and also that while I was in Kent, I should like to visit my old parish of Saltwood where I had been a rector when Thomas was first an archdeacon at Canterbury as there may still be friends there that I had not seen in many years. Prior Edwin said he was happy for me to make the journey and before wishing me God speed," he handed me a letter. This is a letter of introduction which you must hand to one of the Archbishop s clerks on your arrival. It should help you with your wish to meet Thomas in person."

Travelling from Cambridge to Canterbury was a journey not to be undertaken lightly and although I was a monk and in holy orders that did not guarantee me protection from the dangers of the road. The roads were beset by bandits. Often these were soldiers who had no trade to return to during the lulls in fighting

215

against the Scots, Welsh and French. They had a fearsome reputation and it was not really safe to travel alone so I cast about for some willing travelling companions.

I had, of course, made the journey in reverse when my position at Saltwood was ended. At the time, I had thought this was most probably caused by changes made by Thomas of Canterbury in his efforts to reclaim church lands, though I felt no animosity towards him then. I now realise that my loss of position was far more likely the result of Ranulf de Broc and his antagonism to anything to do with the church and those serving it.

Whatever the case, I still had a fervent wish to meet the man who had defended our Church against the King and his Barons through adversity and coercion. Even at the expense of his wealth and status he had stood strong and steadfast and I wanted the chance to meet a man of such faith.

I still had a list of all those places I had passed through on my original journey so all I would have to do now, was reverse the order of the names and with luck should arrive safely at my destination. I would still have to ask the inhabitants of each town or hamlet I passed through for onward directions to the next stop on my route to ensure I was continuing to travel in the right direction.

Prior Edwin said that for safety I should not go alone and therefore he selected two other brothers, Jerome and Matthew, to go with me. He said it would be good for their education to see something of the world outside our small ecclesiastical environs. I was not sure as to whether their company would be a hindrance or a help but accepted the Prior s decision without argument.

With a little money and some basic provisions we set out in the middle of December, not the best time of year to be out on the open road. I decided that we should each carry a satchel with clothing and food and a water skin in case of emergencies. We would also carry a stout stave to aid us with walking but also to act as a weapon should we need to protect ourselves. The king's highways were supposed to be cleared for 200 feet on either side to deny cover to the brigands who preyed on travellers but many country roads did not afford such protection. Sometimes waymarks to show routes through woods and more remote areas would be moved to lead travellers into the hands of waiting robbers. As I have already said, travelling and especially at this time of the year, was a test of fortitude and determination. A test I was willing to undertake though I am not sure that brothers Jerome and Matthew would agree with me.

We were on foot as the priory could not spare any horses or donkeys to carry us and even if they could, we would not have the money to feed both them and us, so we would have to make the best of what we had and trust in the Lord to bring us safely to Canterbury.

If on some parts of our journey we could use what was left of the old Roman roads, that would be a big advantage for us. The main roads were mainly kept in good repair by order of the king, who needed them to get himself and his armies around the kingdom but other roads were often very poor and could be blocked unexpectedly, especially in the winter.

In estimating how long our journey might take, I considered the facts as I knew them. In good weather, someone on foot and in a hurry could travel perhaps fifteen to twenty miles in a day. If the weather was bad or the roads were poor, that might become much less, perhaps only six to eight miles. A cart might manage twelve miles a day, less in winter. A man on horseback might travel twenty to twenty-five miles a day, if he had to use the same horse for the whole journey. Rich men and officials could change horses and managed thirty to forty miles a day. Crucially, the distance covered in a day would depend on the number of hours of daylight, the weather and where the next shelter might be.

In reality our little band would only have about six reasonable hours of daylight in which to travel in relative safety each day. To travel at night would be a risk not worth taking except in the most dire of circumstances. I had the feeling that we would be spending some freezing, miserable nights hidden under trees away from the roadside if we did not manage to find suitable shelter by nightfall.

As luck would have it, providence must have been on our side and the rain of previous days had stopped although the wind still blew and the cold was intense. We trudged for three days huddled in our cloaks with our cowls pulled over our faces to keep the worst of the wind out. For those first three nights we managed to find shelter in priories along the way but these were poor places with little to offer but a friendly face, a straw bed for the night and a bowl of potage in the morning. For these small things, we were grateful.

I suppose we could have used rivers for some parts of our journey but as I had even less knowledge of these than I did of the roads I had decided to remain with that which I knew.

Brother Matthew was a quiet soul and complained of little. Brother Jerome was the opposite and complained every step of the way. His litany kept Matthew and I company throughout our travel.

"My feet hurt, I'm hungry, I need to rest, I'm cold, are we nearly there yet, my back aches?"

"If you don't stop your whining, it will be your backside that aches after I have kicked some sense into it," I told him on one occasion when I could listen no more.

On the fourth morning, the heavens opened and by mid-day the rain had turned to icy sleet which found its way into and onto every exposed piece of skin it could find. The road, more of a track, that we travelled had turned to ankle-deep slush and mud which sapped all bonhomie from my demeanour. Brother Jerome must have sensed this and mercifully desisted with his griping which quite possibly saved his life.

By that evening, bedraggled, wet and frozen we reached Bishop's Stortford, so called because the bishop of London had bought the manor for the princely sum of £8.00. Here we took refuge in a disreputable looking hovel where the crone who lived there charged us a whole half-penny for our night's lodging. We were so cold and wet I think we would have paid whatever she asked just to get out of the weather.

Two days more walking and we came at last to London, halfway on our journey to Canterbury. To the north we passed through tilled fields, pastures, and pleasant, level meadows with streams flowing through them, the watermill wheels turned by their current making a pleasing sound. Not far off there spread out a vast forest, its copses dense with foliage concealing, I am told, wild animals, stags, does, boars, and wild bulls. Around the north side of the City ran a high, wide wall punctuated at intervals with turrets and seven double-gated entranceways. In the past London also had a wall and turrets on its south side but the great river Thames has, through the ebb and flow of the tide, undermined it and caused it and them to collapse.

I had been to London before but my two companions had not seen such a sight and gazed around them in wonder. So many people, so much noise and a smell never to be forgotten. The City of London, where it seems the people of the world were all gathered together. It is the seat of the English monarchy with the great White Tower built on the orders of King William, the first of that name, as a place of safety and to overawe the citizens.

As we trudged through the city streets on our way to the river and the bridge across it we passed a myriad of tradespeople. Brothers Matthew and Jerome looked about them in fascination. If you had the money to spend, everything and anything was available to buy. We neared the river where we could see the masts of ships moored to the quays, the vast storerooms for goods being brought from around the known world.

Now we were passing close by Vintner's quay, near to where the Walbrook flows into the Thames and it was here that we found no shortage of cookshops where we could find something to eat. These shops catered particularly to travellers, and some were even partitioned to create modest accommodations.

Can we afford something to eat?" Brother Jerome wanted to know. I am famished and all we have eaten since the sun came up is a piece of stale cheese and mouldy bread." Although his constant complaining annoyed me to the point of distraction, I could not help but agree with him this time and so we stopped and partook of a bowl of broth each with some kind of meat floating in it. What the meat was, I hesitate to guess at but I have to say that being as hungry as we were, it tasted good. Even Brother Jerome stopped his grousing while we ate.

As we ate, the keeper of the cookshop enquired of us the purpose of our journey. We are going to Canterbury in the hope of an audience with the Archbishop," I told him.

Oh," he said, You have just missed him. He preached a sermon at the Priory of St Mary Overie last week before heading out of London for Canterbury. That might have saved you a journey. Never mind. How is the broth?" All thought of Thomas of Canterbury forgotten.

We were going to cross the river by London Bridge which was cheaper than a ferryman. The bridge had, had a chequered history, having been originally built by the Romans and then by King William, the first of that name, before it was destroyed by a great wind and replaced by King William, the second of that name. Then again, it had caught fire and had to be rebuilt during the reign of King Stephen which was the bridge we were to cross. The elements, as far as the bridge was concerned, were with us on the day we crossed it. There was little wind to blow it down and the rain fell incessantly so it would not burn, thus, we reached the safety of the southern shore of the river at a place called Southwark.

From here it was 60 miles to Canterbury and I suspected that Brother Jerome would remind us at every milestone just how miserable he was and how this journey must be God s punishment for misdeeds unknown to him but not to God. Of Brother Matthew, there was never a sound. If I did not know better, I should have thought him a deaf mute other than the noises he made when eating or when he muttered his prayers morning and evening.

Our road to Canterbury was clear and well used. From the bridge we followed the old Stane Street, until it met Watling Street, one of the fine straight roads the Romans left us. Unfortunately this road is now ruined in many parts and is just mud, especially at this time of the year. Much of the paving and larger stones have been taken and used by local barons for building their churches and manors. Most other habitation along the route was, of course, simple wattle and daub as one would expect, especially of the Anglo-Saxon peasants who live like pigs anyway.

After two days of walking in the cold and rain, which were miserable in the extreme, we came at last to the River Medway. We had found a night s lodging at a small priory near a place called Darenth which gave us some respite from the weather but any benefit had soon vanished We were therefore mightily glad to see the great keep looming across the river with the Cathedral at its side. The prospect of a decent meal and a warm bed heartened us and put a spring in our steps.

There is a bridge which crosses the River Medway just below the castle. This again was a remnant of Roman engineering with nine stone piers constructed on foundations deep below the riverbed. On top of these stone piers was placed a flat timber roadway which allowed us to cross this wide river without getting our feet wet. Well, no wetter than they already were. The monks of the Cathedral chapter gave us a warm welcome and after a meal we were asked to recount the tales of our journey so far which we gladly did. Brother Matthew, of course, just smiled and remained mute whilst Brother Jerome basked in the opportunity to talk incessantly. For my part, I was pleased just to enjoy a seat in good company while my feet warmed by a glowing fire and my stomach enjoyed the sensation of being full for a change. Indeed, the welcome offered us at Rochester was so good that we stayed an extra day.

All good things must come to an end, or so I am told, and so it was that we had to leave the comfort of our new friends' hearth and move onwards to our destination. Two, or perhaps three more days walking should bring us to our destination. All I would have to do then was try to arrange an audience with the Archbishop to make the whole journey worthwhile.

Before taking the last stage of our journey, I had decided that we would seek shelter at the abbey in Faversham which had been founded by King Stephen and his wife Matilda and lay only some 10 miles from Canterbury. Now, both Stephen and Matilda were buried in the Abbey as was their son Eustace, he who at one time had been a pretender to the English throne. Their intention had been to create a royal mausoleum for the House of Blois at Faversham but as fate would have it, they were the first and only royals of that line.

Faversham is a small town that abuts the abbey and is on the main road to Canterbury and thence to Dover so is oft visited by travellers, merchants and royalty alike. There is a small but bustling quay used by fishing boats and merchant ships and a thriving market has grown up around both the Abbey and the quay. Once again, when I made the purpose of our journey known at the Abbey gates we were bade come in" and made welcome. All being well, only one more day and we would reach our goal.

Leaving Faversham in the early morning we climbed a long hill out of the hamlet of Boughton and reaching the top, thought we might catch a glimpse of the cathedral city. The whole area was thickly wooded so all we could see, even from this high vantage point, was the road stretching ahead of us. Still no sight of Canterbury other than a faint smear of smoke to beckon us on.

Oh, a wondrous sight after nearly two weeks on the road and listening to Brother Jerome bemoaning his fate the whole way, Canterbury cathedral in all its splendour stood before us.

I have a letter of introduction to the Archbishop," I told the gatekeeper, to whom should I present it?"

You and about a thousand others," was his churlish, unhelpful reply.

No, I really have. We have travelled a long way to see him. I will show you the letter."

No point Brother, I can t read, but I will find someone who can. Wait here." Then he was gone and we were left standing in the pouring rain at the gate. He returned a few minutes later with a monk whom I took to be one of the cathedral clerks.

Come into the shelter of the archway brothers, out of the weather," he suggested, which we gladly did. Now then, you have a letter of introduction?"

I reached into my satchel and brought out the letter I had been given by Prior Edwin and handed it to the clerk. He broke the seal and read it.

Have you read this?" he asked.

No," I replied, Prior Edwin had it all prepared for when I was leaving. He handed it to me and said I should give it to the Archbishop or one of his clerks when I arrived and that it would, in all likelihood, gain me admission to the Archbishop s presence."

Well Brother, the Archbishop is a busy man but the letter is from a man who was at school with him at Merton Priory and is recommending you to the Archbishop. He is a man who values loyalty to friends both new and old so I would be surprised if after he reads this he does not allow you an audience." This was news to gladden my heart. But first, let me find you and your fellow travellers somewhere warm and arrange something for you to eat while you await the answer to your letter."

Sometime later the same clerk returned. The Archbishop says he would be pleased to greet one of his old friend Edwin s brothers and will see you in the morning. In the meantime I am instructed to offer you our hospitality until then."

Brother Edward wrote a last sentence.

That is how I came to be with Thomas of Canterbury on the fateful day which would change all our lives."

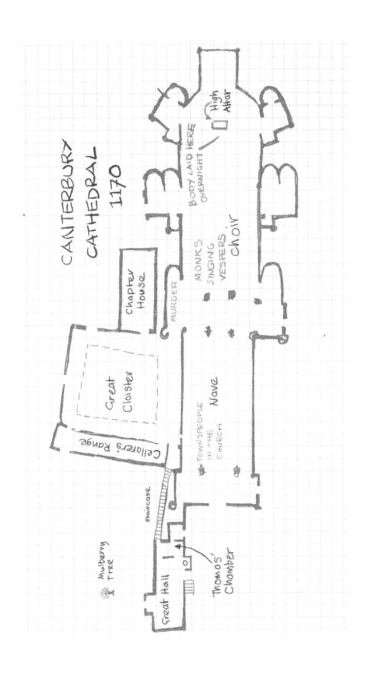

Canterbury Cathedral 1170

224

Chapter 39

The Murder

As Brother Edward sat in the fading light of the scriptorium he knew that his story was reaching its conclusion.

"All that I have written has been leading to this point and my hand trembles at the remembering. What was done was done and as I was one of the few to witness it, the deed must be recorded as I saw it happen."

The day following our arrival at Canterbury, I was shown into the Archbishop's private rooms in the Cathedral precincts.

The Archbishop himself came forward to greet me as I entered.

"Brother Edward," he greeted me, "I take it my staff have looked after you well? You have, I hope, slept deeply and in some comfort after your long journey? Come in and sit. Tell me of my old friend Edwin. It is many years since we shared a classroom at Merton."

Obviously I did as asked and was pleased to tell him that Prior Edwin was indeed in good health and sent his best wished to his old friend. However, I could not help but be shocked at first sight of the man I had travelled so far to see although hopefully that did not show on my face.

I had heard that Thomas of Canterbury was tall and thin but at the same time robust, a man who had at one time, not too long ago, been a warrior, who could hunt and ride with the King all day long. The man I was confronted with was gaunt, pale and somewhat stooped. The adjective I would have used at the time was haggard. Yes, that would best describe the man who was the head of the Church in England, haggard. On his forehead he had deep furrows while his mouth seemed permanently turned down. His once magnificent black beard was now completely white and thinning. I have heard subsequently that Thomas, oddly enough, like King Henry, had suffered for years from some sort of stomach malady and that his diet had always been somewhat restricted because of it. He also suffered constant agony from a disease in his jaw after an operation to remove some of his jawbone. These ailments and the pain they caused him on a daily basis must have, at times, affected his ability to make decisions and think clearly. Perhaps the problem with his jaw was helped when the abbot at Pontigny had insisted that Thomas follow the Cistercian habit of vegetarianism during his stay there and thereafter his diet became even more restricted and frugal. He drank only water from that point on. Not a habit I, myself, would adopt as I think that small beer is better for the digestion and possibly less prone to the onset of the bloody flux but who was I to gainsay an Archbishop?

It is hardly surprising then that after six years of exile, on-going illness, and a constant battle with a vindictive and dangerous King, that he was not looking a picture of rude health. His physical appearance aside, he seemed to me to be in full command of his mental faculties so that his demeanour was soon forgotten.

"As you can imagine Brother Edward I am a busy man with much to attend to so you will forgive me if I cannot devote as much time to you individually as I might like but you are welcome to stay in my circle for a few days and observe the inner workings of the archbishopric. Talking of an inner circle, what has happened to the two other brothers you arrived with?"

"Ah my Lord Archbishop," I replied, "they have decided that they are weary from their travels and beg your indulgence while they recuperate and enjoy the hospitality of your cathedral monks. It is only me who was keen to make your personal acquaintance. They mean no disrespect but I think the truth is that they are somewhat overawed by being here at all. Brother Matthew would be so tongue-tied by meeting you that he would merely dribble and look foolish while his companion would probably try and tell you how to carry out your duties. He has yet to learn the sins of vanity and humility."

"Well, as I have said, your presence is welcome, but now I have work that must be attended to so I wish you good day."

For the next day or two and from a position in the background, I followed Thomas and his entourage around, observing the day-to-day workings of his household and the inner workings of his great office.

In the meanwhile, as I was happily enjoying my discrete observations of an archbishop at work, I was unaware that the four knights, Hugh de Morville, William de Tracy, Reginald fitzUrse and Richard le Breto had landed in Kent. They had left Bur-le Roi and crossed the Channel independently and sailed from different ports but two days later were at Saltwood Castle, the home of Ranulf de Broc and not above 20 mile from Canterbury where they were enjoying his hospitality and planning their next move. The castle was technically part of Archbishop Thomas's demesne but had, during his exile, been given to Ranulf. All the more reason for Ranulf to want to be rid of Thomas permanently. All these knights were well-born of good Norman stock and owned lands in England as well as across the Channel. On reflection it might show that good blood is not always a guarantee of virtue.

On the morning of 29th December in the year 1170 and accompanied by a band of retainers, they set off along the old Roman road from Lymme to Canterbury and to their confrontation with Thomas. Some might tell you that the year was 1171 but that date is based on the fact that the monks of Canterbury have an odd tradition of counting the new year as beginning the day after Christmas. I was there and I can assure you that it was in the year of 1170.

Their first stop on reaching the city was at the Abbey of Saint Augustine where the Abbot was none other than Clarembald, that long time enemy of Thomas. How Clarembald had managed to hold on to his abbacy is something of a mystery although he had, in the past, been a staunch ally of the King. Notwithstanding the support of the King he had incurred the censure of a Papal Commission, been shunned by his own monks, let the abbey buildings fall into a deplorable state of repair and, so it was rumoured, sired 17 illegitimate children in nearby villages. Obviously a man of prodigal appetites.

When they arrived at the Abbey, Clarembald made the knights welcome in his own house where he served them dinner and copious quantities of wine. Over dinner, with the help of the Abbot, they honed their plan of attack. They left the Abbey for the Cathedral in the late afternoon when dusk had already begun to fall.

At first, the knights entered the Bishop's Palace with a small detachment of their men. They made their way through the main gateway to the Archbishop's palace while others of their retinue were combing the city streets ordering any they could find to take up arms in the name of the King and join them in the Palace yard. When the frightened citizens refused to do as they were being ordered, the de Brocs ordered a curfew, instructing everyone "to stay indoors and keep the peace, no matter what they might see or hear". They then stationed their best troops in a house just outside the cathedral walls. At the time this house, opposite the gateway to the archbishop's palace, was owned by a man called Gilbert the Citizen. Whether that is still the case after what subsequently happened I am not sure but I think it unlikely. I do not think that the King would have looked kindly on anyone he thought might have aided these four men.

The rest of their forces they stationed around the city walls and especially at the city gates to ensure that no rescue or escape attempt could be made. If there was one, there would be no way of out from the city into the countryside and so on towards the coast. All these plans they must have made at Saltwood castle before they left for the city.

By now, it was getting later in the afternoon and it would not be long before full darkness fell.

The knights quickly dismounted from their horses in the Palace courtyard and not wanting to alarm those in the Cathedral too much in the first instance, left their chain-mail and weapons stacked up underneath a mulberry tree for safe keeping. To me, this might suggest that all they had intended to do was persuade Thomas to change his mind about the censures and excommunications he had pronounced against the two Bishops and Roger the Archbishop of York for their part in the coronation of the Young King. Things were to go quickly awry.

The four knights then strode into the Archbishop's great hall, where the members of his household were finishing their dinner and the plates were being cleared away. FitzUrse, in a loud voice demanded, "we must talk to the Archbishop immediately. Where is he?"

Just before the knights had entered, making their demands of his servants, Thomas had been eating his meal at the high table on a dais at the far end flanked by his monks and clerks. His cross bearer stood to one side reading from the scriptures. I was much further down in body of the hall with all the lesser mortals. When the Archbishop finished his meal, which was, unusually, one of pheasant, grace was sung and he went up the stairs behind the hall to his private quarters where I was lucky enough to be amongst those invited to join him.

When FitzUrse and his band had thrown out their first demand to know where Thomas was, they were answered by the Archbishop's seneschal, William FitzNigel, who having just finished his meal was guarding the door to Thomas's chamber. He noticed that these knights were the worse for drink and was immediately wary of their intentions.

"My Lord, the Archbishop is in his chamber. What is your business with him?"

"Do not interfere," FitzUrse commanded him, "tell him we are here on the King's business and must speak with him now."

FitzNigel was now caught in a cleft stick. It was his sworn duty to protect Thomas but his duty to the King outweighed that. "Wait here," he told the knights, "I will let the Archbishop know you are here and he can decide whether he wishes to see you or not." FitzNigel went upstairs and explained his dilemma to Thomas saying, "the King might hold it against me if he finds I have obstructed his messengers in carrying out his orders."

"Then, William, you must ere on the King's side," Thomas told him. "go down and let them pass."

When FitzNigel announced the knights they found Thomas sitting on his bed and talking to a group of his advisors and others of the cathedral community. I was among those present in the Archbishops chamber. When they entered the room, Thomas chose to ignore them so they just sat down among those of us already there. I remember thinking to myself that they looked pale and exhausted. I suppose that having travelled from Normandy across the Channel in the midst of winter and then almost straight on to Canterbury it was hardly surprising that they looked this way. It did cross my mind that their physical appearance might also have been caused by suffering from the effects of drinking and eating too much at Saltwood Castle the previous evening and then more at St Augustine's Abbey. An exhausted man and a drunk man can often look the same.

Reginald FitzUrse was not used to being ignored and rudely interrupted the Archbishop's conversation. Without preamble he told Thomas, "we are here by order of the King and have a message from him," which we now know was not strictly true. "Will you hear it in public or in private?"

Immediately, Thomas was on his guard. He had no desire to be left alone with these men so answered without hesitation, "such things should not be spoken in private nor in my bedchamber but in public where all can see and hear what is said and by whom."

Then FitzUrse continued without preamble, "we ask you to absolve the churchmen you have excommunicated and suspended and then you must come with us to Winchester to stand trial."

"Stand trial?" Thomas demanded of FitzUrse, his voice rising "what nonsense is this?"

"When the king made peace with you at Fréteval, he allowed you back to Canterbury but you added insult to injury by breaking the peace and, having obstinate pride, excommunicated those who crowned and anointed the King's son. It is clear that your intention is to depose the King's son and take away his crown. The Young King is to try you and pass judgement on you for attempting to rob him of his crown." FitzUrse had risen from where he had been sitting and Thomas did likewise and looked down at FitzUrse showing that he was taller than the knight come to accuse him. A small but satisfying victory.

"I think not," Thomas told FitzUrse, "the excommunications and suspensions are from the Pope, not I. It is not possible for me to remove them, even if I wanted to. They were imposed for serious crimes including the coronation of the Young King, a duty only I have the authority to perform. The Bishops of London and Salisbury and the Archbishop of York have been offered the right to an appeal to the Pope, an opportunity which they have declined to take."

Thomas resumed his seat on his bed. "I can tell you plainly that I have no wish to annul the Young King's coronation and deprive him of the throne. His coronation is valid and he bears no guilt for it being carried out. Only the Churchmen who presided at the ceremony were in the wrong. It is my fervent wish that the Young King does go on to have a long and successful life and to build on the empire his father will leave to him. Remember, I have a great affection for Young Henry. Was he not brought up and nurtured in my own home? As I am sure you will already know, I tried to visit him on my return to England but for whatever reason, he would not see me. I had brought him a gift of three fine destriers which I had to bring back to Canterbury. I would be very pleased if you would take them with you if you plan to go to London. They are wasted here."

The knights, all shouting at the same time, started berating the Archbishop and making threats towards him. Thomas was so shocked at their loutish, rude behaviour that he covered his ears with his hands until the shouting died down after which he spoke to them calmly, as if to recalcitrant children saying, "I am surprised that you dare to make such noise and threaten me. I made my peace with the King at Fréteval, which you well know."

Rather than be cowed by Thomas's riposte, FitzUrse told him, "We represent the King and it is from the King that you hold your position." By now, Thomas had stood up once again and both men stood face to face. Thomas gripped his accuser by the arm.

"You are mistaken," he told FitzUrse, "I hold my position as Archbishop from God and the Pope. Only my lands and property are what I hold from the King. We must render to the King that which is the King's and to God that which is God's. You were all once my vassals when I was Chancellor but still you attack me in this insolent manner and in my own bedchamber. I should not be hearing from you at all."

FitzUrse broke the Archbishop's hold on his arm and responded angrily, spittle spraying in Thomas's face, "now we serve the King." He looked at the Archbishop's followers gathered in the room, one of whom was me, and commanded us to leave. No-one moved. A silence followed and then FitzUrse, his face contorted with anger, said, "then I command you here present to hold this man prisoner." To which Thomas calmly replied, "No-one will be holding me prisoner as I have no

231

intention of going anywhere added to which, I give the orders in my Cathedral not you. Now, I order you and your men to leave."

As a parting retort, FitzUrse accused Thomas of insulting the king and shouted at him, "you have risked your head by your stubbornness." Thomas remained unmoved and replied, "find someone else to frighten, you will find me steadfast in the battle of the Lord."

The four knights obviously thought that at this point little was to be achieved by talk and withdrew from the Archbishop's inner chamber, retraced their steps through the great hall and into the courtyard. When the knights had gone, John of Salisbury turned to Thomas and asked, "why do you act without thinking? Might it not have been better for a man of your rank and power to act with more tact? Now all you have done is anger these men even more."

It was getting dark and the knights knew they had little time to spare. Robert de Broc, Ranulf's younger brother as well as an apostate Cistercian monk had followed the knights through the main gates and into the gatehouse where he stationed one of his own men in place of the Archbishop's porter. While he was at it, he also brought some soldiers into the gatehouse and closed the street gate. Now, the palace and cathedral were effectively cut off from the city.

The knights themselves, once they had left the hall, positioned two of their men on horseback within the palace porch to keep a close watch that no-one escaped from the palace. At the same time, they were supposed to ensure that the doors into the palace were not locked from the inside. Then, either here in the porch or under a mulberry tree in the courtyard, FitzUrse, with the help of one of the Archbishop's kitchen servants donned his full armour. His three companions did likewise. Once they were ready for the next phase of their plan, FitzUrse ordered the outer gates to be opened and more soldiers poured into the courtyard.

Thomas's enemies planned to charge through the doors of the archbishop's hall, but despite the efforts of the two men posted there, two servants of the Archbishop, Osbert and Algar, managed to bolt and barricade the hall door from inside. It seems that the guards FitzUrse had posted to prevent this very thing had become so fascinated by the preparations that were taking place under the mulberry tree in the courtyard, that they forgot to do what they were supposed to do in regard to the door. Now, despite their efforts, the knights and their soldiers could not break down the door but the noise they made trying to do it caused most of those in the palace, other than Thomas and his companions, to flee into the Cathedral for protection.

Now, in preparation for their final assault, the four knights were wearing full armour, their helmets and carrying their swords. Wearing battle helms covered their faces almost entirely leaving only their eyes visible, thus making it difficult to tell them apart. Now they were girded as for combat as if they expected to do battle with armed knights inside the cathedral rather than an unarmed Archbishop and an assortment of monks and clerks. Certainly, no-one in the Cathedral would be armed.

Perhaps, I remembered thinking, that they didn't really expect any resistance but only put on their armour in the hope that nobody would be able to recognise them. Although, it was growing so dark in the cathedral environs that it would have been difficult to recognise one's own brother.

Because the door to the Archbishops palace had been barred and could not be broken down, Robert de Broc, who as the royal sequestrator had occupied the archbishop's palace for the last six years and so knew all its entrances and hidden passages began to walk round the Palace looking for an alternative way of getting in. He led some troops past the kitchens and through a small orchard where he found a postern door into the Palace. To one side of the door was a set of stairs leading to an upper floor but some of the steps were broken in the middle and were being repaired by two workmen. These two workmen had apparently gone for their dinner but had left a ladder and some tools behind. Robert used the ladder to get to the upper floor and there he used an axe left by the workmen to smash his way through a window and then a door into the Palace. He was thus able to open the postern door to let the soldiers in. They went from there into the great hall where they found Osbert and Algar still there. These two stalwarts offered what resistance they could but were hacked at with swords and fell aside wounded. Robert made straight for the door of the Archbishop's great hall, and threw it open, allowing his fellow conspirators to rush in. The Archbishop's palace was now open to his enemies.

Of course, I only learned of these things much later as while it was all happening, I was still in the upper chamber with Thomas and some of his advisers. I, like the others, heard the shattering of the glass window and clearly heard the shouts and screams of those I took to be the Archbishop's servants as they tried to repel the invaders. I am sure that Thomas must have heard these sounds but he appeared to remain calm and untroubled. Thomas's entourage, unlike their master, began to show signs of panic. "My Lord," they were insisting, "we must leave here and make for the safety of the cathedral. Please we must flee into the church proper."

To everyone's consternation, the Archbishop maintained his insistence on staying where he was. He remained calmly sitting on his bed. "I have told you," he repeated, "I am not afraid of these ruffians and misguided knights and here I will stay."

Soon we could hear the noise of feet as monks and others were hurrying out of the Palace and into the cathedral. Knowing that the bearing of arms in a church was counted as a great sin they no doubt felt that whatever was happening, at least within the sanctuary of the cathedral they would find safety.

As the shouting and other noises of conflict around them grew lounder and closer, we, the Archbishop's friends could hesitate no longer. Staying where we were was not an option any sane man would take. We would have none of these holy heroics and despite his protests and violent struggling, Thomas was forcibly seized by us and physically dragged and carried, protesting all the time, down a staircase, through the cloisters and into the cathedral. We had managed to get Thomas away from his chamber just in time as soon after we had carried him away, the knights burst into the room looking for him.

By this time it was already dark as it was not long after the shortest day of the year. The candles had been lit and cast deep shadows throughout the building. Some cathedral monks had already begun to sing vespers in the choir, and the sound of their voices mixed with the voices of Thomas's advisors pleading with him to bar the doors of the cathedral. 'Let them remain open,' Thomas commanded, "there are people of the town even now coming in to hear vespers. They will not be locked out of this house of God. It is not right to turn the house of prayer, this church of Christ, into a fortress."

A monk arrived with more bad news. "My Lord archbishop you are not safe here. Ranulf de Broc is aiding the four knights who have dared to assault you. They have garrisoned the four castles surrounding the city. There are soldiers in the streets of the City and they have surrounded the cathedral. They mean to trap you here and if necessary, lay siege to you and everyone in here until you accede to their demands. Or" the monk hesitated, "worse."

Thomas, it would seem, was surrounded on all sides.

When he reached what he thought was the safety of the cathedral and entered the chapel dedicated to Saint Benedict, Thomas turned to one of his companions and said, "I must spend a moment and pray on this matter. Roger, you are my servant and long-time friend. I would like you with me when I pray. Let us go quickly to somewhere quiet." Roger had been Thomas's close companion for many years and had become his constant companion. It was he who slept in Thomas's bedchamber at night.

Thomas turned to the man carrying his archiepiscopal cross, a junior clerk named Henry of Auxerre since his faithful cross-bearer, Alexander Llewelyn, had already left for France on an embassy to Henry, and said, "hand me my cross. When I have finished praying I will carry it myself. It stood me in good stead at Northampton in the face of Roger of York. I wish to feel the comfort of its weight if these knights dare to confront me here. They will surely not defy the protection it gives the bearer." Henry of Auxerre was hesitant but did as his Archbishop bid and handed him the cross.

"Come Roger let us have a moment of peace to pray for guidance." The two men ascended the stairs leading to the high alter and went through the small door that led to a private chapel to the left, which was above the altar to Saint Benedict where the others of Thomas's party waited below in fear and trepidation. The noise of angry shouting was growing ever closer as the knights sought out the Archbishop.

A short time later the Archbishop reappeared at the top of the first flight of stairs carrying his cross before him as he had done at Northampton and began to mount the next set of steps to the high altar. It was then that we heard the cloister doors crash open as the knights forced their way into the cathedral. Thomas turned back to face them.

As FitzUrse burst through the cloister door he was in full armour with his sword unsheathed. At first, in the gloom, he did not see Thomas on the stairs. "Where is Thomas Beckette, traitor to the King and the kingdom?' he shouted. He used the archbishop's low-born surname as an insult to remind him that he was very much the social inferior of FitzUrse and his companions.

A few seconds later the other knights came in behind him, also with their swords drawn. These were followed by even more of their retainers amongst whom was a clerk called Hugh of Horsea. Now all was chaos and confusion. Answered by a stunned silence, FitzUrse shouted out again, "Where is the Archbishop?"

Thomas was descending the stairs carrying his cross when he answered, "I am here. What do you want?" To me, he seemed more stooped and his voice sounded strange but I suppose it would be in the heightened state of madness and fear that was beginning to surround him. By this time, Thomas found himself abandoned by John of Salisbury and the rest of his retinue only William FitzStephen, William of Canterbury and me, remained. Why I stayed, I have never been sure. I had only met the Archbishop briefly and there was no good reason for me to be there.

Thomas was wearing a black mantle with a black cap covering his Archbishop's clothing. In the dark of the Cathedral lit only by candles it would have been difficult to differentiate between Thomas and any of the other monks who had by now, returned to the body of the Church although some might have been hovering in the gloom to see what all the commotion was about. The heads and faces of the knights were covered by their mailed coifs, only their eyes showing. I was there and I can tell you that even I, to this day, am still confused as to who was whom.

236

When I met him some years later, I was asked by Gilbert Foliot, "Who struck the first blow?"

"The first blow was more of a slap," I said, "I'm sure it was William de Tracy who had somehow got himself behind the Archbishop and hit him across the shoulders with the flat of his sword. I think this was a warning of serious intent and as he struck he told Thomas that he must come with them as their prisoner."

I told Foliot, "I think the first real blow was struck by FitzUrse. I'd heard Thomas call him by name when he refused to become their prisoner and leave the Cathedral. As I could barely see even their eyes in the gloom I still cannot be sure which of the assailants it was. Whoever it was, I think they acted quickly for fear that the Archbishop might be rescued before they could complete their grisly task. This first blow struck through Thomas's cap and cut a slice from the top of his head. Blood gushed from the wound and flowed over his face obscuring his features."

I think even now that they were afraid to kill the Archbishop in the cathedral and made an attempt to lift him on to the shoulders of one of them. Again, I am not sure which. Although wounded and covered in his own blood, Thomas tried to cling on to a pillar to prevent his being taken. Now his back was to his attackers. The knights must, by now, have realised that they would need to conclude their business here quickly whatever the consequences. There were townspeople and monks in the nave who may have become brave enough to come to their Archbishop's rescue. Then I heard one of the knights say, "you are going to die now."

At this point, I found myself standing slightly to the left side of Thomas. I sensed that a second blow was about to come and without thinking, threw up my arm to shield him from it.

The blow came and cut through my sleeve, it cut away a big piece of my skin and muscle. The sword went right through to the bone. My puny arm was not sufficient to absorb all the force of the strike. It glanced off my bone and hit the top of the archbishop's head loosening a great flap of skin that fell over his face. My pain was intense, I fell to the floor and thought I was about to die. I could do nothing more to help Thomas.

I was to learn later that, that was the sword cut which brought Thomas to his knees. Then William de Tracy hit the kneeling Archbishop so hard on the skull that the tip of his sword shattered when it hit the paving. Perhaps he was trying to behead the Archbishop but missed his mark and Thomas now crashed face down on the paving. Blood poured from the wounds in his head. All the while, the fourth knight, Hugh de Morville, prevented any possible interference from would-be rescuers whilst his companions carried out their deadly mission. A final blow was struck to Thomas's prostrate body by Richard le Breto who said he was there to avenge his friend, the King's brother William, he who supposedly died of a broken heart after Thomas had refused to allow his marriage to Isabel de Warenne.

Still it was not over. The clerk, Hugh of Horsea, called Mauclerk, he who had followed the knights in, stood on the fallen Archbishop's back and using the end of his sword, scooped out the blood and brains which he then spread across the floor. After he had scattered the brains he cried out, "this fellow will rise no more. The traitor is dead." When they had finished with him, I doubt even his own mother would have recognised him. His skull was split open, he had a great gash through his face and a huge flap of skin dropped from his forehead to past his mouth. Then they left, leaving the body of Thomas, the Archbishop of Canterbury lying on the floor of his cathedral amongst the blood and gore of his brains. I lay on the paving alongside the man I had tried in vain to protect, his blood mingling with mine.

Soon, amidst the confusion and shouting some of the cathedral monks began to make their way down the stairs from the knave. They were so horror stricken when they saw what had been done to their Archbishop that for a moment, they were transfixed by inertia. We could hear the shouts of de Brocs men coming from the cloisters and the great hall. We still feared that the danger was not yet over.

Why did I rush to protect Thomas? That is a question I have asked myself ever since that day in the cathedral. Although I hardly knew the man, I was in the place at perhaps the wrong time and somehow could not help myself. It seemed the Christian thing to do. I had only met him for the first time that week yet others who had known him for years had abandoned him to the mercy of his killers. They cowered in the darkness of the cathedral while his murderers slaughtered him like a beast.

The attackers of Thomas had left the way they came, through the cloisters. In the normal way of these things, the next order of the day was looting and before them lay the Archbishop's Palace and all its treasures ready for plundering. Robert de Broc had, however, been left in the Palace to guard it and while the four knights were about their murdering he had already started to ransack the Palace taking away chests full of valuables. Anything of value they took, rings, clothes, spoons, goblets, plates and any silver coin they could find. They took the horses from the palace stables, and those of the servants in the monastic stables. The fine destriers meant as a gift for the Young King disappeared. They took the pack horses and some wagons to carry off all they had stolen. Meanwhile, the common soldiers ransacked the city.

Of all those who were supposedly at the Cathedral that day, I have never heard mentioned the name of Ranulf de Broc as being there. It is said that he had left his castle at Saltwood with the knights and their retainers that morning but then stayed at Saint Augustine's Abbey with Clarembald while his men were about their work in the cathedral. I would think he did this to distance himself from the crime he had set them out to commit. Later in the day he must have slipped back to Saltwood as he was there to welcome back the loot-laden raiding party on their return.

It is horrible to report the speed with which people from the town who were in the cathedral for the service of Vespers began to approach the scene to gawp at the prostrate form lying amidst the blood. While the blood soaked body of Thomas still lay on the pavement, they began to bring bottles and anything that would hold blood to secretly carry off as much of the Archbishop's spilt blood as they could gather. Others tore off shreds of clothing and dipped them in the blood. They were like flies around a corpse. Disgusting. A keening, hysterical howling sound had begun to rise from crowds that had started to gather in the nave as news of the murder spread like wildfire throughout the city.

I cannot recall exactly when but at some point, William FitzStephen had reappeared from behind a pillar where he had been hiding and came to my aid as did some of the monks. He realised there was nothing he could do for Thomas but seeing that I was still alive, ordered some of the monks to take me to a place of safety where my wound could be dealt with.

This is where my story ends. The story from here is well documented. Thomas of Canterbury is now a Saint. He may be dead but his legacy will live on long after both his death and mine.

Chapter 40

Osbert the Chamberlain's Story

I am Osbert. I served Thomas of Canterbury as his chamberlain for many years from his time as Chancellor up until the day he supposedly lay dead in Canterbury Cathedral. Let me explain why I say 'supposedly'.

After we had eaten supper in the great hall and the Archbishop had gone upstairs to his bedchamber, taking his advisors and friends with him, I had remained in the hall to supervise the clearing up as was my duty. I was there when de Broc's knights had come into the room demanding to see the Archbishop and when William FitzNigel had halted them at the foot of the stairs to the private chambers above.

I thought to myself, "this bodes no good." Although the knights appeared not to be armed they looked in no mood to argue and were insistent that FitzNigel should stand aside and let them up. I am an inquisitive man by nature and admit that curiosity got the better of me when caution might have been a more sensible option. I left what I was doing and moved closer to better hear what was going on.

FitzNigel disappeared up the stairs but soon returned saying, "my Lord the Archbishop will see you in his chamber," and showed them up. As I say, I am inquisitive, some might say too nosey for my own good, so I followed behind not wanting to miss out on what was taking place.

I witnessed the confrontation between FitzUrse and my master. Again I was thinking, "this is not good. I wish my Lord Archbishop would use some of those diplomatic skills I know he possess in abundance to keep these men in a peaceful frame of mind. I suppose his sense of the importance of his status would not allow him to make concessions to these interlopers. I felt almost as if he was deliberately angering them."

Of course, events did get out of hand as I had privately predicted. The knights left in high dudgeon but I felt sure they would be sure to return to cause mischief. With this thought in mind, I followed them back into the great hall, where getting Algar, another of the Archbishop's household to help me, took the precaution of locking and barring the doors after they had gone out into the courtyard.

It was not long before my worst fears came true. There was a great hammering and battering at the doors as those outside attempted to re-enter but the doors were solid and remained shut. I could hear shouting coming from the courtyard. "Try at the back," I heard someone shout. The door remained bolted so I made my way back towards the Archbishop's chambers in great fear when there came a terrible crashing sound from the back of the hall. More shouting and cursing filled the air. "Where is the traitor? Find the Archbishop! Let no-one escape!" A sudden rush of armed men poured into the hall and I was hit with something hard and knocked to the ground. A wave of panic rose up in me as soldiers began to ransack the hall. Tables were being overturned, goblets, plates and anything of value was being stuffed into sacks. I lay on the floor feigning death not daring to move. It must have been a sword that had struck me as blood was seeping through my tunic from somewhere.

The chaos subsided as the soldiers, having taken all they could of value from the hall, moved to other parts of the Palace. I crawled out through the back door into a passage used by the Cellarer and from there, managing to stand, into the cloister. All was in darkness, night having fallen and I could hear sounds of hysteria coming from the Cathedral but despite my consternation, I made my way towards it, blood dripping on the paving as I went.

I had been in the employ of Thomas of Canterbury for years and it was to him that I owed my position in his prestigious household. He had always treated me well and while in his service I wanted for nothing. He had my complete loyalty and for that reason it was important that I go to his side. Of course, what I would find when I got there I did not yet know.

As I neared the end of the cloister and the door that led to Saint Benedict's chapel the wailing got louder and I became aware of a great press of people gathered there, all pushing and jostling to look at something. These, I soon found out, were the ghouls trying to catch a glimpse of the body on the paving or worse still, soak up some of the blood with pieces of rag. I knew instantly by the robe that it was the body of my master the Archbishop.

Shoving my way through, all the time shouting, "move aside, move aside" I pushed my way to the corpse. It was obviously a corpse. From the blood and gore spread around there was no hope that there would be any life left.

I took control. I was Chamberlain of the Archbishop's household and was used to having my instructions obeyed. I ordered some monks who were standing uselessly by, "get these people away from here. I do not care where you send them, just get them away from here and while you are at it, bring some benches from the knave to make a barrier. In fact," I added, "empty everyone except your brothers from the Cathedral and lock the doors behind them when you have done it." I think the monks were pleased that someone had taken the burden of responsibility from them for what to do next. They started to shepherd all the people out of the cathedral and as soon as they could, barred and locked the doors as I had instructed.

When the gawpers had been dispersed I took a candle from the altar of Saint Benedict and bent to examine the body more closely. My hands had started to shake and even though it was mid-winter I could fell the sweat running down my face. Even a quick glance showed that the top of the skull was missing. I felt the bile rise in my throat. "Don't despoil the scene even more by being sick all over it," I urged myself.

With great trepidation at what I might find, I gently lifted the head and turned it to one side so I could see the face more clearly. Though the candlelight was better than nothing I nearly fainted with shock at what I beheld. The robes were those of the Archbishop, Thomas of Canterbury but the face was not his. I knew my master's face as well as I knew my own. I had gazed upon it most days for many years past. Even with half the forehead dropping down across it and it being covered in blood, there was no mistake. This was not the Archbishop but his bedchamber servant and companion Roger. The man who slept in his chamber with him at nights and was trusted with the task of whipping him every day. I knew this was part of the Archbishop's efforts to purge his soul and sanctify his flesh but few others were aware of this.

"Think Osbert, think." What should I do? There was a great wave of relief sweeping through me. The man I had come to know and love had somehow escaped the clutches of the evil men sent to murder him. This must surely be a sign from God. Thomas yet lived. "I must keep the secret," I realised, "he needs time to make good his escape. If his killers find he is not dead then they will tear Canterbury apart until they find him and finish the job properly."

Time was moving on and soon monks would return with the benches I had told them to bring. I tore a strip from my surplice and wrapped it around the fallen Archbishop's head and face to cover the fearful wounds but more importantly, its true identity. It was a horribly gory task and by the time the monks returned, my hands were covered in blood.

"Fetch a bier," I ordered, "and we will take the Archbishop's body to a more hallowed place before the high altar until we can decide what is to be done with it." When they went to fetch the bier I said a silent prayer for the safe escape of Thomas. As I was thinking these thoughts, Brother Ernold, who came from a family of goldsmith's in the city, along with some other monks returned to the scene of the murder and gathered up what they could of the congealing blood, brains and pieces of bone into a clean, silver bowl. To stop anyone else walking on the site of the murder, the benches from the cathedral nave were placed to form a barrier around the site. What little spots of the blood that could not be saved pooled in tiny black pockets in dips in the paving stones..

We were just in time.

Early in the morning, Robert de Broc reappeared with a gang of his ruffians for support. As we were busy with Thomas's body, or what everyone other than me thought was Thomas's body, no-one heard his entrance until he started shouting.

"This country is well rid of a traitor who was trying to take away the King's crown. He should be thrown into a pit to rot. He had little fear of God. It is a great blessing that the traitor has been killed." No-one dared to say anything to him. Spittle sprang from his lips as he continued with his rant. "Get his body out of my sight or else I will have it dragged around the city at a horse's tail to a gibbet and hang it there for all to see. It ought to be tossed into a cesspit or chopped up and fed to the pigs."

Now we were all terrified. No sooner had de Broc left, still shouting insults against Thomas over his shoulder, than the decision was taken to bury the Archbishop immediately. The usual washing of the corpse was foregone as it was thought that it had already been washed with its own blood. There was a gasp of shock from some of the watching monks when some of the clothing was cut off to reveal a hairshirt crawling with vermin. "We never knew," someone whispered, "he was a true monk after all." What they did not know but I did, was that Thomas's companion Roger had always worn a hairshirt in sympathy with his Archbishop.

There was a move to remove the covering I had wrapped around the head to cover both the wounds and the true identity of the corpse. "Leave it," I ordered, "we will merely add a clean covering. To remove what is already there with his blood dried onto his face will just cause more damage. Let him rest in peace, he needs no further injury inflicting."

A monk had gone to Thomas's chamber and brought some clean vestments and his pallium which we put on the body. The burial rites were said by the monks, but because the cathedral had been desecrated by bloodshed, no mass was held. Once the service was over, the body was placed in a marble sarcophagus in the eastern crypt which, conveniently, had already been prepared for someone else's burial, though whose, I do not know. There, a marble lid was placed over the coffin. The grave was facing two altars built into the east wall, one dedicated to St John the Baptist, the other to St Augustine, which lay directly beneath the high altar where Thomas had celebrated his first mass.

"At least," I thought, "for now the secret should be safe," and prayed that Robert de Broc was not going to return and despoil the grave and the body, an act of which he was perfectly capable.

On the day after we had buried the body, a woman whose husband had been one of those who had dipped his shirt in the dead man's blood was claiming to have been cured of paralysis by a miracle.

"When my husband returned from the Cathedral and told me of what had happened, I told him to soak the stain from his shirt in a bucket of clean water. When he had done that, I drank the water. The next morning the paralysis from which I had suffered for many years had gone. It was truly a miracle." Word of this soon spread throughout the city and not long after that, the people began calling the dead Archbishop a martyr and a saint.

There and then, I made the decision that wherever he was, Thomas's survival on that day in the Cathedral would be known only to me and God. I would be no Judas. My loyalty has never wavered and he never reappeared in my lifetime. Perhaps he died during his escape attempt and it was kept quiet but we will probably never know unless he wants us to. As a dead martyr, he proved more powerful in his fight for the rights of the Church than he ever would have done as a live Archbishop. I remember his once telling me, Osbert he said, "do not feel obliged to believe that the same God who has endowed us with sense, reason, and intellect has intended us to forgo their use."

Part Three

Chapter 41

Gilbert of St-Sulpice's story

David Hartigan received an email from his team in Canterbury who had been given the task of both opening and then examining the contents of the box they had found in the grave at Mont-St-Sulpice, whatever they may be.

Hi David,

Exciting news. We ve managed to open the box and it contains sheets of manuscript. On first inspection, they look to be well preserved and appear to be written in Latin so we ll start the task of making sure they re stable and then get on with seeing what s written on them. I ll keep you updated.

Susan.

Some weeks later David received yet another email.

Hi David,

You re not going to believe this. I ve attached a translation of the manuscript we recovered from the box you sent us. The contents, if genuine, could change our understanding of what took place in Canterbury Cathedral 900 years ago.

Before you get too excited, it could of course be a very clever and elaborate hoax. Remember the fiasco of the Hitler Diaries and Hugh Trevor-Roper s vehement, initial assertion that they were real. He was soon proved wrong. If at all possible, we are keen to avoid a repeat of that unfortunate situation. I cannot stress this too much. However, we will carry out all the necessary tests as soon as possible bearing in mind that the technologies we are now able to use are much further advanced than those available 40 years ago.

Again, I urge you to say nothing about the contents of this manuscript to anyone, including your team, until much deeper investigations are carried out to authenticate or repudiate the subject matter.

I will keep you updated on progress.

Susan.

Having read the email, David Hartigan found his hands shaking as he opened the attachment and having read what it contained, had to force himself to stop his whole body from shaking. This is what he read:

This is the last confession of Gilbert of Mont-Saint-Sulpice.

I write this as I lie dying in the Priory from which I take my name. I wish to go to my God with a clear conscience.

I have never told of who I really am since the time I escaped from Canterbury Cathedral in the year of 1170. Then I was an Archbishop and known as Thomas of Canterbury and later, Thomas Becket. I had not truly believed that the knights that had come from King Henry were intent on killing me and though I was happy to meet my maker I was persuaded by my trusted servant to change clothes with him just in case.

To begin with on that fateful night in the cathedral I was sure that no real harm would become me but as the evening wore on and the noises from outside my chamber got louder and more insistent, I began to think the perhaps I had underestimated the intentions of the knights who had come to remonstrate with me.

Ranulf de Broc was an evil, dangerous man of whom I had made an enemy and between us there was no love lost. I should have realised that he would be happy to have me removed so he could keep all he had already stolen from Church lands and benefices rightly belonging to the see of Canterbury. The King s rage against me for the excommunications I had pronounced on Salisbury, London and York gave him the excuse he had been looking for. Now he had the opportunity to rid himself of me under the guise of carrying out the King s will. Even then, he could do it at arms-length by getting his henchmen to do it for him so no blood would be left on his hands. In his brother Robert de Broc he had a man who knew the City and my Cathedral intimately and it was he who guided the assassins to me.

I had no fear of dying for my Church and my beliefs and when my friends at first tried to persuade me to flee to the sanctity of the cathedral I resisted. Even when the knights and their followers smashed their way into the great hall, I still resisted but then my followers took matters into their own hands and dragged me protesting into the body of the Church. Even then fear had not gripped me but a realisation that the situation was far worse than I had imagined it could be began to dawn on me.

I wanted to have a moment s calm and peace, away from all the clamour of raised voices from outside, the monks singing vespers and my friends all trying to give me advice at the same time. I needed only a few minutes to gather my thoughts. That is when I retired to the Dean s Chapel taking only my faithful servant Roger with me to help me pray. Roger had been my intimate companion for many years and along with my chamberlain Osbert was a man I trusted beyond all others. It was Roger I had trusted with sleeping in my chamber at nights and with the duty of purging my flesh daily with a scourge. He knew my innermost secrets and darkest thoughts.

As soon as we were alone and I knelt to pray. Roger, his voice full of heartfelt anxiety, spoke to me in a low whisper. My Lord, we have been companions for many years and I have always trusted in your wisdom. Now, you must trust in mine. These knights come with evil intentions and I sincerely believe they mean to kill you. What will your death achieve? I tell you, nothing. If you die then who will shoulder the burden of protecting our holy Church against evil men? I say again, no - one. Did not Saint Peter deny our Saviour three times before he carried on to become our first Holy Father in Rome? You must live to fight on, your death will serve no purpose. You cannot fight the King or evil men like de Broc and his knights from the grave."

What, are you suggesting that I run away," I asked him?

Exactly that my Lord. The night is dark and the Cathedral is lit only by candles. There are many passages and stairways in which you could secrete yourself until the furore dies down. Exchange clothes with me my Lord and let me go in your place. We are of a similar height and build; our beards are old and grey and one tonsured head looks much like another. In the dim light and if I keep my head bowed as if in prayer it is unlikely that these men will know that I am not you. They will see only the robes and cap of an Archbishop with his cross carried before him. They will have no reason to suspect that the man within those robes is not Thomas of Canterbury."

I like it not Roger. There are men out there who know me well, our subterfuge would soon be discovered and anyway, I am no coward."

"No-one doubts that my Lord but come, make a decision, time is wasting. Even if I can give you five minutes, which might be enough for you to slip away in the night to fight another day. I doubt these men will actually kill me but even if they did, my life is of little value whereas you still have much good to do for the Church. Now is your opportunity to escape. I beg you Lord, take it. Do it now," he said, why take the chance if you do not have to?"

I pondered on this for a fraction of a second. The feeling of cowardice that had afflicted me at Clarendon when I weakened and went back on my words resurfaced. It seemed an eternity but was in reality a few seconds only and the decision was made. Now, I thought, was the opportunity to preserve my life and allow me to continue the struggle against Henry and his wicked designs on the Church. Surely that was not cowardice but common sense. But could my conscience allow me to let another take my place in the face of danger?

Now Lord, now," Roger insisted, before it is too late." He was already getting out of his monk's habit, making the choice for me.

He was right. The light in the Cathedral was poor. Dark would be a better description and the few candles there were, cast gloomy shadows over everything which would make it difficult to make out the individual features of peoples faces.

He wore my robes and I, his simple monk s garb. He took my cross to complete the illusion and in the gloom of the Cathedral went to confront those four men of violence in order to give me the chance of escaping.

Our simple plan was for him to confuse the knights long enough to allow me to make good my escape through a passage known to only a few of the monks. It ran from a secret door near the main gates and led under the walls to the Black Boy hostelry in the Bullstake. The monks thought I was ignorant of its existence and their dalliances beyond the walls but little could be kept secret in a small community such as ours within the Cathedral precincts. I had, after all, been both Archdeacon and Archbishop of the Cathedral for many years.

By now, all in the Cathedral was all chaos and mayhem and one more monk wandering in the dark confusion ought not to attract attention. I left the Dean s chapel above the Altar to Saint Benedict by a small staircase and then made my way through from the nave. Now, I walked with an exaggerated stoop to hide my height which would have made me obvious to any monks in the precincts and affected a limp to add to my disguise. Here I mingled with the townspeople who were now being herded out by other monks and I made a play of helping to shepherd them out. When I came close to the main doors, I slipped unobserved through a door which in turn, allowed me access to the passage I sought.

If the Cathedral had been in a state of turmoil, then the city, when I exited into it from the tavern cellar, was no better. The darkness only punctuated by flickering brands and the occasional candle in a lantern. People thronged the streets mixing with soldiers who were everywhere but they seemed more intent on looting and pillaging than they did on taking any notice of a bedraggled, crippled, old monk with nothing obvious to steal. Now I heard shouts of, the Archbishop is murdered. They have killed Thomas. Lord save us all."

Can it be true?" I thought. Have they killed my poor Roger?"

252

My first thought was to get out of the city and make for the coast. Soon I thought, my escape must be noticed and then there would be a hue and cry for my blood. The city gates were supposed to be guarded but now, the guardians were intent on loot rather than on keeping people in or out. Again, as I approached the Burgate, the soldiers there were more interested in seeing what was under a young girl s skirts than they were on a crippled brother. I passed un-noticed.

I thought to avoid Saint Augustine s Abbey and the road to Sandwich as well as the Roman road out through the area known as Wincheape which led to Hythe and thence Saltwood and the de Brocs. Thus, when I left the city, I took the path to Dover in the hope that I might find a boat to take me to France. Once there, I thought, I could hide from anyone who would wish me harm until it was safe for me to reveal my escape.

It was getting late and the rain poured down. I was freezing and the wind made it worse. I needed shelter but needed anonymity more. A lone figure walking in the dark on such a night was bound to attract attention.

I crested a rise and through the trees, off to one side, saw a glimmer in the gloom. Now the smell of woodsmoke came to me on the wind. Shelter I thought.

As I came closer, I could see it was a tiny hovel, not much more than a pile of sticks and mud to afford some shelter from the elements. Off to one side was the source of the smoke. A charcoal kiln. The light came from the small fire inside, around which were three or perhaps four men. Only their eyes showed through their blackened faces, a badge of their lonely, arduous profession as charcoal burners. Local people would shun them fearing that in their austere lives in the woods they would practice evil witchcraft.

Would you allow a poor monk to share your fire? " I asked.

Other than my blessing I can offer you nothing in return, " I told them.

We have little, but what we have we will be happy to share with a man of God, " came the reply. A day before, I had enough

253

to give them to make them rich for the rest of their lives. How fickle is fate.

Far from being evil, these men were kind to me. They were happy to share the food they had which had been provided by the forest. Does the Archbishop know that you poach his rabbits? I asked. I doubt it," Edric the head man told me, and anyway, it is not him we need to worry about. This might be his land but it is the de Brocs who control it now. If they caught us poaching, we would all be hanging from the trees like so much fruit." They all laughed. Most folk think we are wizards and can cast spells so stay away just in case it's true."

I left before daylight the next morning, blessing their humble home before I went. They had cut me a fine, strong staff to help me on my way. There you are brother, that should make your journey easier." Their kindness put me in mind of the parable of the widow s mite. I wished with all my heart that I could have done more. That staff was of more use to me than my Archbishop s cross ever was.

A few miles down the way I was offered a lift from a carter who took pity on my stooped and limping figure as I made my way along the track. Where are you off to this early in the morning brother?" When I told him the Holy Land, he smiled and said, I cannot take you that far but I will be happy to give a pilgrim a ride as far as the hamlet of Shepherdswell. From there, it is only eight or maybe nine miles further to the sea." We sat in companionable silence for a while and watched the swaying buttocks of his ox in front. The Holy Land is it brother? That is a long walk. The furthest I have ever been is, the great city of Canterbury." As I left him, he wished me a good journey" and I limped along through the rain and wind to the coast. Where my answer of going to the Holy Land came from, I have no idea but I realised now that it was an ideal explanation for anyone who asked what I was about. A dishevelled monk on a pilgrimage was a believable disguise.

254

When I came near to the coast, I took the path to down to the harbour area where all was hustle and bustle and where a poor, travel-worn monk would invite no particular notice. It was here that I heard the rumour of my own murder. I sat at the quayside and prayed for the soul of my lost and faithful servant Roger should the rumour be true. If it was true then it made the necessity of escape from England even more pressing. If Henry found I was not dead then he would surely come looking for me and not make the same mistake again when he found me. If Roger was indeed murdered and laid dead in my Cathedral at Canterbury then I could only hope that the subterfuge had somehow remained undiscovered.

I had been away from Canterbury for almost three days. I no longer had to make any effort to look dishevelled; three days living outside in the winter weather had taken its toll on both my body and my clothes. As my stature would always be a clue to my true identity, I made my stoop more pronounced and I shuffled and limped more than ever which my blistered feet made all the more easy to do. I kept my head bowed deep in my cowl so my face could only ever be seen in full shadow. My need to find a ship to take me across the water was now imperative. The longer I lingered in England the more chance there was of my being discovered.

Using my guise of a needy monk with little money I made approaches to boat keepers along the waterside. Brother," I pleaded, I am but a poor pilgrim on a quest to the Holy Land. As you see, I have nothing but God will reward you in heaven if you would but take pity on me and give me passage across the water. In return for my passage I will bless your ship and crew." On my fifth approach my luck changed.

 Bless my ship, you say brother?" The Captain looked at me questioningly, At this treacherous time of the year, we need all the help we can get. Perhaps having a man of God onboard will help keep us safe. Your holy blessing will be a better payment than money. Make it a good one and I will see what we can offer you by way of something to eat. You look like you could use a good meal."

The deal was struck. As his crew busied themselves with preparations to sail, I made the sign of the cross on the bows and said comprehensive prayers for a safe passage. As an ordained priest I felt no sin was being committed by my giving the ship this blessing. As if by some miracle my prayers were answered, the wind died away to a gentle breeze as we sailed and the seas remained calm.

That worked Brother, you have certainly earned your supper," Wulstan, the Saxon captain told me as we sailed on flat waters, you will be welcome to join us whenever you chose to cross in the future." Little did he know that any return trip for me was highly unlikely unless it was to be in chains with the King s soldiers.

For the third time in my life I found myself wading through the surf on a French beach. This time it was a freezing January day and I felt the shingle of the French shore through the thin soles of my sandals. I waved farewell to Wulfstan and his crew and they carried on with life little realising that they had just helped a fugitive escape the King s clutches. It was better for them that they never knew. At least now, I was in France and not in Normandy and I felt just a little safer knowing that within reason no-one alive would know who I was or where I was.

I knew from the experiences of my exile that I had little chance of finding refuge at any of the Cistercian Abbeys and that if I were to keep my real identity a secret then I should avoid anywhere of any size. I will not bore you with all the travails of my journey which were indeed a test but suffice to say, I maintained my ruse of being a pilgrim on a journey to the Holy Land. This proved to be profitable and I was happily given food and refuge along the way and rarely went hungry for want of a piece of cheese or bread.

Whilst on the road I learned of the murder in Canterbury of the Archbishop. So, the subterfuge had resulted in the death of my servant rather than me. I later heard that his brutal murder had so mutilated his face that he was unrecognisable and he was only identified by the fact that he wore Archbishop s robes and had carried the Archbishop s cross. The final sword blow had cut through his skull so it flapped over his face and his brains had been spread over the Cathedral paving. Monks from the cloisters had taken the body and prepared it for burial immediately. By the time anyone could question the identity, the body had been buried and Thomas of Canterbury had ceased to exist in temporal form.

Although the world now considered me dead, I still avoided any large churches or abbeys I came near just in case my disguise failed me and I was recognised. The incident of the Knight and his hawk of years before still haunted me. Now though my demeanour was no longer a disguise, it was who I had become.

As part of the re-invented person I had become I had adopted the name of Brother Gilbert, taking my father s name for whatever time on this earth remained to me. All I had to do now was find somewhere of peace and solitude to see out whatever days the good Lord intended for me.

I wandered the French countryside for what seemed like an eternity but was in fact only a few months and then I found that which I had been seeking. I happened upon it by chance but immediately felt it was to be where I belonged. In a tiny hamlet called Mont-Saint-Sulpice I came to a priory hidden away amongst the trees.

I made my way to the door and was made welcome by a monk even older and more bedraggled than myself. Welcome to our Priory Brother," he said, we do not get many visitors here. Perhaps you would join us at service and then share a meal when you can give us what news you might have of the world outside?"

I doubt I have any news worth listening to," I told him, but what there is I will be happy to share."

The Priory of Mont-Saint-Sulpice had only 5 Brothers and a very elderly Prior who, as good as their word, made me welcome, fed me and said their prayers with me. That was almost 18 years ago and I am still here. One of the younger brothers took over as Prior when the original one died and now, we are *only me, two others and the Prior. Soon I know that number will decrease by one.*

My life here has been beautiful. Simple, peaceful and spiritual. Space to think and reflect. Whilst I tend to my vegetables it is strange to think that there was a visitor here some years ago who told us of the Martyr, Thomas of Canterbury. Of how there is now a shrine to his martyrdom which, I am told, is swollen with gold, rubies, garnets and other precious jewels. No one can confidently say that they will still be living tomorrow but I seemed to have managed it despite evidence to the contrary. Every time I walked a step in my Cathedral, I was walking on a layer of the past. Now others walk on mine.

To my once friend, King Henry, I bear no malice. He has paid the price for his actions in full and if my supposed murder helped the cause of the Church that I love then all has been worthwhile.

I have been both a dead martyr and a living man at one and the same time. I leave this written confession so that history may judge me at some time in the distant future if and when it is discovered. My soul I commend to my maker in whichever guise he chooses to see me and as the light is fast fading on my world that will be very soon now.

Lastly, you may ask, why did I keep myself hidden all these years?

My relationship with Henry of England, the second of that name, was both complicated and toxic. We both believed we were right. Was that the sin of vanity? It is too late now to worry about it. What is done is done.

I have no doubt in my own mind and I have considered it endlessly, that the situation between myself and Henry had reached an impasse whatever we might have agreed at Fréteval. When those knights came to Canterbury all those years ago, they thought that my death was what their King had wanted. True, they were encouraged by wicked men, Roger of Pont L'Évêque and above all, Ranulf de Broc. De Broc was a man I would have excommunicated a hundred times over had I been able. The fact remains that those men killed my faithful servant out of hand and I too must bear the blame for his innocent death.

He was meant only to give me a little time to make good my escape. If I had thought for one second that he would have carried the subterfuge through to such an extent I would never have allowed it. His death weighs heavily and constantly on my conscience

There is also no doubt in my mind that Henry was horrified at what had been done in his name although it took him another three years to make a public penance for the action. By the time he did come to pay for his crime, two things had happened. Firstly, the Church had gained the ascendancy they so long desired over the State, which of course was the main reason for the differences between the King and me in the first place. Secondly, the cult of Saint Thomas of Canterbury has grown beyond belief to the benefit of both the Church in general and Canterbury in particular. Both these outcomes, unexpected as they were at the time, gladden my heart more than I can say.

The re-emergence of a living Thomas would inevitably have quickly destroyed both these things but above all, the cause for which I had fought for during the previous ten years, the Rights of the Church. That was the cause for which I endured royal opprobrium and exile for so long. So, I have kept silent. Let there be no confusion in anyone s mind that I was prepared for martyrdom should it have happened. In this case, the Lord obviously had a different ending in mind for me.

When the time comes for me to face our Lord, I pray he will forgive me my past sins of which I truly repent.

Gilbert of Mont-Saint-Sulpice

Dated this 6th day of July in the year of our Lord 1189.

To say David Hartigan was stunned by the translation of the manuscript would be a gross understatement. Euphoric, incredulous, exultant, exhilarated, would all come into a description of his feelings.

He immediately replied to Susan s email.

Hi Susan,

I can t believe it! I ve re-read it three times and it still hasn t sunk in. What comes next? We need to get all this examined and authenticated by experts better qualified us than or perhaps I should say me. I still can t stop shaking at the thought of what this might mean.

My first fear is that it might be a very elaborate hoax. If it is, it s a good one. It would mean that someone planted , no pun intended, the body and the letter here years ago in the hope that someone might, just might, find it. What an even slimmer chance that would have been if I, or someone very like me, had not bought the property and started digging around in it in the first place.

We need to get the manuscript tested for age and materials to see if they are from the right period. I haven t seen them as they were all sealed up in the box when I sent them to you. What are your initial views? I m so excited I can hardly type this. Can we get the handwriting verified? I know that the archives in Canterbury Cathedral hold original copies of his handwriting. If so, any suggestions as to who we could get that s reputable enough to be believed?

I must chase up the Ministry of Culture and Communication in France to see how they are progressing with tests on the bones in their osteological department as well as radiocarbon dating. If they come up with a skeleton buried last century, we re dealing with a clever hoax which would be a real bugger, excuse the French, it s the excitement getting to me. DNA I suppose would be pointless. His only genetic line would be one of his sisters who possibly had two sons but who knows what became of them. The other one was a nun so I doubt there was any offspring there. He was reputedly celibate so no point in looking in that direction either.

Let s get the ball rolling on everything we can and keep each other updated on progress. Well done on getting the manuscript out in one piece.

Speak soon,
David.

When the results of the osteological examination and the radiocarbon dating came back, the results were consistent with the remains that were found being Thomas of Canterbury. They were dated to the correct period, sometime between 1180 – 1190. They estimated the age of the person to be in their late 60s or early 70s and about 6feet tall, possibly a little taller.

As David had suggested, handwriting experts were brought in to compare the writing on the recovered manuscript with that of known letters written by Thomas held in the Cathedral archives at Canterbury, of which there are many. The consensus of their opinions was that the handwriting on all the documents they examined was that of the same person. They were sure that the letter in the grave was written by Thomas of Canterbury.

The Roman Catholic Church is contesting the findings and insists that the manuscript is an elaborate hoax. Well they would, would they not?

If Gilbert of Mont-St-Sulpice was indeed Thomas of Canterbury and the evidence now shows that he was, then he would have been about 71when he died. It is interesting to note that the date on the recovered manuscript, 6th July 1189, is the same day on which Henry II, his one-time friend and long-time enemy, died.

Part four

Chapter 42

The Aftermath. The History. The Facts

I have taken information about Thomas s life from a variety of sources in an effort to make the story complete. Thomas Becket is perhaps one of the most, if not the most, written about figures in English history so there is a wealth of research material to choose from. Not all of it agrees about the facts. Even those closest to the events such as Edward Grim and William FitzStephens, both of whom were eyewitnesses to the events in the Cathedral, disagree about what actually took place.

Like all history, there is personal opinion, political bias, flawed memory and hagiography involved, which at times makes sorting the fact from the fiction difficult, if not impossible. Sometimes it just comes down to intuition about who one believes and who one does not based on who did the reporting, why they did it and what had they to gain from putting a particular slant on their reporting of what they saw or just as importantly, what they did not see. This was an age when saying the right thing about someone might just keep your head on your shoulders or vica versa.

Thomas and Henry is in essence a novel and not a history book and I have taken the liberty of inventing some of the dialogue in the interests of colour . However, I have, as far as possible, used historically reported conversations to construct those imagined conversations whilst sticking as nearly as possible to the truth. Any errors are mine.

Of course, the last part of the story supposedly written by Gilbert of Mont-Saint-Sulpice is a figment of my imagination, or is it? You have to decide on the evidence.

Consider this. The bones found at Mont-Saint-Sulpice could be tested for DNA and then compared with the elbow bone reputed to have been that of Thomas which was then taken to Hungary at the time of the reburial in 1220. They cannot possibly match. If Gilbert were Thomas, then the bone in the Cathedral could not be his. He was not there. So who was?

What happened after the Murder?

Riders soon set out from England to take the news of Thomas s death to Henry. At the same time, a group of monks were already on their way to the Pope with the news. It was not long before the news was all over the continent.

Arnulf, the Bishop of Lisieux, was with Henry when the news of Thomas's death arrived. In a letter to the Pope, this was how he described the King s reaction: "The king burst into loud cries and exchanged his royal robes for sackcloth. For three whole days he remained shut up in his chamber and would neither take food nor admit anyone to comfort him."

Like all things to do with Thomas, there are varying versions of the same thing. One witness to the scene says that Henry said nothing at all and merely shut himself in his chamber, stunned with grief and shock until he reappeared in the evening.

However, later, once the reality of the situation set in, Henry did go into seclusion for three days apparently living on nothing but a little almond milk. After a short while though any grief about the archbishop s reported demise amongst the courtiers soon turned to anxiety about the King, making some of them wonder if the death of Thomas might lead to the death of the King.

They need not have worried. It did not take Henry overly long to revert to type and start worrying about himself. People will think that I was party to the crime. As God is my witness," he declaimed, this awful deed was not done by my will nor my connivence."

Taking avoiding action and believing that his own couriers could get there first, Henry tried to exculpate himself by composing a shameless letter to the Pope in Rome. In it he maintained that Thomas had not returned to England in a spirit of peace and reconciliation as he had promised at Fréteval. Instead he went, with fire and the sword, stirring sedition, excommunicating royal servants right and left, and behaving so impudently that he made some powerful enemies. These had fallen upon him and murdered him". In other words, the blame was Thomas s alone and none of it could be laid at the door of the King.

Too late! The bearers of the bad news had already flown and were, as we have seen, well on their way to Rome.

William of Blois also wrote to the Pope in condemnation of the murder saying, "I have no doubt that the cry of the whole world has already filled your ears of how the King of the English, that enemy of the angels, has killed the Holy One. For all the crimes we have ever read or heard of, this easily takes first place. Even exceeding all the wickedness of Nero." Pretty strong words.

In spite of all his protestations of innocence, Henry met Alexander III's Papal legates at Avranches in the May following the murder and submitted himself to their judgment. In an agreement that he later signed, he said that he would "at his own expense provide two hundred knights to serve for a year with the Templars in the Holy Land. That he himself would take the cross for a period of three years and depart for the Holy Land before the following Easter. Further, and most importantly, he would utterly abolish customs damaging to the Church which had been introduced in his reign."

Of course, in typical Henry style, he quickly ignored the agreement. He never went on Crusade although his son Richard, known as the Lionheart, made a reputation for himself fighting the Saracens some years later.

In the meanwhile, Pope Alexander, in an act of astonishing speed even for those times, canonised Thomas on 21st February 1173 after which, as Saint Thomas, he became a symbol of Christian resistance to the power of the monarchy. More powerful dead than alive?

Realising that he was never going to win his battle with the Church over the death of Thomas, Henry did concede that, although he never wanted the killing of his old friend, his words may have prompted the murderers to their course of action. Notwithstanding his begrudging words, three years after the event, he did public penance. He traveled to Canterbury and when he arrived at the West Gate of the city he dismounted and walked barefoot all the way to Thomas's tomb in the Cathedral. He wore only a woollen smock as a sign of his remorse. At the tomb he knelt and placed his head through a gap in the tomb and prayed, one assumes for forgiveness, but who knows. It is said that each Bishop present then gave him 5 lashes of the whip after which each of the Cathedral monks, all 80 of them, gave him another 3 each. Given the total number of lashes, about 300, it is highly unlikely that any real force was applied and the act was symbolic rather than punitive. When his flagellation was complete, he spent the night sleeping at the tomb.

All Henry s plans for a new order in England and for the security of his lands were now in disarray. These were the plans he had laid long ago in the days when Thomas was a friend. days when they had ridden and hunted together and perhaps talked of a world where Church and State would be working for the same ends. Thomas Becket the Archbishop was dead and defeated: Thomas Becket the martyr would conquer all Henry s dreams.

Whether Thomas of Canterbury was a saint and martyr is a question that has been fruitlessly debated for centuries. What can be said is that the murder of Thomas in Canterbury Cathedral was an event that caused an earthquake throughout the society of the 12th century and had implications long after the fact. At the time, it had an immediate effect on Henry s international standing and particularly his conflict with the Church. It would be fair to say that it was a, if not the, defining point in his reign. The fact that it is still being written about and debated almost 850 years after it took place is testament to its enduring obsession amongst historians.

To be fair to Henry it has to be said that, at the time, he was not the only ruler was in dispute with the Church. Whilst the Church, at the same time, was engaged in what amounted to a civil war within its own ranks, with two Popes claiming supremacy.

As for Henry s hopes for a smooth transition of power and the continued Angevin dynasty these too came to nothing. Perhaps if Thomas had been around giving sage advice to his one-time friend, things may have turned out differently. Henry s sons, at times in collusion with his wife Eleanor, fought against him and each other, successfully ripping the Angevin empire apart. By the time his younger son John had finished with it, there would hardly be any of it left to argue over, including Normandy from whence William the Conqueror had first invaded England a 100 years before.

By the time of Henry s son John s reign the circle was almost complete. Archbishop Langton had started his reign as Archbishop with resistance to King John and had been exiled. This lead to the whole of England being placed under a Papal Interdict by Pope Innocent III. Something even John s father, Henry, the second of that name, had managed to avoid. John seemed determined to repeat most of his father s mistakes but at least he avoided killing his Archbishop. He did, however, end up backed into a corner to the point where he was forced into signing the Magna Carta. Having signed the Great Charter, he proceeded to ignore both it and its provisions, just like his father would have done.

Now the circle would be closed completely and Henry s grandson, Henry, the third of that name, associated himself and his new Plantagenet dynasty closely with the cult of Thomas of Canterbury, now referred to as Saint Thomas Becket. Presumably, the once slur of the low-born surname having been overlooked.

Soon operating on a fully commercial basis, the shrine quickly built up a lively trade in what turned out to be inexhaustible supplies of watered-down blood known as the water of Canterbury , a liquid said to be so potent, it was able to perform up to as many as ten cures a day. Sold first in small wooden boxes lined with wax, the liquid leaked out so easily that the boxes were soon replaced by small phials moulded out of tin or lead which could be worn loosely around the purchaser s neck on a chain or piece of twine.

Becket was canonized in 1173. Within a short time his shrine at Canterbury became the resort of innumerable pilgrims. Plenary indulgences were given for a visit to the shrine, and an official register was kept to record the miracles wrought by the relics of the saint. Supposed relics of Saint Thomas appeared all over Europe. Some genuine, or at least, genuine if the body they were taken from was in fact that of Thomas. Vials of his blood, small pieces of bone from his skull and even a piece that purported to be his elbow bone ended up in Esztergom, Hungary. It is not known for sure how the relic ended up in Hungary but two prelates from Hungary were said to have been present in Canterbury Cathedral in 1220 after the original grave was opened and Thomas's body reburied in its new tomb. It was brought back to Canterbury in 2016 and put on display there for a short while.

Soon, Thomas s shrine was magnificently adorned with the gold and silver and jewels offered by the pious.

The cathedral monks being afraid that the body they assumed rightly or wrongly to be that of Thomas of Canterbury might be stolen or desecrated by Ranulph de Broc, quickly buried it as I have related in the novel.

Within a very short time following the murder, pilgrims were flocking to the site, and a protective marble case with holes in the sides had to be placed over the original grave to allow the pilgrims to kiss the holy tombstone but prevent them from chipping pieces off as souvenirs.

50 years after the murder in 1220, the body was carefully removed from its tomb in the cathedral's crypt and transferred or to use the correct terminology, translated, to a bejewelled and golden casket in a purpose-built chapel behind the high altar. Moving the bones of the dead may now seem disrespectful, but in the 13th century it was the ultimate confirmation of a saint's exalted status. In subsequent years, the anniversary of the translation of Thamas's bones to their new shrine was the most important and well-attended pilgrimage feast in England.

The date chosen for the event, 7 July 1220, was both symbolic and practical. It was the jubilee anniversary of the martyrdom. Additionally, the date of the anniversary of the martyrdom, 29 December, was awkward as it not only fell during the Christmas celebrations but was at a time in midwinter when pilgrims were unlikely to travel. By establishing another anniversary of equal importance in the middle of summer and therefore at the height of the pilgrimage season ensured that the feast of the translation would become one of the highlights of the English religious calendar as well as a huge source of revenue for the Church in general and Canterbury in particular.

A few days before the ceremony of translation, the saint's grave was opened the holy relics removed. They were placed in a wooden box bound with iron. When this was being done, some of the smaller bones were put aside as presents for the visiting dignitaries which is the most likely reason for the piece of elbow bone ending up in Hungary

The remains, still in their wooden box, were carried in procession through the cathedral, and reverentially placed into a purpose-built shrine in the chapel at the highest and easternmost point of the church. This consisted of a rectangular pink marble base around 7ft high, 7ft long and 3ft wide, with arched niches in the sides where pilgrims could pray. On top was a golden casket, made under the direction of master-craftsmen Walter of Colchester and Elias of Dereham, of gold plate covered in a mesh of gold wire to which gemstones and jewellery, donated from all over Europe in the build-up to the translation, were attached. In prime position on the south face of the shrine was the Regale of France, a huge red gem given to Archbishop Langton by the French king Philip Augustus. Of which more later.

The first tomb, which was, to say the least, simple in appearance, had been in the crypt, distant and detached from the upper parts of the church where the monks performed their daily devotions. Pilgrims had flocked to it, swarmed all over it, and sat around it waiting in the hope of miraculous cures. After the 1220 translation the relics and bones were housed in one of the most spectacular settings in medieval Europe. At the time and for the next 318 years, the new shrine held one of the largest collections of gold and jewels in the world. This necessitated increased security. Pilgrims had to be carefully controlled and supervised so that they would not try to steal jewels from the shrine itself. Soon after the 1220 translation iron grilles were erected around the shrine allowing it to be closed off, and two monks and two clerks were appointed to be full-time custodians of what had become one of the most sacred sites in medieval England.

Three centuries later in September 1538, on the orders of King Henry, the eighth of that name, the shrine was demolished as part of the Reformation. All the treasures it contained were carried off in two large chests 'such as six or eight men could but convey out of the church'. Henry was determined to kill off the cult of Saint Thomas. Becket was declared a traitor and the shrine ordered to be totally destroyed and any remains found in it to be obliterated. He decreed that any bones found should be ignominiously burned. The veneration of saints' relics was condemned by the Protestant king as an idolatrous Catholic practice and was not to be countenanced.

All over the country, iconoclasts would obliterate Thomas's image with hammers, knives or whitewash in cathedrals and parish churches, smashing many of the stained-glass windows containing the stories of his miracles. Even his very name would be carefully excised from missals, psalters and the calendar of saints

The ruby known as the Regale of France which was mentioned earlier, Henry had made into a thumb-ring for himself.

To this day, no-one is certain about what happened to the bones, whether they be those of Thomas or not. Some say that the cathedral monks had warning of the impending arrival of the grave despoilers and removed the bones from the tomb before they arrived. They then re-buried them in a secret location within the cathedral grounds known only to a select few. This secret has, so we are led to believe, been passed down through generations and those cognoscenti still hold a memorial ceremony each year at the site. Other, possibly more realistic suggestions are that the bones were burned and scattered to the winds or were simply thrown into the river Stour. A true mystery.

What happened to Stephen, Matilda and Eustace's bodies?

During the Dissolution of the Monasteries in 1538 Thomas Culpeper was granted Faversham Abbey by Henry VIII. Most of the abbey was then demolished as part of the dissolution and reformation and the remains of Stephen, Matilda and their son Eustace were rumoured to have been thrown into Faversham Creek which lends more credence to the story of Becket s bones suffering a similar fate in Canterbury at about the same time. An excavation of the abbey in 1964 uncovered the empty graves.

What happened to the four Knights?

The murder of an archbishop in his own cathedral was not only sacrilegious but a heinous crime which not surprisingly had far-reaching consequences. It did not take long for the four knights to realise they had made a monstrous mistake in their assassination of who they thought was Thomas. After sharing out their spoils at Saltwood, the four fled north to de Morville's Knaresborough Castle, where they remained for about a year. Here they hunted with impunity in the royal forests and were entertained by sheriffs and royal constables. De Morville also held property in Cumbria and this may also have provided a convenient hiding place, as the men prepared for a longer stay in the separate kingdom of Scotland.

They were neither arrested and nor did Henry confiscate their lands. They did seek the King s advice but he declined to help them. Only after Pope Alexander excommunicated them did the consequences of their foul deed begin to catch up with them. On his orders, they went to Jerusalem to repent for their sins where they had been ordered to serve as knights for the next 14 years in the Holy Lands, though all four were dead by 1182.

Henry, the second of that name, narrowly managed to avoid excommunication but he became a pariah figure throughout Christendom. In 1172, in return for essentially reversing all of the reforms he had tried to enforce on the church in the 1160s he was absolved by the Pope. It would seem that Thomas had won in the end.

271

Who was Edward Grim, Brother Edward of the story?

Edward Grim was a real person and was an eyewitness to the murder of Thomas of Canterbury on Tuesday 29 December 1170 in Canterbury Cathedral. After the murder he wrote his account of it as part of his Vita S. Thomae (Life of St Thomas) in about 1180, some ten years after the murder.

I have chosen to make Brother Edward the narrator of the story but in most other respects have tried to adhere to the historical facts as closely as possible. For the purposes of the book, I decided that Edward Grim would be a monk at a priory in Cambridge.

Despite the fact that Edward witnessed one of the most important events in English history, very little is known about him. He has been variously referred to in the few contemporaneous documents in which he is mentioned as Master , monk or cleric .

If his title of Master is correct and Herbert of Bosham seems to think it was, it is possible that he was graduate of one of the nascent universities springing up at the time. Given that his Life of St. Thomas is written in excellent Latin it suggests that he had a better than average standard of education for the time. He is said to have come from Cambridge as did two teachers who were at the new Oxford University and subsequently returned to teach at Cambridge. They were called John and Geoffrey Grim. Were these two related to Edward? Highly possible.

What about monk or cleric ? Arnulf of Lisieux mentions in correspondence a man who had been granted the church at Saltwood but had been ejected from his living, by the violence of evil men." These evil men were no doubt the de Broc s and it is possible that the man was Edward Grim, the cleric and that he had gone to see Thomas after his return to England in the hope of having his benefice returned to him. Other than those possibilities, Edward Grim remains a mystery.

Facts to consider.

Although his father, Gilbert was known as Gilbert Beckette, Thomas was known initially as Thomas of London and then as Thomas of Canterbury when he became archdeacon. Being called Becket came much later. He is sometimes referred to as Thomas a Becket which is completely wrong and is an attempt to make him sound more French and of a higher status that he was.

William Fitzstephen had been Becket's personal household clerk for ten years and, when Becket became Chancellor of England, Thomas gave his clerk full authority to act in his name in diocesan matters. Fitzstephen became a subdeacon with responsibility for perusing letters and petitions involving the diocese.

Fitzstephen appeared with Becket at the council at Northampton Castle, where the Archbishop was disgraced for agreeing to the Constitutions and then changing his mind, leaving the rest of the Bishops high and dry after they had agreed with his initial stance. When Thomas was forced into exile, after refusing to sign the Constitutions of Clarendon, King Henry accepted a petition, in verse, from Fitzstephen and pardoned him from the banishment meted out to his master. When Becket and the king reconciled, Fitzstephen became his administrator once more. Fitzstephen records that he was among those of Thomas's advisors who cautioned against excommunicating king Henry. Fitzstephen was with Thomas on the day of Thomas's murder in 1170 but by his own admission was hiding behind a pillar when the action took place so could only hear and not actually see what happened.

Excommunication

The power of excommunication was a weapon used liberally by Thomas. Excommunication was and still is, an act of religious censure used to end the communion of a member of the Church with other members of the Church. In Thomas s time it meant realistically becoming a pariah in society and not being able to receiving the sacraments. Some say he used it so often that he devalued it as a viable and credible threat.

An interdict was the most feared ban in the Church s armoury: if an interdict on a country or a diocese was proclaimed, all churches would be closed and religious life would be suspended. Only baptism and the last rites would be allowed, except on the great feast days such as Christmas and Easter, and even then, Mass would be said rather than sung.

How much of a saint was Thomas?

Judging by his earlier life as a pleasure seeking hedonist and then as a ruthless soldier in France advocating mayhem and destruction, Thomas would not have been much of a prime candidate for sainthood.

The process for being declared a saint was ancient, traditional and often, mysterious. A bit like the Masons. Evidence had to be presented to persuade Church officials that the person in question had in fact lived a virtuous life, had faith, and had the support and help of God. Thomas s later life might well have fulfilled those criteria. The Church also looked at miracles as evidence that God was working through that person. However, if a candidate for sainthood was considered a martyr, because they died for their faith, they did not need to be associated with any miracles. Thomas had both going for him, martyrdom and miracles and anyway, if the Pope wished it, he could declare the person a Saint with or without the miracles. As we know, Thomas was well known to the Pope so becoming a Saint was probably guaranteed due to the old boy network operating at the time. More relevant perhaps would have been the political shenanigans of the time and the Pope s need to give Henry a timely reminder of who really held the reins of Power.

What were Thomas and Henry really like?

Stripping away all the partisanship, hagiography and adding the passing of time and the subsequent changing of values, the characters of both Thomas and Henry purely as men appear somewhat different from that portrayed in history.

This is especially true when one takes into account the portrayal of these two in popular myth and culture where Henry is painted as the 'bad guy' and Thomas, the good guy . A good example being the film Becket Good cinema but poor history with powerful images and representations that stick in the mind

More recently these two men have been looked at with a less jaundiced eye by historians. Henry II made some impressive legal reforms but made a couple of big miscalculations in his dealings with Thomas. Had he not committed the Constitutions of Clarendon to paper then things might have gone in his favour. Had he not had his son crowned by Roger of Pont L'Évêque then Thomas may well have been a good deal more conciliatory. Henry was a 12th century King, part of the Devil s Brood. He was hardly likely allow himself, let alone enjoy, being told 'no' by a low-born, ungrateful cleric that he himself had raised to a position of power and wealth.

On the other hand and on closer inspection, there is plenty about Thomas not to like or approve of. At times, even his own clerics accused him of over-ambition, greed, ostentation, ruthlessness and worldly behaviour unbecoming a man in his position. If Henry made mistakes at Clarendon, then Thomas was equally guilty of intransigence when a little humility and diplomacy would have been more appropriate. Thomas was perhaps overly guilty, in modern parlance, of believing his own hype.

From a distance of 850 years it might be a little unfair to make judgements on two men, both exceptional in their own right, based on what others with their own agendas to follow, thought of them at the time. These were men of complex character and ability who have found themselves in the spotlight of history.

Probably what was needed from both of them at the time was more statesmanship. Thomas was, or had been, a professional diplomat so should have been able to achieve his ends without becoming as heavy-handed as he did. Henry had been open-handed at Fréteval and while he had since been slow in returning Thomas's properties and revenues, had acted, eventually, in good faith. In Henry's defence, he had been genuinely distracted by affairs of state in northern France, despite what Thomas might have perceived as a snub and had also, at the same time, fallen seriously ill.

In contrast, Thomas obviously still bore a grudge for sleights perceived, real or not and was out for revenge. It didn't take him long to send a send a servant across the Channel to deliver his sentences of excommunication against the bishops who had challenged his authority. Although on his return to England he

275

did nothing that could be judged illegal, he started to make his presence felt with in an un-necessarily forceful manner.

As we have seen, on Christmas Day during his sermon in the Cathedral Thomas excommunicated all those who, in his opinion, had violated the rights of the Church. At the same time he excommunicated the Bishops who had been involved in the coronation of the Young Henry that year. In some ways it was this that prompted his own death warrant, if of course he was actually murdered. How did Thomas think Henry, a man whom he knew intimately, would act in the face of provocation as blatant as this?

Some have called his behaviour in the final months of 1170 as 'tactless, petty-minded, confrontational and provocative.' What purpose did he think behaving like that would serve, beyond perhaps redeeming his wounded pride and reasserting his authority after having been absent for six years? Maybe, once again, a little diplomacy and tact might have had better results and saved millions of words on all the speculation his actions caused.

Thomas of Canterbury may well have been acting purely on principle but as his struggle with Henry and the State went on, it becomes more difficult not to wonder how much personal motives had a part. As his battle with Henry culminated it would seem perhaps that he lost sight of the original reasons for the rift and that it became less about defending the rights of the Church and more about a personal battle of wills between himself and Henry.

Henry was where he was because of who he was and who his ancestors were, to some extent, one could say he had started at the top and had nothing to prove to anyone. Thomas on the other hand had got where he was through talent and raw ambition and had started at the bottom so had a lot of self-image to accommodate. He would have been regularly reminded in subtle and probably sometimes not so subtle ways, that he was not of the right class. He was a self-made man, proud of it and quite possibly achieved more than he should have in the eyes of many of his contemporaries. Once he fell out with Henry he was seen as fair game to many of his doubters and enemies.

If Thomas was truly motivated by a great passion for justice and a defence of the rights of the Church, he could conceivably gone about his task with more wisdom and understanding. He was and still is, an enigma. Like all figures in history we will never know the real truth about what they were, who they were and what they did or did not do.

Thomas was and still is, hero to Catholics and perhaps a traitor to Protestants and to this day, pilgrims and visitors of all persuasions still flock to Canterbury Cathedral in their thousands. Whether that be for its architectural majesty, its associated history, of which there is much, because it is the centre of the Anglican Communion or just to visit the site of a murder, who knows?

Mont-Saint-Sulpice

There is a village called Mont-Saint-Sulpice in the Yonne region of France. Whether there was ever a priory there, other than in my imagination, I have no idea.

Printed in Great Britain
by Amazon